Conceived by Paul Sochan

About the Author

George Peck has been involved in various IT pursuits for over 35 years. He founded his own consulting and training firm, The Ablaze Group, in 1994 (www.AblazeGroup.com). He has trained, consulted, and developed custom software for large and small organizations throughout the United States, Canada, the United Kingdom, and Puerto Rico.

George works with a variety of Business Intelligence toolsets. In addition to being a certified trainer for Tableau, he consults on Tableau and Tableau Server, as well as SAP BusinessObjects products. George is the best-selling author of several BI books published by McGraw-Hill Education, including multiple editions of *Crystal Reports: The Complete Reference*.

In addition to his software endeavors, George is a broadcaster and voice actor. His voice may be heard on national radio, TV, and web commercials, promotions, and documentaries. He programs his own eclectic music radio station and hosts a regular jazz radio program in Denver, Colorado. He may be reached via e-mail at Author@TableauBook.com.

About the Technical Editor

Molly Monsey is part of Tableau's training team who, since joining in 2011, has developed and conducted customer and partner courses all over the world. Starting at Tableau in 2009 as a product consultant, Molly served as a technical resource, providing support and training for internal and external audiences. Prior to Tableau, Molly worked in finance as a loan specialist responsible for analyzing data for thousands of customers. Molly is a Seattle, Washington, native and a graduate of the University of Washington Business School.

Tableau 8:
The Official Guide

George Peck

New York   Chicago   San Francisco
Athens   London   Madrid
Mexico City   Milan   New Delhi
Singapore   Sydney   Toronto

Cataloging-in-Publication Data is on file with the Library of Congress

Tableau 8: The Official Guide

4567890   DOC DOC   10987654

ISBN: Book p/n 978-0-07-181675-5 and CD p/n 978-0-07-181676-2
of set 978-0-07-181678-6

MHID: Book p/n 0-07-181675-5 and CD p/n 0-07-181676-3
of set 0-07-181678-X

Sponsoring Editor
Wendy Rinaldi

Editorial Supervisor
Patty Mon

Project Manager
Raghavi Khullar,
Cenveo® Publisher Services

Technical Editor
Molly Monsey

Copy Editors
Lunaea Weatherstone
Lisa McCoy

Proofreader
Paul Tyler

Indexer
Rebecca Plunkett

Production Supervisor
Jean Bodeaux

Composition
Cenveo Publisher Services

Illustration
Cenveo Publisher Services

Art Director, Cover
Jeff Weeks

Cover Designer
Jeff Weeks

For Denise
Let's go another 25

Contents at a Glance

1 Introduction to Tableau 8 1
2 Basic Visualization Design 9
3 Data Connection Details 31
4 Top 10 Chart Types 69
5 Interacting with the Viewer 95
6 Tableau Maps 121
7 Calculated Fields, Table Calculations, and Statistics 155
8 Creating Dashboards 187
9 Distributing and Sharing Your Visualizations 211

A Function Reference 231

Index 273

Contents

Acknowledgments   xv
About the Media Included with This Book   xvii

1 **Introduction to Tableau 8**   1
   What Is Tableau?   1
   Tableau User Interface   3
      The Data Window   3
      Shelves and Cards   4
   Basic Tableau Design Flow   5

2 **Basic Visualization Design**   9
   Using Show Me   9
   Choosing Mark Types   12
   Color, Size, Shape, and Label Options   14
      Choosing Color Options   14
      Setting Mark Size   15
      Choosing Shapes   16
      Text Tables and Mark Labels   17
   Formatting Options   20
   Evaluating Multiple Measures   22
      Shared Axis Charts   23
      Dual Axis Charts   26

3 **Data Connection Details**   31
   Connecting to Various Data Sources   31
      Adding and Joining Multiple Tables
         from the Same Database   35
   Customizing Your View of the Data   38
      Modifying Tableau's Default Field Assignments   38
      Hiding, Renaming, and Combining Fields   39
      Changing Default Field Appearance   43
      Using Hierarchies, Groups, and Sets   43
      Saving and Sharing Metadata   53

Extracting Data 55
Data Blending 60
Moving from Test to Production Databases 66

4   Top 10 Chart Types **69**
Bar Chart 69
Line/Area Chart 71
    Tableau 8 Forecasting 73
Pie Chart 74
Text Table/Crosstab 76
Scatter Plot 80
Bubble Chart 83
Bullet Graph 85
Box Plot 88
Tree Map 92
Word Cloud 94

5   Interacting with the Viewer **95**
Filtering Data 95
    Basic Filtering 95
    Interactive Filtering 101
    Quick Filters 103
Parameters 106
    Creating a Parameter 106
    Displaying a Parameter 109
    Using a Parameter in a Worksheet 110
Worksheet Actions 112
    Filter Actions 112
    Highlight Actions 115
    URL Actions 118

6   Tableau Maps **121**
Geocoded Fields 124
    Geographic Hierarchies and Ambiguity 128
    Custom Geocoding 131
Background Maps and Layers 140
    Map Options 142
    Web Map Services 143
Mapping and Mark Types 145
Custom Background Images 148
    Generating Your Own Coordinate System 149
    Adding a Custom Background Image 151

7 Calculated Fields, Table Calculations, and Statistics **155**

Creating Calculated Fields 156

Numeric Calculations 157

String Manipulation 158

Date Calculations 160

Logic Constructs 162

Creating Binned Fields 166

Table Calculations 167

Reference Lines, Bands, and Distribution 179

Single Reference Line 180

Reference Band 181

Reference Distribution 182

Trend Lines 184

8 Creating Dashboards **187**

Creating a Simple Dashboard 187

Tiled Placement 189

Floating Placement 196

Associated Dashboard Elements 197

Advanced Dashboard Elements 198

Layout Container 198

Blank 200

Text 200

Image 200

Web Page 201

Setting Dashboard and Element Sizes 201

Dashboard Actions 202

Highlight Action 203

Filter Action 204

URL Action 207

9 Distributing and Sharing Your Visualizations **211**

Exporting Worksheets and Dashboards 211

Printing to PDF Format 211

Exporting Worksheet Data 212

Exporting Worksheet Images 214

Exporting Dashboard Images 215

Using Tableau Reader 215

Publishing to the Web 216

Sharing on Tableau Public 217

Publishing to Tableau Server and Tableau Online 218

Using Tableau with iPad, Android,

and Other Smartphones and Tablets 221

A   Function Reference **231**
    Number Functions 231
        ABS 231
        ACOS 231
        ASIN 231
        ATAN 232
        ATAN2 232
        COS 232
        COT 232
        DEGREES 232
        EXP 233
        LN 233
        LOG 233
        MAX 233
        MIN 234
        PI 234
        POWER 234
        RADIANS 234
        ROUND 235
        SIGN 235
        SIN 235
        SQRT 235
        SQUARE 236
        TAN 236
        ZN 236
    String Functions 236
        ASCII 236
        CHAR 237
        CONTAINS 237
        ENDSWITH 237
        FIND 238
        ISDATE 238
        LEFT 238
        LEN 239
        LOWER 239
        LTRIM 239
        MAX 239
        MID 240
        MIN 240
        RIGHT 240
        RTRIM 241
        SPACE 241

STARTSWITH 241

TRIM 241

UPPER 242

Date Functions 242

DATEADD 242

DATEDIFF 243

DATENAME 243

DATEPART 243

DATETRUNC 243

DAY 243

ISDATE 244

MAX 244

MIN 244

MONTH 245

NOW 245

TODAY 245

YEAR 246

Type Conversion Functions 246

DATE 246

DATETIME 246

FLOAT 247

INT 247

STR 247

Logical Functions 247

CASE 248

IF 248

IFNULL 249

IIF 249

ISDATE 249

ISNULL 250

ZN 250

Aggregate Functions 250

ATTR 251

AVG 251

COUNT 251

COUNTD 252

MAX 252

MEDIAN 252

MIN 253

STDEV 253

STDEVP 253

SUM 253

VAR 254

VARP 254

Pass-Through Functions 254
    RAWSQLAGG_BOOL 255
    RAWSQLAGG_DATE 255
    RAWSQLAGG_DATETIME 255
    RAWSQLAGG_INT 255
    RAWSQLAGG_REAL 255
    RAWSQLAGG_STR 256
    RAWSQL_BOOL 256
    RAWSQL_DATE 256
    RAWSQL_DATETIME 256
    RAWSQL_INT 256
    RAWSQL_REAL 256
    RAWSQL_STR 256
User Functions 256
    FULLNAME 257
    ISFULLNAME 257
    ISMEMBEROF 257
    ISUSERNAME 257
    USERDOMAIN 258
    USERNAME 258
Table Calculation Functions 258
    FIRST 259
    INDEX 260
    LAST 260
    LOOKUP 261
    PREVIOUS_VALUE 261
    RUNNING_AVG 262
    RUNNING_COUNT 262
    RUNNING_MAX 263
    RUNNING_MIN 263
    RUNNING_SUM 264
    SIZE 264
    TOTAL 265
    WINDOW_AVG 265
    WINDOW_COUNT 266
    WINDOW_MAX 266
    WINDOW_MEDIAN 267
    WINDOW_MIN 268
    WINDOW_STDEV 269
    WINDOW_STDEVP 270
    WINDOW_SUM 270
    WINDOW_VAR 271
    WINDOW_VARP 272

Index 273

Acknowledgments

A book of this magnitude is a combined effort. While the author receives primary credit on the cover, there are lots of other people who have made this endeavor possible.

First and foremost, thanks to Paul Sochan at Tableau Software. Not only did he introduce me to this incredible toolset, but offered up the initial "Hey, you ought to write a book!" thought. Good idea, Paul! Molly Monsey from Tableau is, perhaps, the best technical editor I've ever had the pleasure of working with. Yes, she caught some technical errors. But, more importantly, she brought me back on track, helped me smooth out some awkward language, and just made the book so much more understandable. And, she's just a cool lady!

Francois Ajenstat at Tableau was helpful beyond description. Thanks so much for early alphas and betas, great feedback, and quick answers to every pesky question I asked. Elissa Fink at Tableau has been such a pleasure to work with—let's sell lots of books and software together! And, of course, thanks to Christian Chabot, Chris Stolte, and Pat Hanrahan for coming up with a great idea and founding a wonderful company.

There's a core group at McGraw-Hill Education made up of "behind the scenes" folks that rarely get enough credit. Wendy Rinaldi and I go way back. Wendy, it was great to work with you again, as in the beginning. Thanks to Lisa McCoy for making sense of occasional nonsensical stuff. And Patty Mon and Jean Bodeaux worked so diligently to make this a great final product!

Finally, and most importantly, I give eternal thanks to Denise. You've stood by me and supported me through more of these projects than I can immediately remember, over a longer period of time than I like to remember. I Love You.

George Peck
Author@TableauBook.com
July 2013

About the Media Included with This Book

*T*ableau 8: The Official Guide includes a companion CD that features videos by the author demonstrating key concepts, as well as sample Tableau 8 workbooks that may be opened directly in Tableau 8.

Videos

To view related videos, insert the included CD into your computer's CD drive. If the disc does not auto-start, perform the following steps:

1. Click the Start button.
2. View the list of drives.
   - In Windows XP, select My Computer.
   - In Windows Vista/7, select Computer.
3. Right-click the CD drive icon.
4. View the files on the CD.
   - In XP/Vista, from the drop-down list, select Explore.
   - In 7, from the drop-down list, select Open.
5. Double-click the icon of the Tableau_8 or Tableau_8.exe file.

Sample Workbooks

You may copy workbooks in the CD Sample Workbooks folder to your hard drive, or open them directly from the CD drive (you won't be able to save changes to the CD drive, however).

All sample workbooks are Tableau Packaged Workbook (.twbx) files. You may open these in Tableau 8 without regard to original data source locations. All data sources, necessary images, custom geocoding, and so forth are included in the packaged workbook.

If you wish to expand the content of the packaged workbook, right-click it in Windows Explorer and choose Unpackage. You may also rename the file extension from .twbx to .zip and use a standard ZIP utility to unzip the packaged workbook contents.

Look for any updated or corrected information at www.TableauBook.com. Questions about the content of these sample workbooks may be e-mailed to Author@TableauBook.com.

Note *If you are unable to use the disc that accompanies this book, you can download its content from McGraw-Hill Professional's Media Center at http://www.mhprofessional .com/mediacenter. Some material may require a desktop or laptop computer for full access. Enter this ISBN, 978-0-07-182563-4, and your e-mail address at the Media Center to receive an e-mail message with a download link.*

Ebook Users: Downloading the Media from the McGraw-Hill Professional Media Center

If you purchased the ebook edition of *Tableau 8: The Official Guide,* you can download all of the example material and video included on the print book CD from the McGraw-Hill Professional Media Center. Instructions for downloading are included at the end of the ebook table of contents.

1

CHAPTER

Introduction to Tableau 8

While social networking, cloud computing, and mobility are three of the biggest growth segments of Information Technology in the second decade of the 2000s, Business Intelligence is no slouch. Demand for new and innovative ways for organizations to view the ever-increasing amount of available data continues to grow. *Data Discovery* is a newer niche area of Business Intelligence that concentrates on visual and graphical analytics, as opposed to more traditional text-based reporting. And while an Internet search on the word *dashboard* might have returned a large number of results relating to part of a car interior several years ago, initial search returns now largely relate to some form of computer-based data visualization.

Tableau fits squarely into this Data Discovery/dashboard realm. While standard Business Intelligence tools for corporate and enterprise reporting abound, newer visualization tools, such as Tableau, are just coming of age. Now in its eighth major release, Tableau continues to sit at the leading edge of this growing segment of Information Technology.

Note *Open the Chapter 1 - First Workbook.twbx file in Tableau to see examples that relate to this chapter.*

What Is Tableau?

Tableau Software has its roots in the Stanford University Computer Science department, in a Department of Defense–sponsored research project aimed at increasing people's ability to rapidly analyze data. Chris Stolte, a Ph.D. candidate, was researching visualization techniques for exploring relational databases and data cubes. Stolte's Ph.D. advisor, Professor Pat Hanrahan, a founding member of Pixar and chief architect for Pixar's RenderMan, was the worldwide expert in the science of computer graphics. Chris, Pat, and a team of Stanford Ph.D.s realized that computer graphics could deliver huge gains in people's ability to understand databases. Their invention VizQL™ brought together these two computer science disciplines for the first time. VizQL lets people analyze data just by building drag-and-drop pictures of what they want to see. With Christian Chabot on board as CEO, the company was spun out of Stanford in 2003.

While Tableau 8 improves on the previous seven major releases of the software, the core approach to visual design remains the same: connect to a desired data source, and drag various data fields to desired parts of the Tableau screen. The result is a basic visualization that can then be enhanced and modified by dragging additional data fields to different destinations in the workspace. Beyond this basic visualization approach, Tableau's *Show Me* feature allows quick choices of predefined visualizations by just selecting relevant data fields and clicking a thumbnail. For more advanced requirements, Tableau features a complete formula language, as well as more robust data connection options.

When you first start Tableau, you are presented with the *Start Page*. The largest portion of the Start Page is reserved for thumbnails of recent workbooks you have used. Simply click on any one of these to open the workbook (like Microsoft Excel, Tableau's format for storing data on your disk drive is in a *workbook*, with a .TWB or .TWBX file extension). You may also open sample workbooks included with Tableau 8 by clicking the desired thumbnail at the bottom of the Start Page.

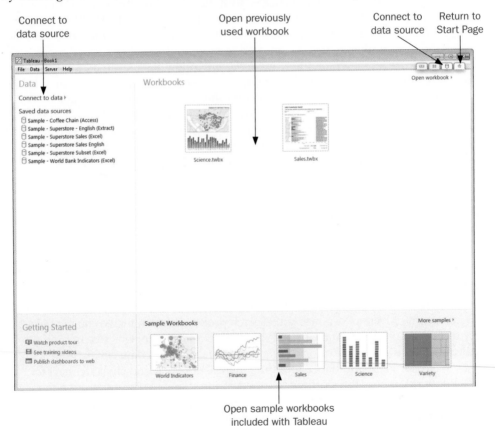

If you want to create a new workbook, you must first connect to a *data source* (types of data sources Tableau works with include industry standard databases such as Oracle or Microsoft SQL Server, Microsoft Excel spreadsheets, text files, and so forth). Unlike spreadsheet or word processing programs, Tableau must connect to some existing data before you can create a visualization. Certain data sources, known as *saved data sources*, will appear on the left side of the Start Page. These "pointers" to an existing data source can be selected by simply clicking them. If you want to connect to a different data source, click the Connect to Data tab (the tab with the "barrel" icon) in the upper right, or click Connect to Data in the upper left under the Data section. Once you've connected to a data source, a new workspace will appear where you can drag and drop desired data fields.

Note *Detailed discussion of data connections can be found in Chapter 3.*

Tableau User Interface

Once you've connected to data, a new worksheet, labeled Sheet 1, will appear. You'll notice that Tableau shares the "multiple worksheets within a workbook" paradigm of Microsoft Excel. A workbook can contain one or more worksheets, with each worksheet denoted by a tab at the bottom of the screen. As with most other standard Microsoft Windows programs, you'll see a series of drop-down menus and a toolbar. Also, many Tableau functions can be selected from pop-up context menus that will appear when you right-click with your mouse.

The left side of a Tableau worksheet contains the Data window, which breaks down data fields in your data source into dimensions and measures. You'll find a blank visualization containing a single column, row, and center area, each labeled "Drop field here." The remainder of the worksheet consists of a series of shelves and cards, where you can drag fields to control certain behavior and the appearance of your worksheet.

The Data Window

Since all Tableau visualizations start with connection to a data source, the first area you'll need to become familiar with is the *Data window*. Fields from your data source appear here, ready for you to drag and drop to relevant parts of the worksheet. In particular, the Data window is broken down into two sub-windows: Dimensions and Measures. *Dimensions* are categorical fields that tie data together into related groups. *Measures* are numeric fields that are aggregated as sums, averages, and so forth, for each occurrence of the grouped dimension. For example, if you want to create a bar chart showing total sales for each region, the region dimension will be used to create a separate bar for each region, with the size of the bar being determined by the sum of the sales measure.

Note *More details on the Data window, including how to reorganize dimensions and measures, along with detailed discussion of various data types, are available in Chapter 3.*

Shelves and Cards

Once you've connected to data and evaluated available dimensions and measures in the Data window, you'll need to decide where to drag desired dimensions and measures. You may choose to drag directly on the visualization area where prompted to "Drop field here." You may also choose to drop on a particular shelf or card. To create a vertical bar chart using the sales-by-region example discussed previously, you would simply drag the region dimension to the top column "Drop field here" area, or the Columns shelf. You would then drag the sales measure to the left of the region columns in the visualization, or the Rows shelf.

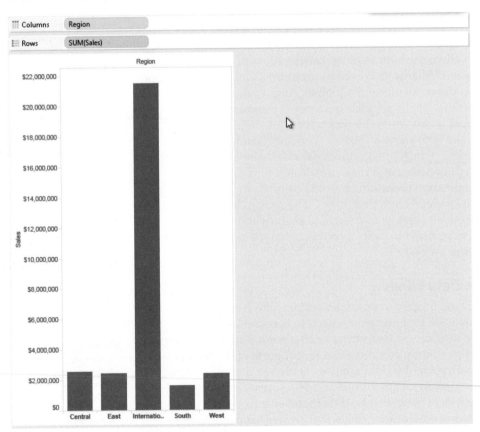

The term *shelf* is unique to Tableau, and refers to a particular part of the worksheet where you can drag and drop a field from the Data window. The most common shelves are Columns and Rows, as dimensions or measures dropped on these shelves determine the basic layout of your visualization. However, other shelves are used frequently as well. The Filters shelf will narrow down data included in the visualization based on a field that you drag to it. The Pages shelf acts as a modified Filters shelf, allowing you to "page" through values within a dimension or measure to quickly see changes in data.

Some parts of the workspace allow more than one function to be modified within the same general area. These are referred to as *cards* (also a term particular to Tableau). In particular, the *Marks card* (which has been completely redesigned in Tableau 8) is a single area of the workspace that contains different parts where you can drag and drop fields. For example, you can change the size of marks of your visualization by dropping a field onto the Size icon on the Marks card. You can also change colors by dropping a field on the Color icon on the Marks card. Once you've dropped fields on the Marks card, the fields will appear below the original icons where you dropped them. You'll be able to tell which part of the Marks card the field was dropped on by the associated icon appearing to the field's left.

Note *It's easy to confuse the terms "shelf" and "card" in Tableau. For example, the Pages and Filter shelves include a "Hide Card" option on their pop-up context menus. And the Rows and Columns shelves include both "Clear Shelf" and "Hide Card" options on their context menus.*

Basic Tableau Design Flow

Consider the basic bar chart illustrated in Figure 1-1. This is a fairly meaningful visualization, illustrating a comparison of sales by region, broken down by department. Notice the various portions of the worksheet discussed previously, such as the Data window, the Columns and Rows shelves, the Filters shelf, and the Marks card. This visualization was created with a few simple steps.

As is always the case with a new worksheet, a data source must be chosen. In this case, the "Sample - Superstore - English (Extract)" saved data source that ships with Tableau 8 is selected. The resulting Data window breaks down available fields into dimensions (that categorize data) and measures (that are aggregated as sums, averages, and so forth).

The illustrated vertical bar chart requires a dimension to appear on the Columns shelf and a measure to appear on the Rows shelf. Re-creating this chart involves simply dragging Region from the Dimensions portion of the Data window to the Columns shelf. This will create one "column," or bar, for each dimension value, or each region.

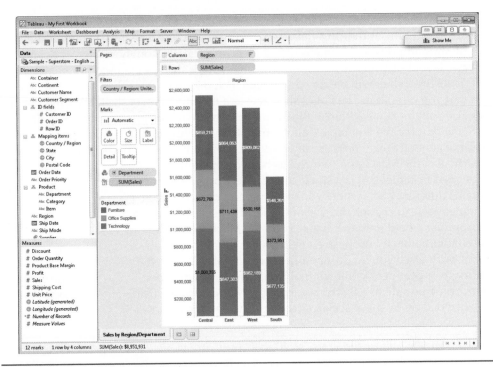

Figure 1-1   Basic Tableau visualization

Then the measure used to determine the height of the bar (in this case, Sales) is dragged to the Rows shelf. By default, Tableau aggregates this measure as a sum, representing total sales as a bar.

Note   *You may also begin this bar chart by using Tableau double-click options. If you initially double-click the desired measure, it will automatically be placed on the Rows shelf. Then the desired dimension can be double-clicked, which will place it on the Columns shelf, resulting in the same bar chart. Note that the order in which you double-click is significant. If you double-click on the dimension first and the measure second, the result will be a text table and not a bar chart.*

As the data in the sample data source includes international customers, a large International bar initially appears. As the desire is to only include the four regions of the United States, data must be *filtered* to include only U.S. sales. This is accomplished by dragging the Country/Region dimension to the Filters shelf. The resulting dialog box allows only United States data to be selected.

Notice that the region bars are broken down into three different colors (this is often referred to as a *stacked* bar chart). This is accomplished by dragging the Department dimension onto the Color icon on the Marks card. Note that this field now appears below the icons on the Marks card with a corresponding icon indicating that it was dragged onto Color. The resulting color legend appears on its own card.

To help annotate the values represented by each bar stack, the Sales measure is dropped onto the Label icon on the Marks card. The resulting sales amount appears on each stacked bar. As with the Department dimension, the Sales measure is aggregated to a sum and appears below the icons on the Marks card with the corresponding label icon appearing to the left.

You may notice that the regions are not appearing in alphabetical order (which is default behavior when initially creating a visualization). Instead, they are appearing in high to low order, based on sum of Sales. While there are several ways to accomplish this, the Sort Descending toolbar button is a very quick way to sort a visualization on its primary value.

And, last but not least, don't forget to give your worksheet a meaningful name. As with Microsoft Excel, Tableau's default sheet names are the word "Sheet" followed by a number. This is hardly meaningful when dealing with a workbook containing many worksheets. Just right-click on the sheet tab at the bottom of the screen and choose

Rename Sheet from the context menu. Or just double-click on the tab and type in the desired sheet name. A nifty Tableau 8 new feature is the ability to color worksheet tabs. Just right-click on the tab and choose Color from the context menu and choose one of several colors to assign to the tab.

Tip *Make sure you save Tableau workbooks early and often. Unlike some other applications, there is no auto-save or recovery option in Tableau. If the power fails, or your computer experiences a freeze or hang and you must reboot, you will lose any unsaved work.*

 Video *Introduction to Tableau 8*

2

Basic Visualization Design

One of the compelling benefits of Tableau is how easily and quickly you can visualize your data. By providing a combination of automatic visual best practices, along with quick, shortcut approaches to visual design, you can create meaningful Tableau visuals in, literally, minutes. And, the more familiar you become with Tableau, the quicker it becomes to create more sophisticated and advanced visuals as well.

One of the first choices you'll make for many visualizations is which basic design method to use. The first option, briefly introduced in Chapter 1, simply involves dragging fields to shelves or double-clicking fields in the Data window. The second option, *Show Me*, provides a quick way of choosing from a list of predefined visualization types after selecting desired fields in the Data window.

Note *Open the Chapter 2 - Basic Visualizations.twbx file in Tableau to see examples that relate to this chapter.*

Using Show Me

Any time you're editing a new or existing worksheet, you'll notice the Show Me tab at the upper right of the screen. Clicking that tab will expand the Show Me dialog box (to close the Show Me dialog box, just click the title bar of the dialog again). Show Me will display a series of thumbnail images representing the different types of charts you can create with just a few clicks. You can use Show Me anytime you want—whether you've already created an existing visualization or not. If you've already created a chart, Show Me will replace the existing chart with the type you choose in the Show Me dialog box (and, you can undo using the toolbar button or CTRL-Z key combination if you want to

9

Exactly What's a Dimension and What's a Measure?

One of the first decisions you make when you create a Tableau visualization is which fields from your chosen data source you'll use to compose the graphic. The Data window at the left of the Tableau screen automatically places these fields into one of two categories: dimensions and measures. This may raise the question, "What's the difference?" or "What determines whether a field becomes a dimension or measure?"

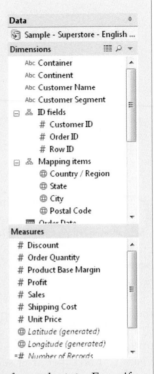

There's no designation in the original database or data source (unless it's a cube data source, such as Microsoft SQL Server Analysis Services) that indicates "dimension" or "measure." Instead, Tableau makes a fairly basic distinction when examining the incoming fields from your data source: whether the field is numeric or non-numeric. Numeric fields are automatically assigned as measures, and non-numeric (text, date, and so forth) are automatically assigned as dimensions.

A *dimension* is a field that organizes data in Tableau in categories, or "buckets" (Tableau uses the term *member* to refer to different dimension values). For example, if your data source contains United States data and includes a State field, "State" would become a dimension (it's not numeric) and would potentially contain 50 members... one for each state. Even if the data source contains lots of records (far more than 50), there would still only be 50 unique state values, or "members," of the State dimension.

A dimension creates distinct divisions on a chart, such as separate bars for all 50 state members. These divisions typically display labels (Tableau refers to them as *dimension headers)* for each dimension member. Furthermore, Tableau typically treats dimensions as *discrete* values, consisting of specific, categorical members. You may notice light blue coloring for dimensions in the Data window and field indicators on shelves. While you may think this blue coloring indicates a dimension, it actually indicates a discrete value.

As the name implies, a *measure* is a field that returns a numeric value for measuring something, such as a sales amount or order quantity. Expanding on the previous U.S. data discussion, a Sales Amount measure in the same data source could return far more than just 50 distinct values. In theory, many records could contain a variety of small sales amounts correlating to the smallest items your company sells (maybe even one cent), up to very large amounts for multiple high-priced items. As such, the Sales Amount measure isn't considered by Tableau to have "members," but instead contains a range of values, from the very minimum (potentially one cent) to the very maximum (potentially millions of dollars, or more), and every value in between the minimum and maximum.

A measure is usually aggregated to a single value (by default, measures are summed) for each corresponding dimension on a chart. So, using the previous Sales Amount by State example, a bar chart might consist of 50 bars, one for each state dimension member, with the size of the bar represented by the sum of Sales Amount for that state. And, while it's easy to distinguish discrete dimension members, a measure can have a much larger variety of values. As such, Tableau treats measures as *continuous* values, consisting of a minimum, maximum, and everything in between. You'll notice a light green coloring on continuous measures in the Data window and on shelves.

go back to the original chart). If you haven't created a chart yet, Show Me will create one for you in the current blank worksheet.

While Show Me is designed to be a simple, quick way to create a chart, there are a few fine points you'll need to know to make the best use of Show Me:

- If every thumbnail in Show Me is dimmed and unable to be selected, you probably are creating a new worksheet and no fields have been selected in the Data window. Select fields you wish to include in your chart, and associated thumbnails in Show Me will be enabled.

- If fields are selected, or you already have a chart created that you wish to change, Show Me will only show chart types that are appropriate for fields that are in use with your current chart or that have been selected in the Data window.

- Depending on the number and type of fields selected, Show Me will highlight the recommended thumbnail with a blue box (this is yet another example of Tableau's attempt to employ visual best practices for you). To use this recommended chart type, just click the thumbnail. If you prefer to use another chart type, just click the desired thumbnail.

- If you hover your mouse over a Show Me thumbnail, the bottom of the dialog box will show the name of the chart type you are hovering over, as well as the number of dimensions and/or measures that are required for that chart type. If you want to use that chart type, just CTRL-CLICK the desired dimensions/measures in the Data window until the desired thumbnail is enabled. Then, click the thumbnail to create the new chart.

Choosing Mark Types

 Video *Using the Marks Card*

No matter which approach you use to initially create a visualization (the drag-to-shelves approach or Show Me), Tableau will make some default assumptions about the type of chart created, or more specifically, the *mark type* that will be used. For example, if you initially use a date dimension for a chart, you will find a line chart (and thus, a line mark type) being chosen by default. Use of a geographic dimension (a dimension with a small globe icon next to it) will typically result in a circle mark type placed on a map background. If you choose no dimensions, but instead choose more than one measure (resulting in a scatter plot), you'll find the mark type defaults to an open circle. And, a bar mark type will typically result in other combinations of nondate, nongeographic dimension/measure combinations.

In all these cases, a mark type of "Automatic" will appear on the *Marks card* (the dialog box that appears to the left of your finished chart). Again, this is Tableau's approach to visual best practices; estimating the proper chart type and mark type based on the number and type of dimensions and measures chosen. However, there may be situations where you prefer to alter Tableau's automatic choices.

A very common requirement comes with date or date/time dimensions. As discussed previously, Tableau will choose a line mark type if you choose a date or date/time dimension. Line charts lend themselves to "trend over time" visualizations for a range of dates or date/times—this is a visual best practice. However, if you have a small number of distinct date dimension members you wish to compare (perhaps a "this year versus last year" or "four previous quarters" requirement), you may prefer an alternative to a line chart, such as a bar chart. Accomplishing this is as simple as changing the mark type on the Marks card from Automatic to Bar.

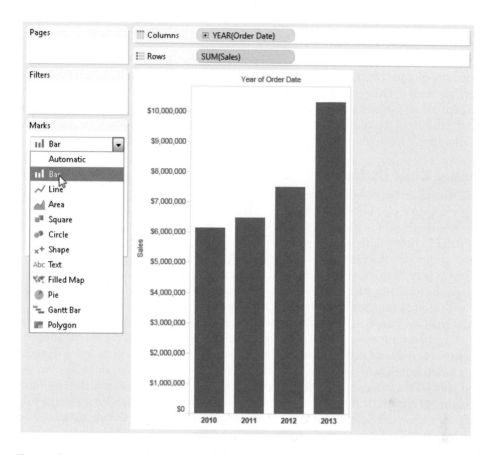

Depending on the mark type you select, other parts of the Marks card may change and require your attention. For example, if you choose a Pie mark type, an additional Angle option will appear on the Marks card. By placing a relevant measure on Angle and a desired dimension on Color, a pie chart wedge will be created for each member of the dimension placed on Color, with the wedge size based on the measure (with the largest aggregated measure value resulting in the largest "piece of the pie").

Maps also have interesting additional Marks card choices. While the default automatic mark type is a filled circle, you may desire some other mark type on a map background, such as a square or shape (a hollow circle being the default shape displayed). You may even prefer to display a filled map, whereby Tableau shades the entire area of a geographic region, such as country or state, by using the Filled Map mark type.

Choosing different mark types can result in some interesting (but sometimes ineffective) charts. Feel free to experiment, but keep visual best practices in mind. Remember that you want to effectively convey information about your underlying data. Think about what combination of mark types and chart organization will accomplish this.

Color, Size, Shape, and Label Options

In addition to mark types, the Marks card provides other options to customize the appearance of your chart. The first is color. Again, Tableau builds in visual best-practice adherence with default colors that are chosen for you (in fact, Tableau has hired experts in human visual interpretation to help identify the default color palettes and behavior that are built in to the product). You may choose your own colors, however, by using the Color item on the Marks card.

Choosing Color Options

If your visualization consists of only one color (a single-dimension bar chart, a map, or so on), clicking Color on the Marks card will display a color palette dialog. Choose a different color from the palette, or click More Colors to display the standard Windows color palette dialog with precise color choices. You may also set transparency options, as well as choose colors for borders of marks. A halo option is even available that provides a way of shading the edges of certain mark types to make them easy to distinguish (typically, this is useful for large numbers of marks in a chart, such as a map with a large number of circles, or a busy scatter plot).

You may also drag a dimension or measure to Color on the Marks card to color your chart based on relevant data. Coloring on a dimension will create distinct color values for each dimension member. As such, you'll probably want to use a dimension with a small number of members for color (trying to color a "sales by year" bar chart based on a 50-member state dimension will probably prove to be of little use—a four-member region or five-member product type dimension may be more useful). Dragging a measure onto Color will create a shaded-variance color result based on the "continuous" behavior of numeric measures. For example, a profit measure will color the mark in a shaded variation based on whether profit is negative or positive— highly unprofitable bars may appear in a heavy shade of red, while very profitable bars appear as deep green. Moderately profitable bars will appear with a lighter shade of green, and bars that represent products sold at cost will appear with a neutral gray shade. The heat map illustrated in Figure 2-1 is another example of a mark colored via a measure.

Regardless of whether you drag a dimension or measure to Color, a color legend will appear below the Marks card. Clicking the small arrow on the legend and choosing Edit Colors from the resulting menu, or clicking Color on the Marks card, will present options for customizing color behavior. Depending on whether a discrete dimension or continuous measure is on Color, the set of available colors will be reduced to those maintaining visual best practices. Furthermore, a set of predefined color palettes will be available for you to use as alternates. For example, the automatic red/green color palette discussed earlier used to distinguish profit may be better replaced with a blue/ orange palette more appropriate for a color-blind audience.

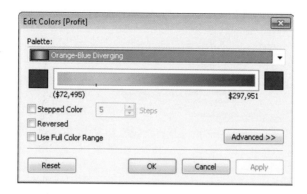

Tip *You may add more than one dimension to Color on the Marks card to create combined color variations. Just* CTRL-CLICK *or* SHIFT-CLICK *the dimensions you wish to add in the Data window. Then, drag the group of dimensions to Color. Tableau will create a unique color for every combination of dimension member (because of this, you'll probably want to use dimensions that have a relatively small number of members to avoid too many colors on the chart). You'll notice that all dimensions you dragged will appear on the lower portion of the Marks card, each with a color icon. If you later wish to reduce the number of color dimensions, simply drag the desired color dimensions off the Marks card.*

Setting Mark Size

Depending on the mark type, you may wish to change the size of the mark, either consistently across all marks, or variably, based on another dimension or measure. Clicking Size on the Marks card simply displays a size slider that you may use to adjust the mark size. This is handy if you want to reduce or increase the white space between bars, make circles on a map larger, and so forth.

However, by dragging another dimension or measure on Size, you can vary the mark size based on another field. This is handy when you wish to size-encode a mark—perhaps vary the size of a circle on a map based on sales, population, or something similar. Some chart types are based on variable mark sizes by design. The *Heat Map* is available in Show Me, or it can be designed manually. This alternative to a cross-tab or text table (similar to a spreadsheet) helps analyze a large number of measures in a row/column matrix. However, rather than showing the actual measure value at the intersection of each row and column, the Heat Map displays a shape (typically a square) that represents the value of the measure. By varying the size of the mark by placing a measure on Size, you can make quick comparisons by simply glancing at the size of a mark. Figure 2-1 illustrates the benefit of variable mark sizes.

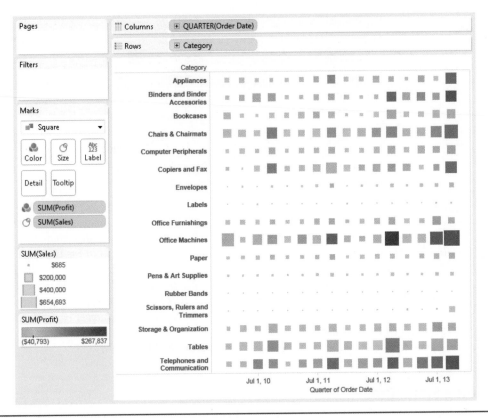

Figure 2-1 Heat Map

Choosing Shapes

As discussed earlier, Tableau provides an automatic mark type based on the types of fields you drag to shelves or the type of chart you choose in Show Me. One chart type, the *scatter plot* (available in Show Me, or resulting from initially using measures on rows and columns in your chart), results in a shape being chosen for the automatic mark type. If you don't create a scatter plot, you may find certain situations where changing the mark type to *Shape* may be of benefit.

By default, an open circle will appear as the initial shape and an additional Shape area will appear on the Marks card. If you click it, a default shape palette will appear, where you can choose an alternative shape. Clicking More Shapes in the shape palette will display the Edit Shape dialog box, where additional shape palettes are available for selection. The default open circle will be replaced by the selected palette/shape combination. The true power of shapes, however, becomes apparent when you drag another dimension or measure onto Shape on the Marks card (generally, you'll find the most benefit from adding dimensions instead of measures). Tableau then assigns a different shape to each mark to delineate different dimension members or measure values. In addition, a shape legend will appear, showing assigned shapes.

To further customize shapes, click Shape on the Marks card, double-click the shape legend, or click the small arrow on the shape legend, followed by Edit Shape. The Edit Shape dialog box will appear with the currently assigned shapes displayed, as well as palette choices. If you wish to assign a different shape from the current palette to any existing dimension or measure value, select the dimension/measure value under Select Data Item and click the desired shape from the palette. If you wish to use a different palette, select it from the drop-down list. If you wish to assign all new shapes from the just-selected palette, click Assign Palette. Or, you may just choose one shape from a new palette for a particular dimension/measure by clicking the value and then the desired shape; shapes from more than one palette may be assigned this way.

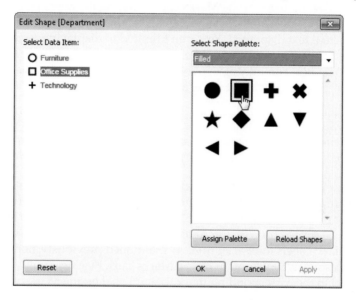

Tip *You're not limited to just using the available shapes in the palette drop-down list. To add your own custom shapes, obtain or create a series of image files in .png, .gif, .jpg, .bmp, or .tif formats. Generally speaking, you'll benefit if the images are "icon size," or around 32 by 32 pixels. And, if you want to color-code the shapes with Color on the Marks card, you'll benefit from using .png or .gif format with background transparency enabled. Place the images in their own folder (the folder name will be used to name the palette in Tableau) within My Documents\My Tableau Repository\Shapes. If Tableau is running when you add shapes, click Reload Shapes in the Edit Shape dialog box to read the new shape folder.*

Text Tables and Mark Labels

Although Tableau is designed to present graphical representation of your data, sometimes plain text comes in handy (as proven by the continued popularity of the ubiquitous spreadsheet program introduced in the early 1980s). For these cases,

Tableau provides the *text table* (also known as a crosstab). A text table is available in Show Me, or is created automatically if you just double-click two dimensions and then one measure, in that order. The key to a text table is the Text area of the Marks card, which appears automatically with the two dimension, one measure scenario just discussed. Text will also appear on the Marks card if you explicitly replace some non-text mark type, such as bar or circle, with a Text mark type (Label appears in place of Text on the Marks card for non-text mark types, as discussed later in this section).

By default, the field displayed at the intersection of each text table row and column is placed on Text on the Marks card. A field appears in the lower portion of the Marks card with the associated text icon. If you wish to display a different field on Text, simply drag the existing field off the Marks card and drag the new one onto Text. You may also click Text on the Marks card and adjust the alignment of the text, as well as customize the actual text displayed. You aren't limited to displaying a single field in a text table either. Simply drag additional fields onto Text, and they'll appear next to previously chosen ones. You may also invoke Measure Names and Measure Values to display multiple measures on a text table, as described later in the chapter.

Tip *While using Measure Names and Measure Values automatically labels multiple measures, Chapter 4 discusses an innovative way to label multiple fields placed on Text without using Measure Names and Measure Values. Look for the sidebar "Using More than One Measure."*

When using a graphical mark type, such as a bar or line, you may find it helpful to still show text around a mark indicating the actual value it represents (to show the value of a bar or point on a line, for example). This is possible using *mark labels*. Basic mark labels can be turned on with the Analysis | Show Mark Labels drop-down menu option, or the Mark Labels toolbar button. As mentioned previously, non-text-mark types will also display a Label option on the Marks card. Placing a field on Label will add a mark label to the corresponding mark. Using Label on the Marks card provides additional flexibility beyond the toolbar button option.

You may place more than one field on Label. For example, you may wish to annotate a pie chart with not only the dollar value of the measure represented, but also the percentage each wedge contributes to the total. Or, you may choose to hide the standard color legend and add the dimension name to Label to place the label on top of each bar of a bar chart, as well as the value the bar represents. Simply drag more than one field onto Label. Changing the order in which fields display is as simple as dragging and dropping the order of fields in the lower part of the Marks card.

You may also click Label and customize the mark label display in a number of ways. An edit box allows complete customization and formatting of all chosen labels. And, you may choose which marks to label (all, minimum/maximum only, and so forth) and when to display labels (always, or only when marks are selected or highlighted). And, an option appears allowing labels to overlap adjoining marks.

Tip *You may change the property of any existing field on the Marks card. For example, if you mistakenly drop a field on Color but actually want it on Label, there are two quick options. First, you may just drag the field from the lower portion of the Marks card onto the desired icon. Or, you may click the icon to the left of the desired field on the lower portion of the Marks card. A pop-up menu of available Marks card properties will appear. Choose the desired property you wish to move the field to (in the case of this example, choose Label). The icon next to the field, and the visualization, will change accordingly.*

Customizing Tooltips

Tooltips are small pop-up text boxes that appear when you hover your mouse over a mark. By default, tooltips show values for all relevant fields included somewhere on your visualization, as well as clickable action links to create inclusion or exclusion filters, create a group or set (groups and sets are discussed in Chapter 3), and view the underlying data making up the mark.

There are several ways of customizing tooltip appearance. First, you may right-click any field used on the worksheet (on a shelf, on the Marks card, and so forth) and toggle the Include in Tooltip option (this option will not appear if you have customized the tooltip in the Edit Tooltip dialog box, described next). You may also choose the Worksheet | Tooltip drop-down menu option, or click Tooltip on the Marks card to display the Edit Tooltip edit box. You may format various parts of the tooltip text, add more fields (including an All Fields option), and choose whether or not to include the previously described action links in tooltips.

Formatting Options

So far, customized formatting has been limited to options available in text edit dialog boxes. These dialog boxes permit you to select various parts of text and change font and color formatting. However, Tableau also includes complete formatting options for other parts of your visualization, such as marks, headers (column or row headings that appear for each dimension), axes, and so forth.

There are several ways to initiate formatting in Tableau. You may choose options from the Format drop-down menu. You may also right-click virtually any kind of Tableau element (fields on shelves, marks, labels, legends, axes, and so forth) and choose Format from the context menu. The Data window will be replaced with a Format Window, as illustrated in Figure 2-2.

You'll notice several small icons at the top of the Format Window. Click the desired icon to change font, alignment, shading, borders, and lines on your worksheet. These icons

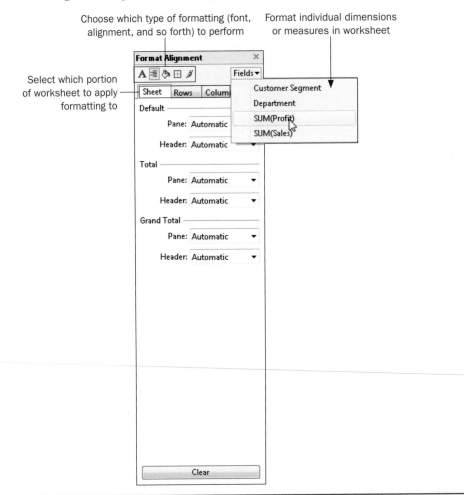

Figure 2-2   The Format Window

equate to the first five options on the Format drop-down menu. Below the icons are three tabs: Sheet, Rows, and Columns. Click the desired tab to format the overall worksheet, or just row and column items.

A small Fields drop-down arrow appears at the upper-right area of the Format Window. Clicking this arrow will expose a list of all dimensions and measures in use on the worksheet. Selecting an individual dimension or measure will allow you to format just occurrences of that field, as opposed to overall formatting for all fields. The previously described Sheet, Rows, and Columns tabs will be replaced with Header/Axis and Pane tabs. Header/Axis formatting applies to dimension labels (or headers), which appear for each member of a dimension. Axis formatting applies to a numeric axis that is associated with a numeric dimension. Pane formatting applies to the actual graphical or text items within your chart. In particular, charts based on more than one dimension will create a series of "panes" within each other, which are formatted via the Pane tab.

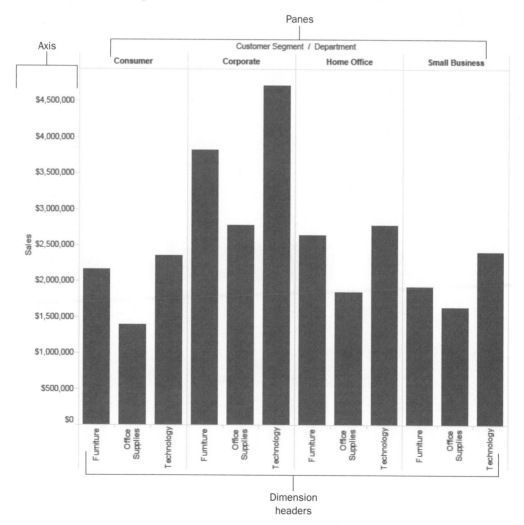

Formatting in Tableau may require some getting used to, as the organization of the Format Window is different from many other standard Windows applications. Just experiment—if you don't see the expected outcome, try choosing other combinations of tabs or formatting icons until you achieve the proper results. There is no OK confirmation button in the Format Window, so formatting happens on-the-fly as you choose options. You'll be able to see the results of your choices immediately and reverse them if they're not correct. And, you can always resort to the Undo button on the toolbar.

Evaluating Multiple Measures

With most basic visualizations illustrated so far, a single measure has been analyzed (with the exception of the scatter plot, which analyzes the relationship between two measures). However, it's often helpful to compare more than one measure—either comparing two measures on two different "panes" in a visualization, or within the same pane using the same axis.

There are several ways of comparing more than one measure. The first is accomplished by simply dragging two or more measures onto the Rows or Columns shelf. The result will be multiple rows or columns, with each representing one measure. Consider the chart shown in Figure 2-3. Here, product category is contained on the Columns shelf, with the

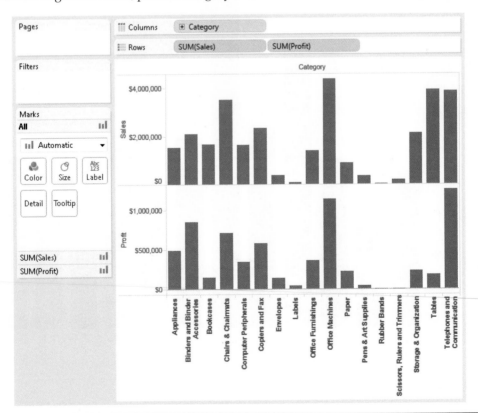

Figure 2-3   Multiple measures on a shelf

sales measure and profit measure appearing on rows. This creates two different rows, with a separate axis, for each measure. This approach provides several benefits: Each measure can be compared across a single row, and the measures can be compared to each other by evaluating the two bars within each product category column. This type of chart is helpful if the two measures are drastically different in values or minimum/maximum scale, as each axis is automatically scaled to accommodate its specific measure.

Shared Axis Charts

While the example presented in Figure 2-3 may be appropriate for certain measure comparisons, you may prefer a more direct comparison of multiple measures in the same "pane," using the same axis. The *shared axis chart*, illustrated in Figure 2-4, accomplishes this. Here, both sales and profit share the same axis. This provides for a more direct comparison of not only the trend sales and profit take over time, but how profit and sales compare.

Creating a shared axis chart, while simple, requires a specific approach. After creating a chart with the first measure, drag the second measure from the Data window *onto the existing axis in the work area.* Look carefully—you'll see a "dual axis" icon (two side-by-side green bars) appear in the existing axis. When you see this icon, drop the

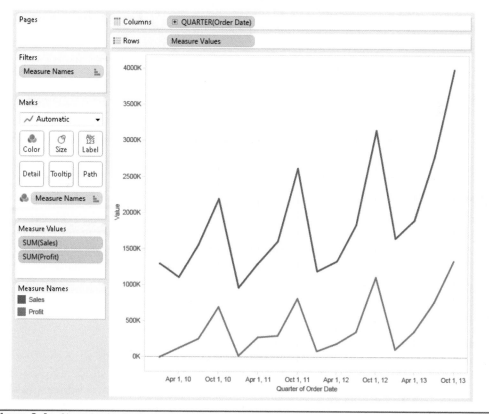

Figure 2-4   Shared axis chart

second measure. Both measures will now appear on the visualization in the same pane, sharing the same axis. You may do this as many times as necessary (as long as too many measures don't render the chart unusable). Just drag additional measures onto the shared axis.

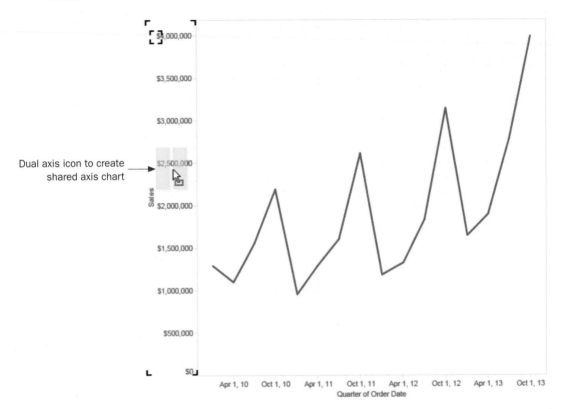

Best Practice *While Tableau permits multiple measures of drastically different values and scales to share a single axis, you'll probably find these visualizations to be of limited use. The drastic difference will require Tableau to scale the shared axis for the larger measure, which may make comparison to the smaller measure difficult. As such, you should only use shared axis charts if the measures are not dramatically different in scale.*

Measure Names and Measure Values

Shared axis charts are simple to create—simply drag another measure to an existing axis. However, various shelves and cards in the Tableau workspace suddenly show lots of changes based on this simple drag-and-drop. You'll now notice several Measure Names and Measure Values fields appearing in various parts of the workspace.

In summary, *Measure Names* and *Measure Values* are a way of allowing more than one measure to appear in the same place. Measure Names exposes the names of multiple measures (in the example shown in Figure 2-4, there are two names: the word "Sales" and the word "Profit"). Measure Values exposes the actual values of the measures. In the example shown in Figure 2-4, the two values are sum of sales and sum of profit. You'll notice that Measure Names is automatically placed on the Filters shelf, even though no data is actually being filtered from the underlying data source. Instead, the Measure Names filter is limiting the measures exposed to just sales and profit—all other measures in the data source will appear in the Measure Names filter, but only sales and profit are checked. And, you'll notice Measure Values is placed on a shelf to actually expose multiple measures on the same shelf, without creating a new row or column for each measure. Furthermore, Measure Names has been placed on Color on the Marks card in the example illustrated in Figure 2-4 to create different colors for sales and profit.

Another helpful use of Measure Names and Measure Values is when you wish to use more than one measure in a text table/crosstab (text tables are discussed earlier in this chapter). While you may drag more than one measure on Text on the Marks card to add multiple measures to a text table, you may consider Tableau's automatic double-click capability to add more measures. For example, if you drag desired dimensions to Rows and Columns shelves and then simply double-click a measure, the measure will automatically be placed on Text and will appear at the intersection of the row and column dimensions. Instead of dragging a second measure to Text, simply double-click the second measure. Tableau will invoke Measure Names and Measure Values, placing

Measure Values on Text to show multiple measures in the same place, and Measure Names on Rows to create a separate row for each measure. The added benefit of this approach, when compared to dragging individual measures to Text, is that a single set of headers appears containing the names of the measures. No special effort is required (such as a calculated field or manual editing of the text value) to properly label multiple measure rows or columns.

			Region			
Customer Segment		Central	East	International	South	West
Consumer	Profit	$64,281	$61,174	$866,929	$26,558	$54,547
	Sales	$404,292	$480,805	$4,075,355	$329,780	$620,338
Corporate	Profit	$210,126	$144,866	$2,084,506	$23,243	$127,303
	Sales	$1,042,483	$818,102	$8,035,475	$569,904	$838,901
Home Office	Profit	$136,231	$78,402	$1,157,495	$40,036	$29,201
	Sales	$709,259	$506,332	$5,087,195	$427,010	$526,351
Small Business	Profit	$109,187	$93,124	$1,296,110	$14,364	$99,799
	Sales	$384,308	$617,565	$4,284,500	$270,652	$405,849

Note *While you'll see Measure Names and Measure Values items in the Data window, it's typically better to let Tableau invoke them automatically with drag-to-axis or double-click functionality described earlier. While you may drag them to shelves and cards directly from the Data window, you'll probably find lots of additional (and often confusing) effort will be required to achieve the desired end results.*

Dual Axis Charts

One of the potential pitfalls with shared axis charts discussed earlier is an unacceptable difference in scale of values of the compared measures. Sharing a single axis becomes useless in these cases, as the axis scale required for the larger measure renders comparison to the smaller measure impractical. Tableau solves this problem with *dual axis charts*, charts that actually can display separate left and right axes.

Figure 2-5 shows such an example. Here, sales and order quantity can be reasonably compared in the same physical space. However, there are two separate axes on the chart: the sales axis appears on the left, the order quantity axis on the right. Note the two different scales of the axes, which avoids the issue of comparing dissimilar measures on the same axis. As with shared axis charts, creating a dual axis chart is simple, but requires one of two specific steps. First, drag the second measure from the Data window *onto the right side of the existing chart in the work area.* Look carefully— you'll see a "single axis" icon (one green bar and a dashed line) appear on the right of the chart. When you see this icon, drop the second measure. You may also drag the second measure to the Rows or Columns shelves directly after the first measure. This will initially create a second row or column for the new measure. Now, right-click or select the drop-down menu arrow on the second measure indicator and choose Dual Axis from the context menu. This will place the second measure on its own axis on the right side of the chart.

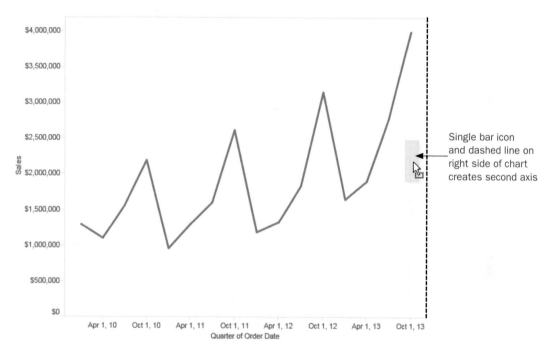

Single bar icon and dashed line on right side of chart creates second axis

Note *As mentioned earlier, dual axis charts allow dissimilar measures to be analyzed in the same physical space. There is a potential pitfall, however. Since the different measures are displayed using separate axes, data "confusion" may result when comparing them. For example, if the scale of the left axis is showing millions of dollars, while the scale of the right axis is showing hundreds of orders, it may appear that orders being displayed are in the millions, or dollars being displayed are in the hundreds. While you may right-click the right axis and choose Synchronize Axis to set the scale for both axes to be identical, you have then eliminated one of the benefits of a dual axis chart by scaling both measures' axes identically. You'll need to consider the benefit of a dual axis chart against the possible data confusion of different axis scales in the same physical space.*

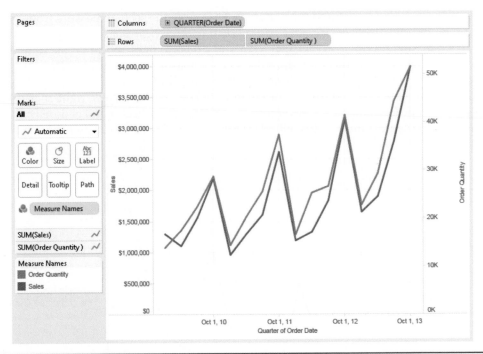

Figure 2-5   Dual axis chart

Multi-Measure Marks Card Fine Points

In the dual axis example presented earlier, you may have noticed invocation of Measure Names but not Measure Values. In this case, Tableau automatically placed Measure Names on Color on the Marks card to set individual colors for the two measures. However, a closer look at the Marks card in this example reveals something new: a *Multi-Measure Marks card*. The previous example of two separate measures on the Rows or Columns shelf will also result in the same situation.

When multiple measures are used on a visualization (with the exception of a shared axis chart), the Marks card will expand to show an All option, as well as options for individual measures. Click All or the desired measure you wish to modify. A separate Marks card will appear for your choice. All measures will be affected by choices you make in the All card (Measure Names sets separate colors if used on the All card). However, only the chosen measure will be affected when you select its corresponding Marks card.

Multi-measure Marks cards come in handy for creating a variation of the dual axis chart known as a *combination chart*. Like a dual axis chart, a combination chart displays more than one measure on separate axes. However, each measure uses a different mark type. For example, by selecting the Marks card for the second measure and choosing something other than an automatic mark type, you may maintain the default line chart for the first measure on the left axis, but display a bar chart for the second measure on the right axis. Color options may be set separately as well.

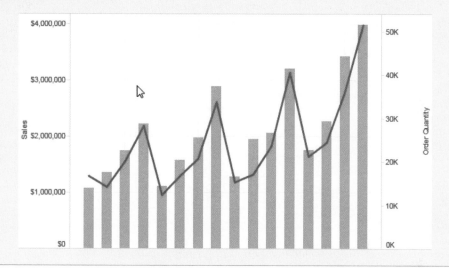

CHAPTER

Data Connection Details

As discussed in Chapter 2, the very first requirement when creating a new Tableau workbook is choosing a data source. Unlike traditional spreadsheet and word processing programs, Tableau can't start with a "blank slate"; it must connect to some existing database, data file, or data source before you can begin to design a chart or graph. Tableau's entire paradigm is visualizing data—the first thing you have to do is pick the data!

Note *Open the Chapter 3 - Data Connections-Groups-Sets-Blending.twbx file in Tableau to see examples that relate to this chapter.*

Connecting to Various Data Sources

When you first start Tableau, you are presented with a wide array of "places to start," including the ability to pick a previously used workbook from a series of thumbnails, open an existing workbook from either the recent file list or Open entry on the File Menu, or select existing sample workbooks from the bottom of the home screen.

There are several approaches to creating a new workbook as well. The File | New drop-down menu option will display a new workbook in the Tableau workspace, but without any fields appearing in the Data Window—you will have nothing to drag to shelves. In this instance, you'll need to click the Connect To Data option at the top of the Data Window, or use the corresponding Data | Connect To Data drop-down menu choice. You may also create a new workbook based on a chosen data source directly from the Tableau home screen. Just select Connect To Data in the upper left, or click the data tab (the tab displaying a small barrel icon) in the upper right. In all cases, the Tableau workspace or home page is replaced with the Connect To Data Window.

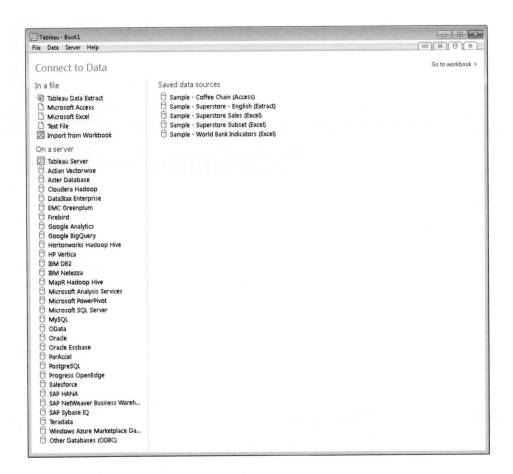

Tip *If your version of Tableau only presents the "In a file" selection of data sources and not the "On a server" selection, you have probably purchased Tableau Personal Edition. This version of Tableau is designed specifically for analysis of a limited set of PC-based "local" data sources, such as text files, Microsoft Excel and Access, and Tableau Data Extracts. If you need to analyze data located in standard corporate databases, such as Microsoft SQL Server or Oracle, or web-based data sources, such as SalesForce.com or Google Analytics, you'll need to purchase Tableau Professional Edition. Only Professional Edition presents the "On a server" list of data sources.*

Tableau supports connections to many different databases and data sources, including standard corporate databases; newer "big data" data sources, such as various versions of Hadoop and Google Big Query; and web-based data sources, such as Salesforce.com and Google Analytics. Even if the particular database you wish to connect to isn't in the list of existing data sources, Tableau will connect to data via Microsoft's Open Database Connectivity (ODBC) connection type. If your data source includes a standard ODBC driver, Tableau can probably connect to it.

Select the type of data source you wish to connect to. An associated connection dialog box will appear, prompting you to choose various data source properties. Depending on the data source, you'll need to provide a user name or e-mail address, password, server location, database name, and so forth. For example, to connect to Microsoft SQL Server, you'll need to specify a server name, user ID and password (if not using Windows Authentication), and database name.

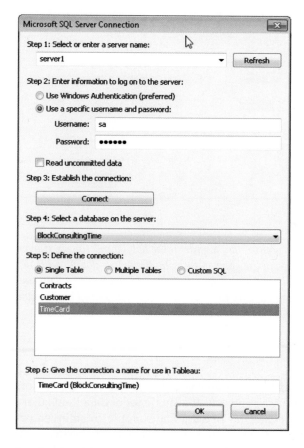

A different type of connection dialog will appear when you connect to web-based data sources. For example, connecting to Salesforce will present a significantly different dialog. You are still prompted for a user name, password, and server, but the list of database/table options is different than that presented by a standard corporate database.

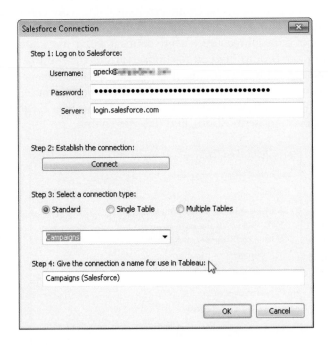

Note *Although a data source may appear in the list, connecting to it may require downloading additional drivers from the Tableau website. If a driver download is necessary, a dialog box indicating such will appear when you attempt to connect to a data source. Visit TableauSoftware.com/drivers to find additional drivers and try the connection again after the proper driver has been downloaded and installed.*

 Video *Choosing Data Connections*

Regardless of which data source you use, Tableau eventually organizes data into one or more tables. A *table* consists of a single set of data items that relate to one particular function or category of data. For example, in an inventory database, there may be tables dedicated to ReorderLevel, OnHand, MasterInventory, and similar inventory-related functions. A payroll database may present Employee, Paycheck, Deduction, and PayPeriod tables. Choosing the proper table or tables is key to getting the right data for your charting need. Various data sources present table choices somewhat differently. In the SQL Server example presented previously, a Single Table choice allows you to add just one table to your workbook. However, the Salesforce connection dialog illustrated previously offers a Standard choice, which will add multiple related tables automatically, or a Single Table choice to permit adding just one table. Once you pick a table and click OK to close the connection dialog, the Tableau workspace will appear with the Data window breaking down fields from the chosen data source as dimensions and measures (a complete discussion of dimensions versus measures, and how Tableau chooses them, appears in Chapter 2).

Adding and Joining Multiple Tables from the Same Database

While it may be possible to create meaningful charts and graphs with a single database table, it's not uncommon to require several (and sometimes many) tables to gather all the necessary data for your visualization. For this purpose, you must add more than one table and *join* the tables together on one or more common fields.

When you connect to your data source, the connection dialog box will provide several radio buttons that allow you to choose a single table or multiple tables. The

Single Table option is simple; just pick one of the available tables from the table list and click OK. That table will be added to the Data window, where you may choose fields to chart. However, if you need to use more than one table, the Multiple Tables radio button presents more advanced choices, including the requirement to join tables together.

Begin by choosing the first table you want to add to the Data Window before you click the Multiple Tables radio button (you may remove a table later if you accidentally start with the wrong table, but it will save time if you pick the desired table first). Click Multiple Tables. The existing table will continue to appear, but additional buttons (Add Table, Edit, Remove, and Preview Results) will also appear.

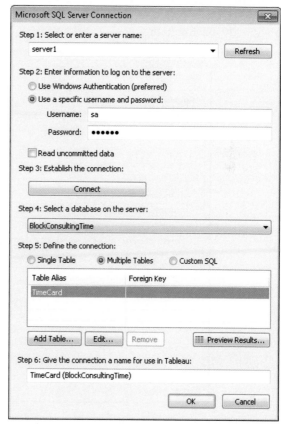

Caution   *In addition to Single Table and Multiple Tables radio buttons, some data sources will allow you to create custom SQL with a corresponding radio button. While there may be benefits (and sometimes a requirement) to base a Tableau visualization on a custom Structured Query Language query, you may see significant performance degradation as you interactively drag and drop fields in the workspace. In these situations, you may consider extracting the results of the custom SQL (extracting data is covered later in the chapter) for improved performance.*

Click Add Table. An Add Table dialog box will appear showing additional available tables in the data source. Click each table to see a list of fields available in that table. Once you've found the table you'd like to add, you may optionally change the *table alias* (a substitute name you can use for the table if the default table name conflicts with another table or is difficult to understand), as well as select or deselect fields from the table that you want included in the Data window. You may also assign a *field alias* (a substitute field name you can use for a particular field if the name conflicts with a field in another table or is difficult to understand) by double-clicking the field in the Table Fields list. Once you have made these choices, click the Join tab to join the new table to an already existing table.

Tableau will attempt to join your selected tables automatically on a common field name—you'll see a join clause already appearing that ties the two table fields together. However, it's possible that fields that are named identically in the two tables aren't the proper fields to be used for the join (date and timestamp fields are often named the same, but aren't proper join fields). It's also fairly common that the proper join field (or fields—joins may require more than one field) is not named identically and won't be automatically chosen by Tableau. If the existing join clause is incorrect, select it and click the Delete button. Then, examine the two tables and available fields under the Add Join Clause section of the dialog box. Make choices based on these considerations:

- What common field exists between the two tables? Both fields should be the same data type (string, number, date, and so forth) and should contain similar values. If you need to browse table data, click the browse button to the right of each table name.

- Select the correct matching fields under each table.

- Choose a join operator from the drop-down list. Typically, you'll leave the default equals sign as the join operator, which will match data from the two tables when the common fields are equal to each other. However, in some specialized cases, you may need to return data from the tables when the first join field is less than the second field, greater than the second field, and so forth. Make the desired choice from the drop-down menu.

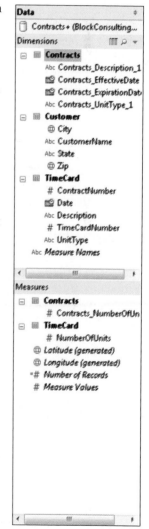

- Choose a join type from the Join Type drop-down menu. By default, Inner is chosen, which will return a combined record when the join field matches in both tables. If you choose Left, all records will be returned from the left table (the table that appears in the join clause first), as well as matching records from the right table. If there is no matching data from the right table for a left table record, right table fields will be null. If you choose Right, all records will be returned from the right table (the table that appears in the join clause second), as well as matching records from the left table. If there is no matching data from the left table for a right table record, left table fields will be null. Full, which is not supported for all data sources, will return all combinations of matches from both left and right tables. If there is no match from one table to another, fields from the mismatched table will be null.

Once you've made all choices, click OK. The Add Table dialog will close and you'll notice the table you just added in the multiple tables list. If you need to add and join more tables, click Add Table and make table/join choices as many times as necessary. When you have finally added and joined all necessary tables, click OK to close the connection dialog box and display all chosen tables and fields in the Data window.

Note *In some cases, you may benefit from gathering data from tables from different databases. This requires data blending, which is discussed later in this chapter.*

Customizing Your View of the Data

It can be said that there are two fundamental requirements to successful data analysis in Tableau: learning to use Tableau to its fullest potential, and learning the underlying data source or database. While you may be very familiar with Tableau's features and capabilities, a new database that you haven't worked with before can be very daunting and complicated. A standard corporate database may consist of hundreds of underlying tables, each containing a significant number of fields. Depending on how the database is designed, the table and field names may be cryptic and unfamiliar. And, required fields for joining tables may be ambiguous. This complexity can cause even the most experienced Tableau analyst to shy away from a visualization project, as the underlying database may prove too complex.

One of the ways that database designers and vendors simplify the organization of complex database structures is through the use of metadata. *Metadata* is a broad term that generally covers a simplified view of a complex database. By reducing the number of database tables to only those required for typical analysis (and by renaming them to be more intuitive), by pre-joining tables in advance, and by only including fields necessary for typical analysis (and renaming them to be meaningful), metadata can make complex databases easy to understand and analyze. While you may consider Tableau to be primarily a data visualization tool, it features many metadata capabilities that can greatly simplify the complexity of an underlying data source.

Modifying Tableau's Default Field Assignments

As discussed in Chapter 2, Tableau uses a field's data type to determine whether to categorize a field as a dimension (non-numeric field) or measure (numeric field). While this automatic assignment is usually appropriate, there are times that you'll need to override Tableau's defaults. For example, a numeric key field may be more appropriately categorized as a dimension instead of a measure, as it will act as a unique key. Recategorizing a measure as a dimension is as simple as dragging it from the Measures area in the Data window to the Dimensions area.

Recategorize a dimension as a measure using the same approach. Just drag it to the Measures area. The dimension will be moved to the Measures section of the Data Window with a default aggregation of Count. If a numeric value has been interpreted by the underlying database, and Tableau, as a text field (you'll notice the small ABC icon next to it), converting it to a measure alone will not convert it to a numeric value that can be summed. You'll need to also right-click and choose Change Data Type | Number from the context menu, and then choose the desired default aggregation from the same menu.

Hiding, Renaming, and Combining Fields

Even though the ability to change table and field aliases exists when first connecting to a data source, you may find a need to rename fields even after a data source connection has already been made. For example, a field with the same name may appear in more than one table and, as such, has been annotated with the table name to avoid ambiguity. Or, field names may simply be unintuitive, as database designers may not always keep simple field-naming concepts in mind when databases are initially designed. And, fields may have been added en masse with a number of tables that later are not required for common analysis tasks. These unneeded and hard-to-understand fields don't lend themselves to common data analysis tasks.

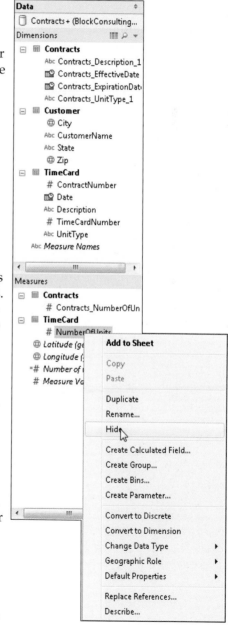

To hide a field that you no longer wish to use, simply right-click the field in the Data window and choose Hide from the context menu. The field will simply disappear from the Data window. You may hide as many fields as necessary, even CTRL- or SHIFT-clicking multiple fields and choosing Hide from the combined context menu. You may even hide all fields that aren't being used in a worksheet once you've completed your chart. Just right-click a blank portion of the Data window (make sure no fields are selected) and choose Hide All Unused Fields.

If you later wish to redisplay fields that were previously hidden, you must perform a two-step process. First, right-click a blank portion of the Data window (make sure no fields are selected) and choose Show Hidden Fields. All previously hidden fields will now appear in the Data window, but will be dimmed. Select one or more hidden fields, right-click, and choose Unhide from the context menu.

Renaming fields is very straightforward. Simply right-click a field you wish to rename and choose Rename from the context menu. A Rename Field dialog will appear. Just type in the desired field name and click OK. If you later decide to restore a field to its original name, right-click again, choose Rename, and then click Reset in the Rename Field dialog.

If you need to combine the contents of more than one dimension into a single value (sometimes referred to as *concatenation*), it's easy.

Just CTRL-click or SHIFT-click the dimensions that you wish to combine. Then, right-click and choose Combine Fields from the context menu. A new dimension will appear in the Data window, initially named based on the field names of the combined fields. If you wish to rename the new dimension, right-click it and select Rename from the context menu. When the combined dimension is used in your worksheet, every combination of members from the source dimensions will result in a new combined member.

Using Clipboard Data Sources

When you look at the list of available data sources on the Connect To Data screen, you may be under the impression that the only way to make use of data is to ensure that it is in one of these formats. In fact, it's possible to "cut and paste" data directly into Tableau via the Windows Clipboard.

Consider the World Population web page illustrated here. Note that a standard "table" organization exists, with each country comprising a row, and country name and population for four years spread across five columns. Notice that the table has been highlighted, including the first row containing labels for the country and year columns.

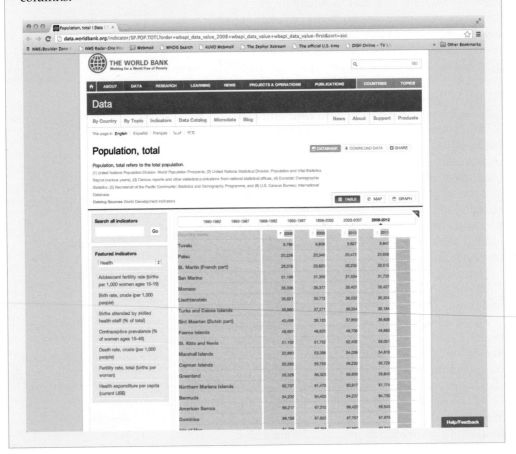

Making use of this data in Tableau is as easy as copying the highlighted data to the Clipboard via the browser's Edit | Copy drop-down menu option or CTRL-C keyboard shortcut. Then, choose an existing workbook where you wish to use the data, or just display the Tableau home screen. Then, choose Data | Paste from the Tableau drop-down menu, or simply press the CTRL-V keyboard shortcut. Tableau will create a new data source in the Data window (labeled Clipboard, followed by a unique number) and display all pasted fields in a new worksheet, as illustrated here.

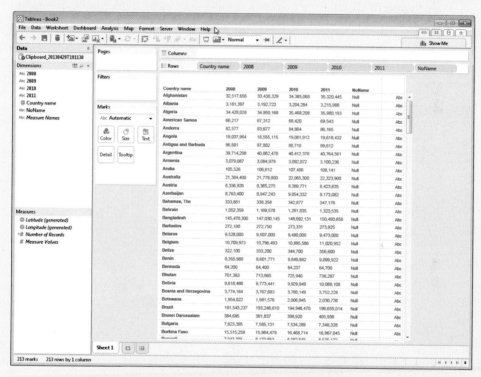

In some cases, Tableau may perfectly interpret data in the pasted table and properly identify data types and dimension and measure assignments. However, in other cases, misinterpretation may occur. In this example, notice that while the general row and column format of the pasted data is intact, there are several issues that will prevent the data from being properly used in Tableau:

- An extra column was copied from the web page that contains no usable data. It has been named "NoName" by Tableau.

- Population values have been identified by Tableau as strings instead of numbers, and have therefore been classified as dimensions instead of measures.

(continued)

Fixing these issues is fairly straightforward, making use of previously described techniques for customizing a data source:

- The NoName field has been removed from a shelf and then hidden via the right-click | Hide context menu.
- The 2008, 2009, 2010, and 2011 fields have been reclassified as numeric fields instead of strings by using the Change Data Type option that appears when right-clicking the field name. Once converted to numbers, these same four fields have been reclassified as measures via the same context menu.

The result is a far more usable data source, allowing a population map to be created by use of the geographic country field and one of the yearly population measures.

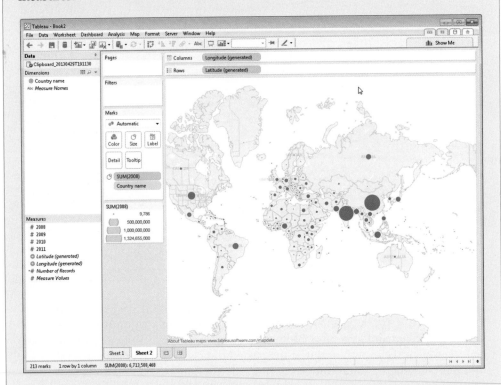

Once you've done any necessary data source modifications and saved the associated workbook, the Clipboard data source will be saved in a tab-delimited file. You may then reuse (or extract) that file for further use in other workbooks. A dialog box will confirm saving of the Clipboard data source.

Clipboard Data Saved

Your clipboard data has been saved to the following location:

C:\Users\George\Documents\My Tableau Repository\Datasources\

Clipboard_20130429T191130.tab

OK

Do not show again

Changing Default Field Appearance

Tableau provides several default properties and behaviors for a field, depending on its data type. For example, numbers take on a certain default number format, dates are automatically formatted with a certain month/day/year organization, numeric measures are automatically summed when added to the worksheet, and dimensions are assigned default colors based on Tableau's built-in visual best practices.

If you wish to change any of these defaults, make choices from a field's context menu Default Properties option. For example, you may change the default colors that Tableau will assign dimension members. Or, if you prefer a different default date format, choose Date Format. If you'd rather display the average for a numeric measure by default instead of a sum, select a different Aggregation option. And, you may add a descriptive comment that will appear when you hover your mouse over the field in the Data window. The Comment option is helpful for providing descriptive background information for a field.

Using Hierarchies, Groups, and Sets

So far, this section of the chapter has discussed fairly straightforward ways of modifying the view of your underlying data source (the *metadata*) to make the data source easier to understand and analyze. There are more advanced options, however, to customize the way the data source is organized. While these advanced options aren't strictly considered to be part of the custom metadata, they can be saved in a customized data view (discussed later in the section "Saving and Sharing Metadata"). As such, they are important to consider when you are customizing metadata for your use or to be shared among other Tableau users in your organization.

Building Field Hierarchies

A *hierarchy* is a from-the-top-down organization of related dimensions. By default, Tableau displays date or date/time fields in a hierarchy. So, if you drag a date field to a shelf, the date will initially be rolled up to year. You can then click a plus sign on the date field indicator to expand the date hierarchy from year, to quarter, to month, to week, to day, and if time is included, from hour, to minute, to second.

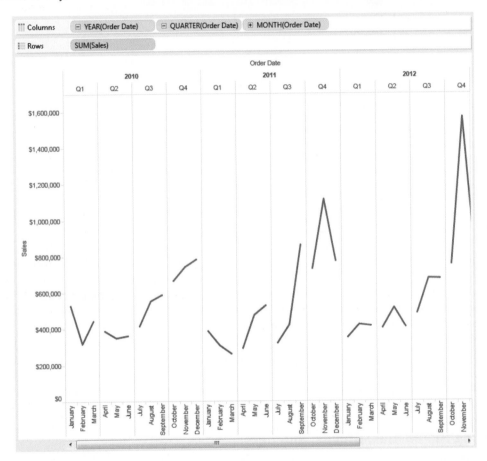

You may have other related nondate dimensions that lend themselves to a hierarchy. For example, you might have a series of separate geographical fields, such as country, state, county, city, and ZIP code, that lend themselves to a natural hierarchy. Or, you may prefer to create a hierarchy to navigate from division, to region, to sales team, to salesperson.

Creating your own hierarchies in Tableau is surprisingly easy. Simply drag the "inner" dimension on top of the "outer" dimension. For example, if you are creating the geography hierarchy discussed previously, drag State on top of Country. The Create Hierarchy dialog box will appear, prompting for a name for the hierarchy (with the default name being the fields you dragged and dropped). Give the hierarchy a more meaningful name (such as "Geography") and click OK. Notice that the Data window now contains the hierarchy you created, preceded with a plus sign. Click the plus sign to expand the hierarchy and expose the dimensions within it. Drag additional dimensions inside the existing hierarchy. If you happen to drag the dimensions in the wrong order, simply drag and drop within the hierarchy to reorder dimensions properly. If you drag a dimension into the hierarchy by mistake, just drag it back out. To completely erase a hierarchy, right-click the hierarchy name and choose Remove Hierarchy from the context menu.

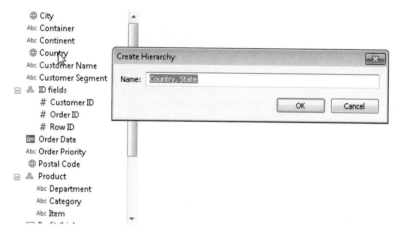

Once you've created your own hierarchy, drag the hierarchy name onto a shelf. Notice that the top-level dimension in the hierarchy is displayed on your visualization and that a plus sign appears on the field indicator on the shelf. As with the previously illustrated date hierarchy, plus and minus signs on the field indicators can be used to navigate through the hierarchy. You may also drag an inner field from the hierarchy to a shelf. Navigation will be available from that field on down.

Creating and Modifying Groups

Although not purely a metadata function, groups allow you to organize data in a more logical fashion, as well as accommodating certain types of data inconsistencies, perhaps resulting from data entry errors. Any custom groups you create are saved with a custom data connection so that they may be reused and shared within your organization.

A *group* is a reorganized set of dimension members. For example, your data source may contain data broken down by state, but a data entry error places some data in a state labeled CO and other data in a state labeled Colorado. These may be combined into a single dimension member. Or, if you wish to analyze data by salesperson territories (and these territories don't exist in your data source), you can create salesperson territory groups based on state. You could highlight Montana, Wyoming, Colorado, Utah, and Arizona and create a "John Doe" group. California, Oregon, Washington, Nevada, and Texas could be placed in a group named "Jane Smith," and so forth. You may then use either the original state field or the new group to analyze data. And when you save the data source, the group is saved with it for use in other workbooks.

There are two ways to create these kinds of groups: by selecting dimension headers on an existing worksheet, or by using the Create Group option in the Data Window. To use an existing worksheet, CTRL- or SHIFT-click the group member headers you wish to combine (it's important that you click the names of the members—the headers—and not the actual marks, as you'll see later in this section). Then, with your mouse hovered over one of the selected headers, click the paper clip icon in the tooltip. You may also click the group (paper clip) button on the toolbar. Or, you can right-click the header and choose Group from the context menu.

The selected dimension members will be combined into a new single member consisting of the names of the original dimensions and a new group dimension will be created in the Data window (the group will be named the same as the original dimension with a group designation appended to it). In addition, the original dimension on any worksheet shelves will be replaced by the new group dimension. From this point forward, you may analyze either the original dimension by dragging it to an appropriate shelf or the new combined group by dragging it to a shelf.

Several options are available to customize the new group:

- To ungroup the just-combined members, select the header of the combined member and click the paper clip again. Or, right-click and select Ungroup from the context menu. While this will return members to their original separate locations, the group will remain in the Data window and on a worksheet shelf.

- To change the name of the new combined group rather than maintaining the list of original member names, right-click the new member header and choose Edit Alias from the context menu. Type in the new name you wish to appear for the combined group.

- To add a combined member to the group, select additional original members as you did previously and use the same paper clip or context menu options as before. A combined member will be added.

- To add original members to an existing combined member, select the original members you wish to add, as well as the existing combined member. Use the paper clip or menu options to add.

- To combine one or more already combined members, select the combined members and use paper clip or menu options. They will be combined into yet another new combined member consisting of everything in the original combined members.

In addition to manipulating groups on the worksheet, you may create and modify groups in the Data window. Begin by selecting the original dimension you wish to group. Then, right-click and choose Create Group from the context menu. The Create Group dialog box appears, displaying the original dimension members for the chosen dimension. Select the existing members you wish to combine with SHIFT- or CTRL-clicks (if the dimension has a large number of members, you may wish to click the Find button and add search criteria to find the members you want to select). Then, click the Group button. The selected members will be combined into a new member consisting of the names of the selected members. If you wish to rename the new combined member, simply hold your mouse button down on the name for a second or so, or select it and click the Rename button. Type in the desired name for the combined member. You may also change the default name of the group (initially, the name of the dimension the group is based on, followed by the word "group") by selecting the Field Name portion of the dialog box and typing in a new name.

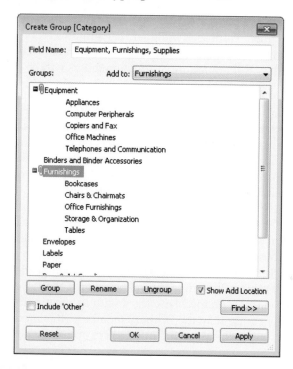

When you've finished customizing the group, click OK. The new group will be added to the dimension list in the Data window. You may now analyze with the original dimension by dragging it to a shelf, or the new group by dragging it to a shelf. When you first create a group, or if you select an existing group in the Data window, right-click, and choose Change Group from the context menu, there are several fine points that can help you maximize use of the group dialog box:

- To expand or contract combined members, double-click the plus or minus sign to the left of the combined member. When expanded, you'll see the original members that have been combined into the new member.

- To ungroup a combined member, select the combined member next to a plus or minus sign and click the Ungroup button.

- To create another combined member, select additional original members as you did previously and click the Group button again. A new combined member will be added.

- To add original members to an existing combined member, select the original members you wish to add. Then, either drag them inside the existing combined member, or choose the existing combined member you wish to add them to from the Add To drop-down list at the upper right of the dialog box.

- To combine one or more already combined members, select the new combined group members and click the Group button again. They will be combined into yet another new combined member.

- To create an "Other" combined member that contains all original dimension members that weren't placed in any combined members, click the Include "Other" checkbox. All remaining original members will be combined into one last combined member named Other.

There is a third variation on grouping (referred to informally as *visual grouping*) that you may prefer for quick visual delineation of group members. As mentioned earlier in this section, when creating combined group members on the worksheet, you should select the actual member names/headers, *not* the marks (bars, circles, and so forth). If you do select marks instead of headers (with CTRL- or SHIFT-click, or by dragging over multiple marks), then Tableau behaves somewhat differently.

Once you've selected desired marks, click the group (paper clip) button in the tooltip that appears, click the group (paper clip) toolbar button, or right-click and choose Group from the context menu. As discussed previously, the selected dimension members will be combined into one new member in a new group, which will be placed in the Data window. However, contrary to earlier steps when headers were selected, the new group *will not* replace the original dimension on a shelf. Instead, the new group will be placed on Color on the Marks card with the originally selected members now showing a different color than the "Other" members (this method of group creation uses the previously discussed Include Others option by default).

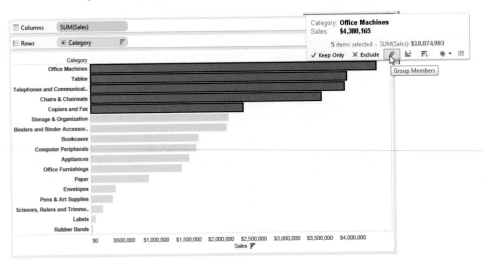

As before, the name of the new combined member will be a list of the original member names. You may edit the newly created group in the Data window to provide a more appropriate name. Or, you may simply select the name in the color legend, right-click, and choose Edit Alias. Type in the new name for the combined member.

There are some fine points for using this "visual" method of grouping as well:

- To ungroup the just-combined members, select one or more of the already grouped marks. When the tooltip appears, you'll notice that the previous group paper clip icon now displays a small x, indicating that it now functions as an ungroup button. You may also right-click and select the Ungroup option from the context menu.

- To add a combined member to the group, select additional original members' marks as you did previously and use the same paper clip or context menu options as before. An additional combined member will be added to the group, which will create an additional color.

- To add original members to an existing combined member, select the original marks you wish to add, as well as at least one mark from an existing combined member. Use the paper clip or menu options to add.

- To combine one or more already combined members, select *all* the marks from existing combined members and use paper clip or menu options. They will be combined into yet another new combined member consisting of everything in the original combined members.

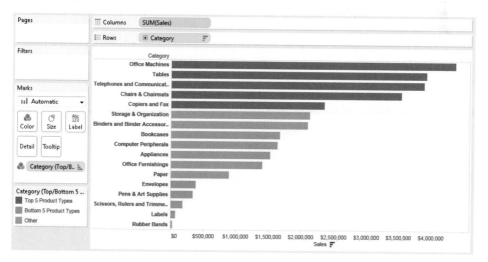

Working with Sets

Although not purely a metadata function, sets are a way of narrowing down analysis to subsets of all the data in your original data source. Any custom sets you create are saved with a custom data connection so that they may be reused and shared within your organization.

A *set* is a smaller subset of all the data in your underlying data source. For example, a set may consist of just five salespeople that are underperforming. Or, another set could contain all products that have an on-hand quantity at or below a reorder level. While you may confuse sets with groups, it's important to understand that groups *combine* multiple dimension members into one combined member, whereas sets simply *narrow down* to the selected dimension members—they are not combined. Once sets are defined, they can be used as filters, placed on the Color shelf or other parts of the Marks card, and so forth to help analyze the subsets of data that you've defined.

There are two types of sets you can create in Tableau. The first, a *constant set,* contains a specific set of dimension members. An example of this type of set is one that specifies five salespeople who are underperforming. You may use this constant set to analyze, color, filter, and so forth, based on the five specific salespeople you've added to the set. Even if one of the salespeople improves their sales dramatically, they'll remain in the set until you manually edit the set and remove them. The second type, a *computed set,* uses a conditional formulaic expression to define what the set contains. For example, a set can be defined that determines products that need to be reordered by comparing the Quantity_On_Hand database field to the Reorder_Level database field using a less-than operator. Any product dimension members that meet that condition will be included in the set. As data changes, different dimension members may be added to or removed from the set automatically based on changing on-hand quantities or reorder levels.

There are several ways of creating a constant set. If you already have a chart defined in your worksheet, you may select as many marks or headers as you'd like to add to the set via CTRL- or SHIFT-click, or by dragging to highlight a series of marks (in a scatter plot, for example). From the tooltip, click the Create Set button. Or, right-click and choose Create Set from the resulting context menu.

The Create Set dialog box will appear with the dimension members you selected appearing as a list (if your visualization contains multiple dimensions, they will appear in separate columns). If you wish to remove an entire dimension in a multidimension set, hover your mouse over the column heading of the dimension and click the red X.

And, any dimension members may be removed by hovering over the row and clicking the red X. Give your set a meaningful name by typing it in in the Name area. If you wish to immediately filter your worksheet by the new set, check the Add To Filters shelf. Click OK to create the set. The new set will appear in the Sets area of the Data window. Like any other field in the Data window, you may drag the set to a shelf or to a portion of the Marks card to analyze only the data included in the set.

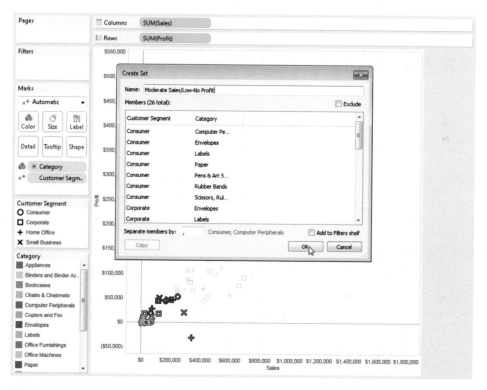

You may also create a set by right-clicking an existing dimension in the Data window and choosing Create Set from the context menu. The Create Set dialog box will appear containing three tabs: General, Condition, and Top. The General tab will simply list all the members of the dimension. Just click as many members as you wish to add to the set and click OK. However, if you want to create a computed set, select either the Condition or Top tab and select some sort of condition, based on the dimension itself, or a measure. For example, to create a set containing all products whose on-hand quantity is below the reorder level, click the Condition tab, click the By Formula radio button, and enter the proper comparison formula in the text area (you may also click the ellipsis button to display the Calculated Field Editor).

Note *Details on calculated fields and formulas may be found in Chapter 7.*

One feature of sets that you will find handy in overall set analysis is the In/Out feature. Depending on where you use a set (dragging a set to Color on the Marks card is a prime example), your chart will break data down into "in set" and "out of set" delineations. For example, if you create a text table that includes Product Name, On Hand Quantity, and Reorder Level, you may place the previously illustrated set on Color to highlight which items are "in" the set (need to be reordered) and "out of" the set (those that have sufficient quantity on hand). If you prefer to highlight the actual members that make up the set rather than whether items are in or out of the set, click the context arrow on the set's field indicator on the shelf and choose Show Members In Set.

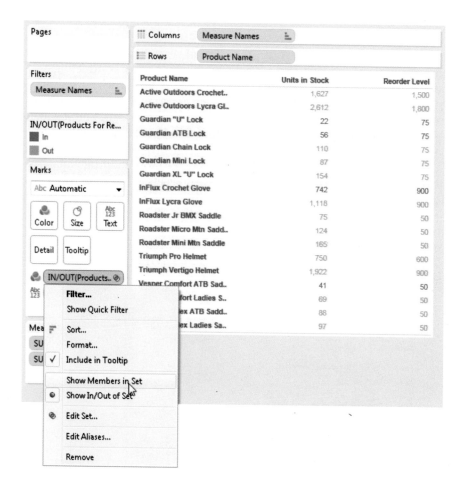

Caution *The "in set" and "out of set" capabilities just described, as well as the ability to use sets in calculated fields, are not available with Microsoft Excel or Microsoft Access data sources. If you wish to use these capabilities with an Excel or Access data source, extract the data source (as described later in this chapter), as these set capabilities are available with Tableau Data Extracts.*

Saving and Sharing Metadata

So far, this chapter has discussed myriad ways of modifying the "view" of your data source (the metadata). When you save the workbook, this metadata is saved within it—the next time you open the workbook, the Data window will appear just as it was when the workbook was saved. However, once you've expended a fair amount of effort customizing this metadata, you very probably would like to save it for use with new workbooks you create in the future. In fact, if more than one person in your organization uses Tableau, you may want to share it with them as well. Enter the *Tableau Data Source File.*

Combined Sets

If you remember math class from your grade school years, you may remember the teacher drawing intersecting circles on the whiteboard while conducting a discussion of sets. That knowledge may come in handy as you work with Tableau, as Tableau allows creation of combined sets. A *combined set* is a set that uses two existing sets to create some combination of members from both sets. Perhaps you wish to analyze customers that order high dollar amount products, but that also are responsible for significant returns. If you have created two distinct sets for each of these customer categories, you may combine them for more thorough analysis.

To create a combined set, CTRL-click the two existing sets in the Data window. Right-click and choose Create Combined Set from the context menu. The Create Set dialog box will appear, but with a different organization than previously illustrated. Give the combined set a meaningful name, and then choose the intersection of the two original sets that you wish the combined set to return (the four icons will take you back to those school days). Click OK when finished. A new combined set will appear in the Sets area of the Data Window that you may drag and drop onto your visualization.

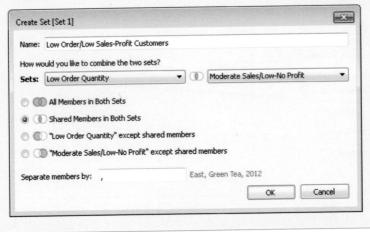

A Tableau Data Source File is a separate file saved on your hard disk with a .tds extension. This .tds file contains the "view," or metadata, you have created, including renamed fields, hierarchies, groups, and sets. The original data source file, or database, that the .tds file is based on remains unchanged in its original location. You may then connect to the .tds file in the future to reconnect to the original data source or database it references, but with your customized view of the data.

To save a .tds file, right-click the data source name at the top of the Data window and choose Add To Saved Data Sources from the context menu. You may also use the Data | <data source name> | Add To Saved Data Sources drop-down menu option.

A standard Windows Save As dialog box will appear, prompting you for a filename. Notice the default .tds extension. By default, the directory will be My Tableau Repository within your personal Windows folder.

Tableau Data Source Files placed in My Repository will automatically appear on the Tableau home screen from that point forward. However, since others in your organization will be using their own personal repository folders, you may choose to save the .tds file in another shared location, such as a shared network drive. In that instance, you (and others in your organization who want to use the shared .tds files) will need to use the File | Open drop-down menu option in Tableau to open .tds files not in their repositories.

If your organization has access to Tableau Server, you may also save .tds files there for sharing among your other Tableau users. Right-click the data source name at the top of the Data window, or use the Data pull-down menu option, and select Publish To Server. You'll be prompted to log on to Tableau Server. Supply necessary logon credentials and click OK. The Publish Data Source To Tableau Server dialog box will appear. Choose the desired project, name, and other values, and click OK to publish the .tds file to the server. Anyone who has access to Tableau Server may now use the custom data source by selecting Tableau Server in the "On a server" category of the Connect To Data screen, just as they would select another data source.

Extracting Data

If you use standard corporate databases, such as Microsoft SQL Server or Oracle, you may find situations where it's inconvenient (or impossible) to perform data analysis. The first possible issue may be poor performance. If the database is very large or has not been fully optimized by the database designer, real-time analysis with Tableau may be difficult. Or, you may wish to continue to work with a centralized database when you're away from your office (perhaps, on an airplane) and connection to the database simply isn't possible. And, you may encounter a situation when using something other than a desktop database (Microsoft Excel, Access, or a text file) when you attempt to save a Tableau Packaged Workbook (a .twbx file). Because a packaged workbook incorporates all the workbook's underlying data sources, you'll receive an error message when you attempt to save it if you're using other than a desktop data source.

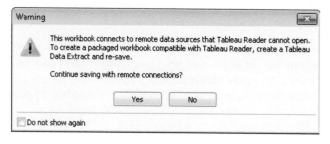

These are the types of situations that call for a Data Extract. A *Data Extract* is a Tableau-proprietary file that contains the imported contents of another database or data source. A Tableau Data Extract file (you'll notice the .tde file extension) consists of a very compact, high-speed data file that Tableau attempts to store in your computer's memory. As such, analysis with an extract is typically very, very fast. Also, an extract can be stored in a stand-alone packaged workbook for distribution to users of Tableau Reader or other Tableau designers who may not have access to the underlying source database.

Note *Some data sources, such as Salesforce.com and Google Analytics, will create extracts automatically when they are first accessed. This is because these web-based data sources may perform slowly if interacted with natively. Also, frequent web-based data source interactivity may exceed service limits placed on users by the data source vendor.*

Your first opportunity to create an extract is when you initially connect to most data sources. Once you specify any necessary data source properties, you're presented with a dialog box prompting you to either choose a live data connection or create an extract. If you wish to create an extract here, you may select Import All Data to create a complete extract of every field and row in the underlying data source, or select Import Some Data to display the Create Extract dialog box, where you can narrow down your extract to a limited set of data from the underlying data source.

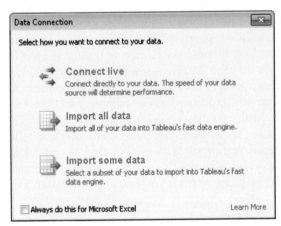

To create an extract from an existing data source in your workbook, right-click the desired data source in the top portion of the Data window and choose Extract Data from the context menu. You may also use Data | *<data source name>* | Extract Data from the Tableau drop-down menu. The Extract Data dialog box appears.

To simply extract all data from your underlying data source, just click OK. But, if you want to narrow down the extract to only include a subset of the original data source's data, select various options in this dialog box:

- To narrow down your extract to a limited set of data (perhaps only for the past year or only for your region), add one or more filters. Filters are specified identically here as they are in Tableau when dragging a field to the Filters shelf.

- If you check the "Aggregate data for visible dimensions" box, Tableau will summarize (or "roll up") the underlying data source based on the dimensions that have not been hidden. This will reduce the size of the resulting extract file. You may also choose to roll up dates. If you choose this option, select the level of date detail you wish to retain in the extract. For example, if you select Month, the underlying data source will be summarized ("rolled up") to the month level. Using the extract from that point will allow you to display dates at the month, quarter, or year level, but not the week or day level.

- You may choose to extract all rows from the underlying data source (any filters or roll-ups you specify will still be applied) or select an incremental extract. Checking Incremental Refresh will permit the extract to be updated at a later time with only new data that's been added to the underlying data source. For large extracts, this may significantly speed up extract updates in the future. Select either a date dimension or unique ID/key in the underlying data source to base the incremental refresh on. The next time you refresh the extract from the Data Source context menu or Data drop-down menu, only rows that contain a date or key later than that of the last refresh will be imported.

- If you select the Top radio button, you may further narrow down to a number or percent of rows from the underlying data source. This type of extract may be helpful when you wish to use a limited set of data from the underlying data source for "on the road" or initial development, with the expectation that you will eventually return to the full underlying data source for production analysis.

Once you've completed the dialog box, click OK to create the extract. You'll be prompted for a location to save the Tableau Data Extract (.tde) file. Specify the location and filename and click Save. The extract file will be created and any worksheets in the current workbook using the original underlying data source will be converted to use the extract (you'll notice a checkmark next to Use Extract on the data connection's context menu or the Data drop-down menu).

One of the initial concerns you may have about using an extract is the "disconnection" from the underlying data source, particularly in terms of currency of data. For example, if the initial data source is a transactional database that is updated frequently, you may be concerned that you will now be analyzing on an extract that's out of date. Tableau provides a simple way to *refresh* extracts from the underlying data source to update the extract with new data. A full refresh will read all data from the underlying data source again with filters and rolls-ups applied. While this assures that your extract will fully match the underlying data source, a full refresh can be time consuming. An incremental refresh (discussed previously) will only import new records from the underlying data source into the extract. To perform either kind of refresh, just right-click the data source at the top of the Data window, or select Data | *<data source name>* from the drop-down menus, followed by Extract | Refresh. If you initially chose to import all rows when the extract was first specified, a full refresh will occur. If you selected an incremental refresh when the extract was first specified, you'll notice the word "Incremental" will be appended to the Refresh menu option and an incremental refresh will occur. If you wish to change an extract refresh from an incremental to a full, or vice versa, simply perform a new extract using the original menu option described earlier. Changes to the All Rows/Incremental refresh options will be applied to future refreshes.

Tip *If you are using Tableau Server, you are able to store extracts on the server and schedule automatic refreshes at regular intervals. This powerful feature can often bridge the gap between currency of data and speed of analysis that extracts sometimes present.*

Once you have extracted data, several menu options are enabled to help you maintain extracts and switch between the original data source and the extract. Right-click the data source at the top of the Data window (which will now exhibit a two-barrels-with-arrow icon, indicating that an extract is active), or choose Data | *<data source name>* from the drop-down menu. The first option is to return to the underlying data source by unchecking Use Extract. You may easily return to the previously generated extract by selecting this option again. When an extract is being used, the Extract sub-menu provides additional options:

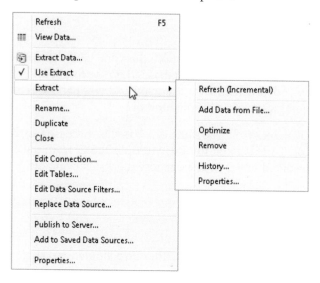

- **Add Data From File**   You may add data to an existing extract from an external desktop-type file (Excel, Microsoft Access, text, comma-separated values), as well as other existing extract files. The columns in the external file must match those in the extract.

- **Optimize**   If you have created any new calculated fields since an extract was created, this option will evaluate the results of the calculations and write them to the extract file. This may improve performance with large extracts, as calculated fields won't have to be reevaluated "on the fly."

- **Remove**   You may remove the extract and return to the underlying data source. When you choose this option, you'll be provided an additional option to delete or retain the .tde extract file.

- **History**   Displays a dialog box indicating dates the extract has been refreshed.

- **Properties**   Displays a dialog box providing overall information about the extract, including location of the extract file, filters used, and so forth.

Caution *When you initially create an extract based on an existing data source in a workbook, Tableau will maintain the relationship between the original data source and the extract in that workbook. This will permit you to uncheck the Use Extract option to use the original data source, refresh the extract from the underlying data source, and so forth. However, if you create a new workbook based only on the resulting .tde file, the relationship to the original data source won't be available. You will be unable to switch back and forth between the original data source and the extract, refresh the extract, and so forth.*

Data Blending

 Video *Data Blending*

It's not uncommon to require data from more than one table within a database/data source, or maybe even more than one database/data source, in a Tableau workbook. Depending on how your workbook is organized and what analysis requirements you have, there are several ways of accomplishing this:

- Join multiple tables from the same database, as discussed earlier in the chapter in the section "Adding and Joining Multiple Tables from the Same Database" and use the joined tables in one or more worksheets in your workbook.

- Create several worksheets, each using various data sources (including joined tables), and combine the worksheets on a dashboard. The dashboard can provide links between the worksheets via filters and so forth (creating dashboards is covered in Chapter 8).

- Tie more than one data source together on a single worksheet using data blending. This is what this section of the chapter will cover.

In traditional relational database analysis, joining tables from the *same* database is a common practice. However, when data needs to be combined from *different* databases, complications often arise. As most database vendors don't provide easy methods of combining data from other vendors (if they provide it at all), this task is often left to the analysis tool itself. Tableau's approach to this predicament is called *data blending*. Data blending provides a way to combine data from more than one data source on a single worksheet. In short, Tableau connects to multiple data sources, sends independent queries to those data sources, and then combines (or "blends") the aggregated results of the independent queries on a single worksheet.

Note *It's important to keep the "independent queries/aggregated results blended" paradigm in mind when considering whether data blending will work in your environment. Remember that data blending is not the same as a table join, or the same as more common single-database combining techniques, such as unions. The key to blending is identifying a common dimension in both data sources that can be aggregated to.*

Despite the somewhat-complex concepts of data blending, it's very easy to implement. Consider a fairly common requirement where existing transactional or sales data is contained in one database and goal data is contained in another. For this example, transactional data is contained in the "Sample - Superstore - English (Extract)" file that is included with Tableau 8. Because Sales Goal data is absent from this file, a text file has been created that contains goal data. In order to calculate the difference between actual and goal and display actual and goal side by side on the same worksheet, data blending must be used.

Consider the chart illustrated in Figure 3-1. This chart, based on the "transactional data" extract, is based on a single data source. This data source is considered the *primary* data source, as it was the first data source used to generate the worksheet. This is confirmed by the small blue checkmark that is displayed on the data source name at the top of the Data window. However, notice that another data source also exists in the workbook. This other connection is used by another worksheet.

Since more than one data connection can exist in a workbook, yet another connection will need to be made to the text file containing the goals. Simply add a new data connection using already covered approaches. Once the new connection is added, you may view its underlying data to see that goal records exist for each matching region. However, since a primary data source has already been used for the existing worksheet, notice the orange line that appears in the Data window when the second

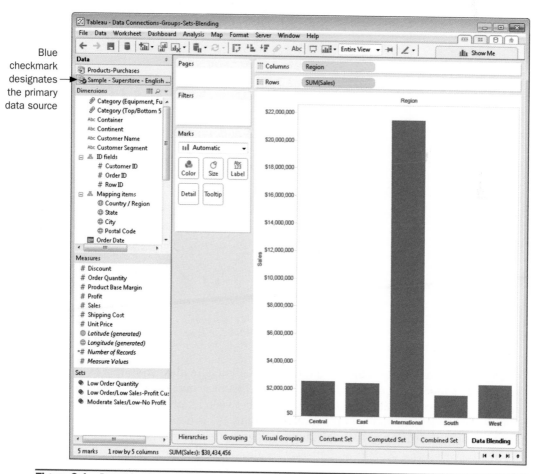

Figure 3-1 Data blending candidate

data source is selected. This indicates that this data source will become a *secondary* data source—primary and secondary data sources will be connected via data blending.

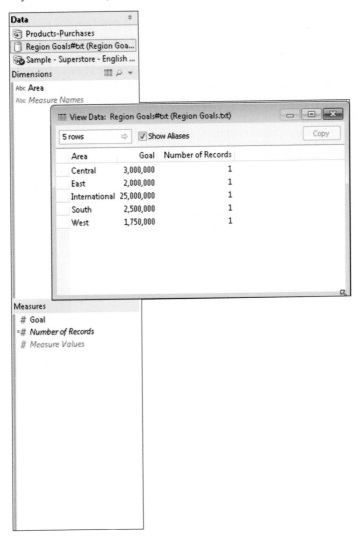

One other consideration that may not be immediately evident from this example is the lack of an identically named dimension in the primary and secondary data sources (Tableau will automatically create a relationship between identically named fields). Specifically, the aggregated field illustrated in Figure 3-1 is named "Region," while the matching field appearing in the secondary data source is named "Area." If you simply try to drag a measure from the secondary data source onto the existing chart based on the primary data source, this lack of matching dimensions results in an error. Even though the measure will appear on the chart, it is not properly aggregated to match up to the primary field.

There are two ways to solve this problem. Probably the simplest is to merely rename the field in either data source to match that of the other. After right-clicking the Area dimension in the secondary data source, choosing Rename from the pop-up menu, and renaming the field to Region, examine the Data window. Note the orange link icon next to the field. This indicates that a matching dimension exists in the primary data source and that this field will be used as the common field between the data sources.

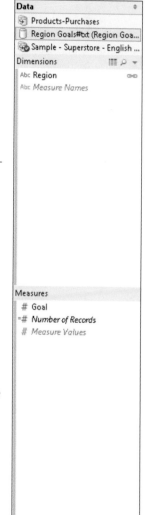

Tip *If multiple link icons appear in the secondary data source, more than one field name matches in the two data sources. "Broken" link icons indicate data blending candidate dimensions. Determine which dimension you wish to use to blend and click it. The icon will change to a "closed" link and that dimension will be used to match to the other data source.*

If, for some reason, you prefer not to rename a dimension in one data source to match the other, you may specifically tie the two dimensions together by choosing Data | Edit Relationships from the drop-down menus. This will display the Relationships dialog box. First, ensure that the proper primary data source is displayed in the first drop-down list. Then, choose the desired secondary data source in the list to the left. If Tableau has performed any automatic by-field-name matches, you'll see them when the Automatic radio button is selected. If Tableau has not been able to do a proper match, click the Custom radio button, followed by the Add button at the bottom of the dialog box. The Add/Edit Field Mapping dialog will appear.

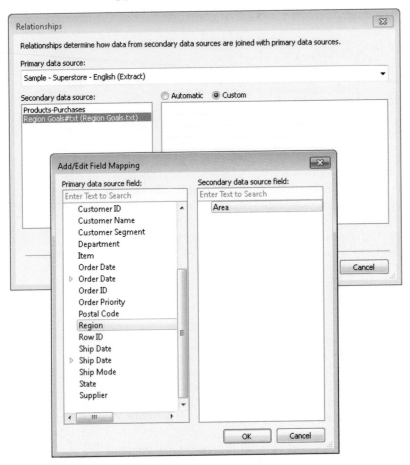

Select the desired dimensions to match in the left and right lists. Click OK to add the relationship. If you need to add relationships because more fields need to be matched, click Add however many times you need and choose additional sets of matched dimensions. When you have specified all matching dimensions, click OK to close the Relationships dialog box. The Data window will return with the orange link icon appearing on the selected dimension.

Once you have successfully matched the primary and secondary data sources, simply drag measures from the secondary data source onto the existing visualization. The data from both data sources will be blended, with all dimension members from the primary data source appearing on the chart, and matching members from the secondary data source appearing on the chart (data blending performs the equivalent of a left outer join—any members from the secondary data source that don't exist in the primary won't appear on the chart). You may also create calculated fields using fields from both data sources. Figure 3-2 shows the resulting chart.

Tip *Not only can you resolve data blending dimension name mismatches by just renaming a field in the Data Window, but you can resolve dimension member mismatches by editing a member's alias. For example, if you are blending on state and one data source returns Colorado, while the other returns CO, just right-click the incorrect member name in the worksheet header and choose Edit Alias from the context menu. Change the member name to match the other data source. The two data sources will then properly blend.*

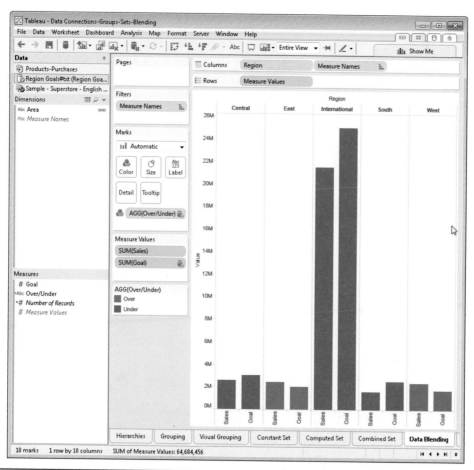

Figure 3-2 Completed data blending chart

Moving from Test to Production Databases

It's not uncommon to initially develop a workbook using one data source and then eventually need to migrate that workbook to another similar data source. A very common example of this is developing against a test database and then migrating the workbook to a production database. In some cases, these databases may be on similar database platforms. But, in others, the test database may be a desktop system, such as Microsoft Access, with the production database being SQL Server. Regardless of the underlying types of data sources, Tableau makes it easy to migrate a workbook from one data source to another.

Consider this Data window, based on a Microsoft Access "test" database. In particular, it's significant to note that the current worksheet is using the Country dimension and Order Amount measure.

For this example, assume that a "production" database exists on SQL Server. The first requirement is to connect to the SQL Server as you would any other data connection. Add and join any necessary tables. When complete, the SQL Server data source will appear in the Data window. Then, right-click either of the data sources at the top of the Data window, or choose the Data drop-down menu and select Replace Data Source.

The Replace Data Source dialog box will appear, showing drop-down lists where you may choose the existing (test) data source and the data source you wish to replace it with (production). Choose the desired data sources and click OK.

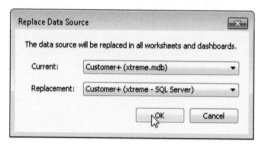

All worksheets in your workbook that were using the original test data source will now be directed to the new production data source. Provided all field names in the new data source match the original data source, all worksheets will immediately reflect the new data source. However, if field names aren't identical, portions of your visualization may be dimmed and an "invalid" icon (an exclamation point) may appear on any fields that aren't found in the new data source.

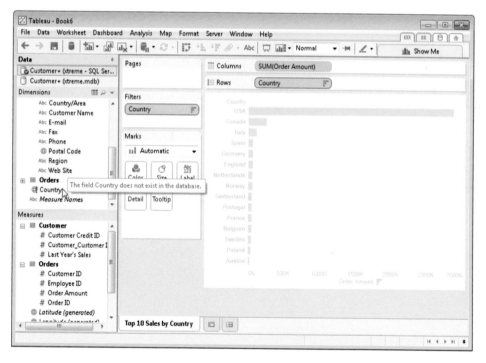

Resolving these field name mismatches is a straightforward process. Right-click the "invalid" field in the Data window and choose Replace Reference in the context menu. The Replace Reference dialog box will appear, prompting you to replace all references to the now-invalid field with the field chosen in the new list of fields. Just select the proper field in the new data source and click OK. Any worksheet using the invalid field will now refer to the new field from the new data source. You may now right-click the invalid field and choose Delete from the context menu to delete it from the Data window.

Top 10 Chart Types

Tableau can create many different chart types. While Show Me (covered in Chapter 2) provides a number of charts you can create very quickly, it's hardly the limit of Tableau's capabilities. Still, there are ten chart types that you'll probably use more than others, if you are performing standard visualization and analytical activities. Some of the charts discussed in this chapter can be created very quickly with Show Me. However, in order to provide fuller knowledge of Tableau, manual steps to create each chart are covered here.

Note *Open the Chapter 4 - Top 10 Chart Types.twbx file in Tableau to see examples that relate to this chapter.*

Bar Chart

Despite all the visualization possibilities, and the plethora of tools to create charts and graphs, the basic *bar chart* is still probably used more than any other type. This is very useful for comparing many different types of measures, including dollars, quantities, number of phone calls, web page hits, and so forth.

In many cases, leaving the mark type on the Marks card set to Automatic will result in a bar chart (charts based on date/time dimensions being a notable exception). Just drag your desired dimension to the Columns shelf and desired measure to the Rows shelf to create a vertical bar chart (you may also double-click a measure first, then double-click a non-date/time dimension for the same results). If you want to change another chart type to bar (for example, if the default line chart for a date/time dimension isn't what you want), select Bar in the Mark Type drop-down on the Marks card.

Tip *While you can re-drag dimensions and measures to different shelves to change from a horizontal to vertical bar chart, try using the Swap button in the toolbar instead.*

You can enhance a basic bar chart using any number of Tableau features. To create a stacked bar chart, where each bar is broken down by portions of another dimension, drag the second dimension to Color on the Marks card (this is illustrated in Figure 4-1).

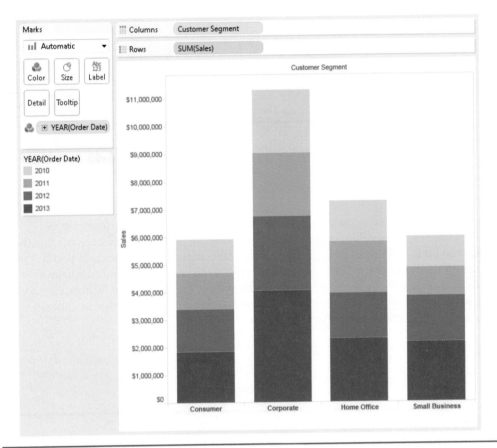

Figure 4-1   Stacked bar chart

Or you can create a graduated-color bar chart, where each bar is shaded with a variation of a color range based on a different measure. Drag the desired measure to Color on the Marks card. You can even create some interesting variations of a bar chart by utilizing both Color and Size on the Marks card, as well as unstacking bars by choosing Analysis | Stack Marks | Off from the drop-down menu. This results in two bars appearing on top of each other, but with different size and color.

Best Practice *If you are charting a single dimension, you may be tempted to add the same dimension the chart is based on to Color on the Marks card to assign each bar a different color. Reconsider this. The different colors may not benefit, and may actually confuse, your audience. Which is a more effective, less confusing visualization?*

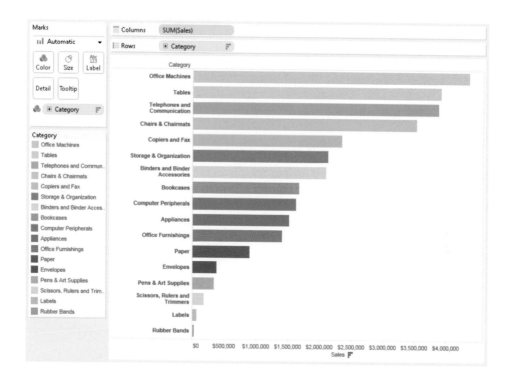

Line/Area Chart

Another popular chart, the *line chart*, shows a trend over time. For example, sales plotted for the past 12 months or number of web hits by time of day benefit from a line chart. If you initially add a date or date/time dimension to the Rows or Columns shelf, and a measure to the other shelf, a line chart trending the measure over time will result. (Though a line chart will be created either way, vertical line charts based on a dimension on the Rows shelf may be of limited use.)

As with other chart types, a basic line chart can expand with placements on Color on the Marks card. If you place another dimension on Color, a different colored line will appear for each member of the dimension. Alternatively, if you add a different measure to Color, the existing line will take on a graduated color indicating the variation of the measure placed on Color. While you can also place measures or dimensions on Size on the Marks card, you may find the results to be more confusing than useful with a line chart.

Best Practice *It's easy to convert a chart initially created as bar to line or area. Just choose Line or Area from the drop-down on the Marks card. This is helpful if you have a dimension that Tableau doesn't automatically determine to be a date/time dimension, but that still can be used to show a trend.*

A variation on the line chart is the *area chart*. Like a line chart, an area chart is best used to trend data over time. However, rather than just showing a single line to represent the path of the trend, the area chart fills in the entire portion of the chart from the bottom of the chart with a shaded color. This often results in a "mountain range" look. Simply select Area from the drop-down on the Marks card to create an area chart.

Like line charts, area charts can be enhanced by dragging a dimension to Color on the Marks card (using a measure on Color will have no usable benefit). This will create a stacked area chart with each member of the dimension placed on Color creating a separate colored stacked area (this is illustrated in Figure 4-2).

A variation of an area chart is an unstacked area chart. Create this by dragging a desired dimension (with a minimal number of members) to Color on the Marks card. Initially you'll see a stacked area chart. Then select Analysis | Stack Marks | Off from the drop-down menu. The areas that were previously stacked will now overlap each

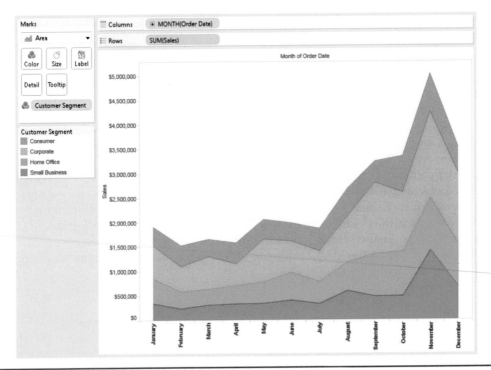

Figure 4-2 Stacked area chart

other, and Tableau will change the colors to make them easier to distinguish. This may not always be desirable. Even though Tableau displays the color dimension with transparency, it's still easy to miss certain valleys in the "mountain range" if other peaks occlude them.

Tableau 8 Forecasting

 **Video** *Forecasting*

Tableau 8 introduces *forecasting*, the ability to examine data and trends in existing date- or date/time-based data and forecast what trend may occur in the future. The first requirement to forecast in Tableau 8 is to create a chart based on a date or date/time dimension. If you choose to change the default discrete Year date level of the dimension, you must choose a continuous date level—discrete date levels other than Year won't permit forecasting.

Once your initial chart is displayed, you can forecast by using the Analysis | Forecast | Show Forecast drop-down menu option. Or you can just right-click on the visualization and choose Forecast | Show Forecast from the context menu. Tableau will look at the existing time-based data and forecast future trends based on it. The chart will be extended to show the forecast data, and a forecast icon (a slanted up arrow) will be added to the forecast measure's field indicator. Also, a forecast indicator will be placed on Color on the Marks card to distinguish existing data from forecast data.

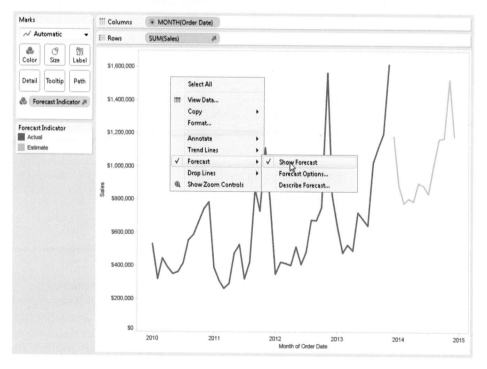

You can also use two other options from the Analysis | Forecast drop-down or Forecast right-click menus to customize or document the forecast. Forecast Options will display the Forecast Options dialog box, where you can change the duration of the forecast, change the date level granularity used for aggregation, choose to ignore a specified number of periods at the end of the actual data range, elect whether or not to fill missing values with zeroes, and choose from a variety of forecasting models. Describe Forecast will display a dialog box exposing details about the way the forecast was calculated via both Summary and Models tabs.

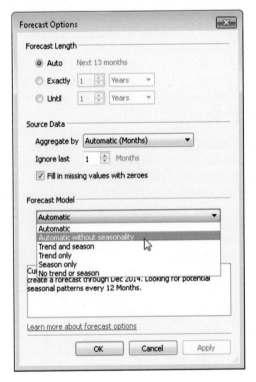

Note *Although line or area charts are typically used to trend data over time, forecasting will work equally well with other chart types based on date or date/time dimensions, such as a bar chart showing sales by year.*

Pie Chart

Although some authorities in visual design decry them (preferring, for example, stacked bar charts), *pie charts* remain a fixture of the visualization world. They are used to show a single measure for a smaller number of dimension members (probably not more than six or eight), illustrating what "piece of the pie" each member has. Tableau provides the ability to populate a worksheet with a single pie chart, with multiple pie charts organized for different combinations of dimensions or measures, and even as a chosen mark type for other types of visualizations, such as maps.

To create a pie chart worksheet, choose Pie from the drop-down on the Marks card. Then drag the measure you want the pie to represent onto Angle on the Marks card (Angle will only appear after you choose a Pie mark type). Finally, drag the dimension that you want to use to create pie wedges to Color on the Marks card (again, the dimension should have no more than six to eight members to not create too many pie wedges).

Tip *To add a percentage label to each pie wedge, drag the same measure used on Angle on the Marks card to Label on the Marks card. Then choose Analysis | Percentage of Cell or Analysis | Percentage of Table from the drop-down menu. Tableau allows multiple items to be included on mark labels. For example, you can also drag the dimension used to set pie colors onto Label on the Marks card along with the measure to show both the percentage and dimension at the same time.*

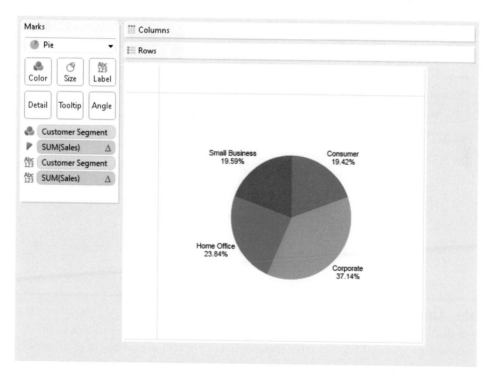

Multiple pie charts can be created by just dragging a dimension you'd like to subdivide by onto the Rows or Columns shelf. Be careful, as subdivided pies can quickly become difficult to interpret. Consider stacked bar charts or other easier-to-interpret chart types if you find that subdivided pie charts are difficult to understand.

Tableau also features the ability to choose the Pie mark type on other visualizations. One example is using a pie on a map. A Pie mark type can add context to a map that would otherwise just show a single circle for a state or country. After creating the map, change the Automatic mark type to Pie from the drop-down on the Marks card. Then drag a dimension onto Color on the Marks card to subdivide into pie wedges (the fewer dimension members, the better). The result will be individual pie charts on each country, state, or other geographic dimension used to create the map.

Tip *Placing another measure on Size may enhance the effectiveness of Pie mark types, especially when used on maps.*

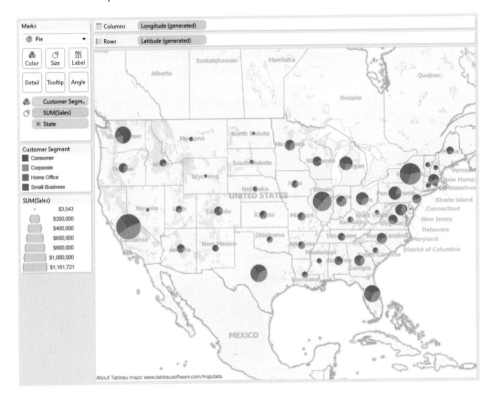

Text Table/Crosstab

One of the original applications that made personal computers popular was the spreadsheet program. Decades later, spreadsheets are still used widely in all aspects of virtually every type of organization. Even after the introduction of leading-edge visualization tools such as Tableau, numbers organized in rows and columns are still often used when analyzing data. For these requirements, Tableau provides the *text table* or *crosstab* (with the term *crosstab* being used for the remainder of this chapter).

Like a spreadsheet, Tableau displays rows and columns of numbers, with one or more dimensions appearing on the Rows and Columns shelves, and one or more measures appearing on Text on the Marks card. In fact, a crosstab is created automatically using Tableau's default double-click behavior if one or more dimensions are initially double-clicked and a subsequent measure is double-clicked. You can also drag dimensions to the Rows and Columns shelves, and then drag a measure to Text on the Marks card. If you include more than one dimension on the Rows or Columns shelf, a hierarchy of "panes" will be created showing the second dimension organization within the first dimension (make sure the dimensions have a logical hierarchical relationship if you do this).

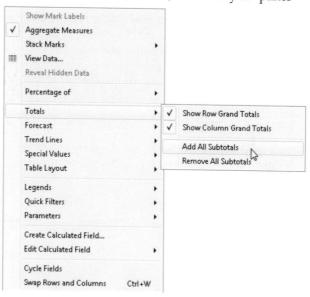

In the case of a crosstab based on more than one dimension on a shelf, you may want to show subtotals on the crosstab at the end of each outer dimension. Even if you don't use multiple dimensions, you may want to see grand totals for rows or columns in the crosstab. Options from the Analysis | Totals drop-down menu will add these totals.

Note *The Totals options from the Analysis menu, while probably most appropriate for crosstabs, can be used with any visualization type. Just be careful if you use totals beyond crosstabs. For example, a total bar at the end of a bar chart may introduce confusion when trying to compare individual value bars while a total bar appears in the same chart.*

By default, a crosstab will display measures on the Text shelf in black. As with spreadsheet programs, certain numbers may need to stand out based on their value. Tableau facilitates this by allowing another measure or dimension to be placed on Color on the Marks card. If a measure is placed on Color, the range of measure values will create a color range that will automatically color-code cells in the crosstab (typically a graduated color palette will result). A dimension (or perhaps a calculated field that returns only two values) can also be placed on Color to create a more stark "this color or this color" coding for the crosstab.

As discussed earlier, the numbers-in-rows-and-columns spreadsheet metaphor is still popular. A request to "just see the numbers" when viewing a non-crosstab visualization can be easily resolved by right-clicking on the worksheet tab. Simply choose Duplicate As Crosstab from the context menu. A new sheet will be created containing a crosstab representation of the dimension/measure organization from the original worksheet. Any worksheet (whether it contains a crosstab or not) can be copied to the Windows clipboard as a crosstab of numbers in rows and columns for pasting into another application.

Using More than One Measure

While a simple crosstab may be perfectly useful when showing just one measure, comparing more than one number will often be a requirement. Tableau versions prior to 8 required invocation of Measure Names and Measure Values to include two measures in a crosstab. With the new organization of the Marks card in Tableau 8, however, you may prefer to drag additional measures to Text on the Marks card to include multiple measures in the crosstab.

Though dragging multiple measures to Text is a quick, simple way to include multiple measures in a crosstab, it will not automatically add labels to the crosstab to distinguish one measure from another. You may want to create a calculated field that returns text values to label measures you've added to Text. For example:

```
"Sales" + CHAR(10) + "Profit"
```

will return the word Sales, followed by a carriage return, followed by the word Profit. This calculated field can be placed on a shelf to add labels for a multiple-measure crosstab.

Department	Category	Sales/Profit Label	Consumer	Corporate	Home Office	Small Business
Furniture	Bookcases	Sales	$350,559	$692,337	$342,327	$289,556
		Profit	$64,654	$90,691	($31,115)	$20,219
	Chairs & Chairmats	Sales	$730,091	$1,272,000	$877,018	$652,081
		Profit	$143,573	$212,755	$217,400	$138,641
	Office Furnishings	Sales	$247,356	$461,574	$453,504	$240,632
		Profit	$63,067	$103,960	$126,340	$62,154
	Tables	Sales	$629,960	$1,396,208	$959,447	$742,336
		Profit	$14,881	$57,791	$12,253	$83,871
Office Supplies	Appliances	Sales	$240,387	$621,219	$345,988	$312,453
		Profit	$71,392	$210,469	$105,907	$105,659
	Binders and Binder Accessories	Sales	$328,918	$845,522	$484,810	$458,253
		Profit	$132,929	$363,811	$148,916	$203,725
	Envelopes	Sales	$67,448	$118,190	$75,362	$123,855
		Profit	$18,301	$43,594	$27,525	$50,012
	Labels	Sales	$12,111	$28,200	$15,091	$18,887
		Profit	$5,902	$16,888	$10,033	$9,087
	Paper	Sales	$167,538	$331,041	$213,301	$182,156
		Profit	$43,116	$81,655	$46,238	$46,844
	Pens & Art Supplies	Sales	$72,027	$121,015	$73,753	$71,430
		Profit	$4,654	$17,603	$7,961	$10,784
	Rubber Bands	Sales	$5,637	$10,000	$9,219	$7,392
		Profit	($451)	$1,381	$773	($846)
	Scissors, Rulers and Trimmers	Sales	$72,772	$40,391	$59,145	$10,316
		Profit	($113)	($1,193)	$1,002	($2,010)
	Storage & Organization	Sales	$429,847	$656,613	$593,065	$447,016
		Profit	$44,178	$75,250	$55,055	$54,984
Technology	Computer Peripherals	Sales	$250,521	$647,487	$417,796	$315,455
		Profit	$52,110	$135,834	$68,373	$86,845
	Copiers and Fax	Sales	$498,546	$753,716	$540,046	$557,497
		Profit	$87,140	$159,435	$111,018	$209,316
	Office Machines	Sales	$935,642	$1,776,157	$871,260	$797,106
		Profit	$127,874	$522,309	$217,293	$267,434
	Telephones and Communication	Sales	$671,210	$1,533,196	$945,014	$736,452
		Profit	$190,283	$497,813	$316,392	$255,864

By default, Tableau 8 will still use Measure Names and Measure Values to create a multiple-measure crosstab as previous versions did. The easiest way to use this method is to simply double-click on additional measures. Tableau's default double-click behavior will add Measure Names and Measure Values to appropriate places on the worksheet and include the additional measures you click. In this case, Measure Names will be placed on the Rows or Columns shelf, which will automatically label measures in the crosstab.

Just right-click on a measure or mark in the visualization and choose Copy | Crosstab from the context menu. The resulting crosstab on the clipboard can be pasted into another application as a row-and-column-with-numbers matrix.

Product Category	Product Sub-	Sales/Profit	Label	Customer Se Consumer	Customer Se Corporate	Customer Se Home Office	Customer Segment Small Business
Furniture	Bookcases	Sales Profit	Profit	-32	-9,145	-16,391	-7,602
Furniture	Bookcases	Sales Profit	Sales	184,348	292,854	194,718	150,062
Furniture	Chairs & Cha	Sales Profit	Profit	44,300	38,325	41,663	25,650
Furniture	Chairs & Cha	Sales Profit	Sales	373,903	660,781	403,420	306,040
Furniture	Office Furnis	Sales Profit	Profit	12,311	27,579	41,987	15,002
Furniture	Office Furnis	Sales Profit	Sales	113,940	226,389	219,624	105,959
Furniture	Tables	Sales Profit	Profit	-1,672	-31,589	-20,836	-7,175
Furniture	Tables	Sales Profit	Sales	439,609	658,171	463,059	326,375
Office Suppli	Appliances	Sales Profit	Profit	15,501	50,961	25,343	6,218
Office Suppli	Appliances	Sales Profit	Sales	112,337	306,807	187,463	140,726
Office Suppli	Binders and I	Sales Profit	Profit	47,850	125,757	71,674	61,893
Office Suppli	Binders and I	Sales Profit	Sales	167,218	405,003	255,582	196,719
Office Suppli	Envelopes	Sales Profit	Profit	7,260	15,083	10,848	15,520
Office Suppli	Envelopes	Sales Profit	Sales	30,692	57,963	35,613	52,030
Office Suppli	Labels	Sales Profit	Profit	1,359	5,609	3,076	3,645
Office Suppli	Labels	Sales Profit	Sales	6,215	15,152	7,806	9,869
Office Suppli	Paper	Sales Profit	Profit	9,032	10,539	12,105	14,311
Office Suppli	Paper	Sales Profit	Sales	85,450	154,710	113,350	95,986
Office Suppli	Pens & Art S	Sales Profit	Profit	2,563	1,717	1,581	1,692
Office Suppli	Pens & Art S	Sales Profit	Sales	37,098	61,203	33,383	35,841
Office Suppli	Rubber Band	Sales Profit	Profit	274	-354	-70	72
Office Suppli	Rubber Band	Sales Profit	Sales	3,054	4,759	4,087	3,339
Office Suppli	Scissors, Rule	Sales Profit	Profit	-558	-3,331	-2,844	-1,066
Office Suppli	Scissors, Rule	Sales Profit	Sales	29,405	23,110	23,643	4,838
Office Suppli	Storage & Or	Sales Profit	Profit	4,059	-2,988	-554	2,000
Office Suppli	Storage & Or	Sales Profit	Sales	236,919	336,052	303,651	223,153
Technology	Computer Pe	Sales Profit	Profit	14,153	45,339	17,771	17,271
Technology	Computer Pe	Sales Profit	Sales	123,514	320,480	202,771	149,789
Technology	Copiers and I	Sales Profit	Profit	41,310	28,654	29,283	68,113
Technology	Copiers and I	Sales Profit	Sales	233,017	364,176	248,344	284,825
Technology	Office Machi	Sales Profit	Profit	41,349	170,733	33,086	31,422
Technology	Office Machi	Sales Profit	Sales	538,623	891,427	409,378	331,914
Technology	Telephones	Sales Profit	Profit	49,781	120,597	86,789	59,785
Technology	Telephones	Sales Profit	Sales	348,268	721,989	458,870	360,186

Tip *Crosstabs are particularly useful for "just show me the numbers" types of user requests. Not only can you quickly "just show the numbers" when designing a workbook, crosstabs provide drill-down capabilities in dashboards. By adding a crosstab to a dashboard with filter actions, you can show related numbers when a user clicks on a particular dimension in another portion of the dashboard. Filter actions are covered in more detail in Chapter 8.*

Scatter Plot

Although more esoteric than many of the standard chart types discussed in this chapter so far, the *scatter plot* can provide very meaningful visualization of two related numeric measures. There are, generally speaking, two different analyses that scatter plots help consider: comparison/correlation of the two measures, and existence of outliers. In most cases, one or more related dimensions are also used in a scatter plot.

For example, a scatter plot may be ideal in looking for correlation between number of web ads placed and number of hits to your website, with further analysis on dimension data, such as where the web ad was placed, day the ad ran, or known demographics of the person who visited your website. Or your candidate may want to see if the number of outgoing phone calls asking for campaign contributions can be correlated to the number of contributors or the amount of contributions. Certain outliers, such as a few contributors who contributed large amounts, will stand out on a scatter plot, allowing for targeted analysis.

A particular scatter plot example that may be close to home if you've compared other business intelligence (BI) tools to Tableau is the BI Magic Quadrant issued by Gartner. This scatter plot evaluates BI vendors by two measures: completeness of vision and ability to execute. While not all scatter plots share the Magic Quadrant's "both farther to the right and farther up is better" approach, many scatter plots make analysis easy by automatically indicating preference to higher or lower areas on either or both axes.

A scatter plot in Tableau begins with numeric measures placed on both the Rows and Columns shelves. You can either drag them there individually or simply double-click on one measure after the other, with the first measure becoming the row and the second the column. Initially, this will simply place one mark (a blue open circle) on the scatter plot indicating where the aggregation of both measures appears. While this may be somewhat helpful for a very quick analysis of how the measures relate, you'll typically want to place additional dimensions "in play" to make the scatter plot more useful.

Tip *If you initially add measures to the wrong shelves, you can undo the addition or manually move them to the proper shelves. But you may find it faster to CTRL-click on both measure fields on the Rows and Columns shelves to select them. Then right-click and choose Swap from the context menu, or just click the toolbar Swap button.*

Dimensions (or other measures that help broaden scatter plot analysis) can be added to additional areas of the Marks card. For example, to simply add additional blue open circles for every member of a desired dimension, drag the dimension to Detail. While you can change the shape from the default open circle to another shape by choosing a different mark type from the Marks card drop-down, you may prefer to have different shapes appear for different members of a desired dimension. Just drag that dimension to Shape. You can have different colors appear for different dimension members or measure ranges by dragging the desired dimension or measure to Color. Marks can be sized by dragging a dimension or measure to Size. Figure 4-3 shows an example of the effects of these different Marks card options.

Since scatter plots display a mark for every combination of measure and dimension added to the worksheet, they can quickly become busy with different combinations of marks. In some cases, you may want to show an even denser series of marks if you choose to use a scatter plot to deduce broader generalizations, rather than correlations for a smaller number of marks. In that case, you may want to *disaggregate data*, which will retrieve individual values from the underlying data source, instead of aggregated sums, averages, and so forth (which Tableau provides by default). To disaggregate, uncheck Analysis | Aggregate Measures from the drop-down menu. You may need to

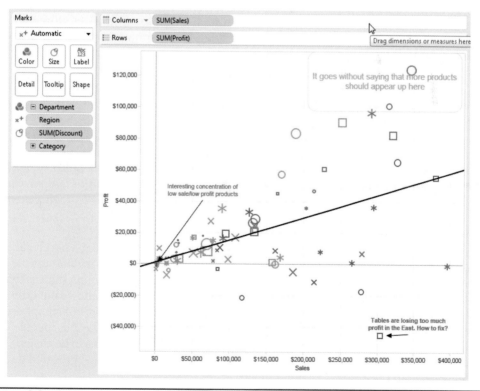

Figure 4-3   Scatter plot with Marks card features, trend line, and annotations

add filters (covered in detail in Chapter 5) to reduce the large number of marks that can result from disaggregation. Hovering your mouse over an individual mark on a disaggregated scatter plot may be of limited use, as no dimension information will appear for the individual mark. Drag desired dimensions to Detail or Tooltip on the Marks card to include that dimension on the tooltip that appears when you hover over a mark.

While not required, trend lines generally add interpretive value to a scatter plot. Just right-click on the visualization and choose Trend Lines from the context menu, or choose Analysis | Trend Lines | Show Trend Lines from the drop-down menus. If necessary, edit the default trend line (from the Analysis drop-down menu or right-click context menu) to change various trend line properties (trend lines are covered in more detail in Chapter 7).

And, while annotations are available for any visualization type, they come in particularly handy for scatter plots. Add annotations by right-clicking on the workspace and choosing Annotate from the context menu. A *mark* annotation will add text and an arrow pointing to a particular mark (unique combination of measures and dimensions) on the plot. If that particular mark later moves elsewhere on the scatter plot, or is eliminated via a filter, the associated annotation will either move or disappear. A *point* annotation will add text and an arrow pointing to a specific x/y coordinate on the scatter plot whether a mark appears there or not. As the scatter plots axes change with variations in data or filters, the annotation will follow the original x/y coordinate. An *area* annotation, like a point annotation, will add text to a particular x/y coordinate. However, rather than displaying an arrow, an area annotation will draw a rounded box containing the text. You can resize the box to set not only the originating x/y coordinate for the annotation, but the width and height of the annotation as well. Like a point annotation, the area annotation will move as the underlying data changes the dimensions of the scatter plot.

Best Practice *Effective scatter plots include either a small enough number of marks following a general trend to draw quick conclusions about the individual measures, or a large concentration of marks (perhaps due to disaggregation) to draw general conclusions.*

An effective variation of many Tableau chart types (scatter plots being a particularly good example) is commonly known as a *small multiples* visualization. Small multiples make use of one or more dimensions added to the Rows and/or Columns shelves that result in multiple scatter plots on one or more rows or columns. This allows not only individual conclusions to be drawn from individual scatter plot analysis, but comparisons to other dimension members with identical scatter plots. Best practice dictates that the individual scatter plots display either a small enough number of marks to be easily interpreted at first glance, or a large number of marks (perhaps via disaggregated data) to draw general conclusions at a quick glance.

Here, as in the previous example of a modified scatter plot, bubbles are sized based on sales and colored based on profit. It's fairly easy to compare sales and profit, noting categories that sell similarly (with similar-sized bubbles) but that are far different profit-wise (very different coloring).

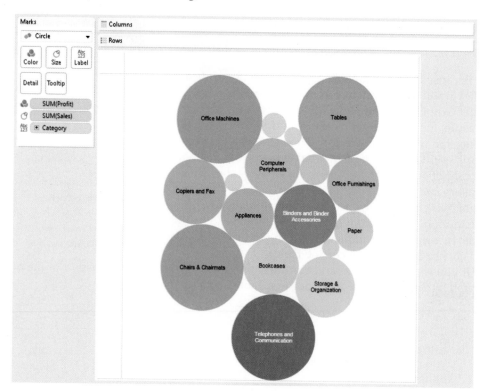

Bullet Graph

A common requirement in visualization is to compare two measures. Often, those two measures are an actual number and a target or goal. Depending on other elements of the comparison, a bar chart (sales versus quota by salesperson) or line chart (sales by month compared to monthly goal) may suffice. However, Tableau includes another option that provides an effective comparison method that takes up a minimal amount of space. The *bullet graph* was created by visualization author and lecturer Stephen Few to provide just such an "actual to target" visualization.

The basic portion of a bullet graph is a bar chart (typically, a horizontal bar chart), which denotes the actual or base measure for comparison. Each bar is then paired with a reference line, which denotes the goal or target. The compact combination of bars and reference lines not only allows a quick comparison of the actual values to each other, but a quick determination of how actual value bars compare to target reference lines.

The bullet graph even provides for good comparison of goals/targets by allowing, at a glance, analysis of relative positions of the reference lines. An optional portion of a bullet chart is a reference distribution, which shows a shaded area extending above and below the actual bar to indicate relative comparison of the actual measure to the goal or target.

Note *More detail on reference lines and reference distributions can be found in Chapter 7.*

Because there are several steps required to create a bullet graph from scratch, you may prefer to use the Bullet Graph option in Show Me. Simply select the actual measure, the goal/target measure, and the desired dimension in the data window. Then click the Bullet Graph option in the Show Me dialog box. Note that Show Me cannot automatically determine which is the actual measure and which is the goal/target, and may assign the target to the bar and the actual to the reference line/ distribution. Tableau provides a quick shortcut to fix this issue. Just right-click on the axis for the incorrect measure and choose Swap Reference Line Fields.

If you want to create a bullet graph from scratch, or modify some aspect of the one created by Show Me, make use of these Tableau features:

- The dimension used to create individual bars is placed on the Rows shelf (or Columns shelf, if you prefer to create a vertical bullet graph).

- The actual measure is placed on the Columns shelf (or Rows shelf, if you prefer to create a vertical bullet graph).

- The target/goal measure is placed on Detail on the Marks card (in order for reference lines/distributions to make use of the target/goal, it must be in use on the worksheet).

- A reference line is created from the right-click context menu of the worksheet's axis. Line is chosen, per cell, showing the average of the goal/target measure, with Label set to None, and a black bar color.

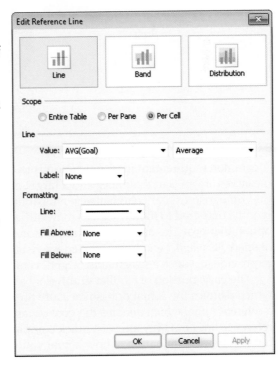

- If a "range of performance" distribution band is desired, another reference line can be created from the right-click context menu of the worksheet's axis. Distribution is chosen, per cell, showing 60%, 80% of the average of the goal/target measure, with Label set to None, and with Fill Above and Fill Below checked.

- If the distribution band is difficult to see, the size of the bar can be reduced by clicking Size on the Marks card and moving the slider to the midpoint.

- Optionally, another dimension or calculated field can be applied to Color on the Marks card to denote actual values that are above and below the goal/target.

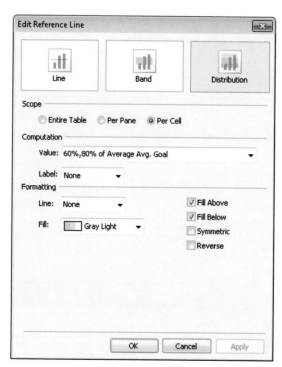

Where Are the Gauges?

If you're used to other BI toolsets, you may spend a fair amount of time looking around Tableau trying to find a gauge Show Me option or mark type. Search as you might, you won't find one. While some people may consider this a shortcoming of Tableau, the gauge is missing for a very good reason: it's generally not a visualization best practice. As Tableau works very hard to help you create meaningful visualizations as you design your worksheets and dashboards (the Automatic mark type being an example of this approach), other visualization types are available in Tableau as replacement for gauges. The bullet chart is an example.

Figure 4-4 shows a comparison of gauges and a bullet chart, with each visualization showing the same set of salespeople, their actual sales, and sales goals. Look closely and ask yourself the same questions a sales manager who was charged with evaluating his or her sales team would ask. Which is a more effective visualization of sales versus goals? Which salesperson is highest and lowest in sales? How close is each salesperson to goal? Which salesperson is over or under goal, and by how much? Which is a more efficient use of precious dashboard space? You'll probably find that bullet charts, and other available Tableau visualizations, will provide more effective analytics for your audience.

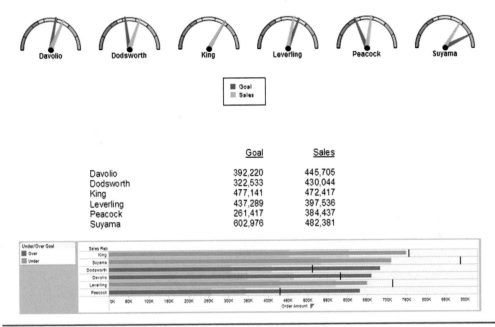

Figure 4-4   Gauges versus bullet chart

Box Plot

Although it may not be found as frequently as bar, line, and pie charts, the *box plot* is a very useful visualization when circumstances demand it. Introduced in the mid-1970s by the statistician John Tukey, the box plot excels at displaying the distribution of data over a range. You can easily determine where the heaviest concentration of data elements is in the range, and optionally, you can easily identify outliers. Although there are variations of a box plot, there are a few common elements in all cases:

- There are indicators of the maximum and minimum value in the range. The maximum and minimum, as well as all values in between, can be represented as individual marks or as a solid line connecting them.

- The "box" portion of the box plot consists of lines indicating the 75th percentile (or upper quartile), the 50th percentile (or median), and the 25th percentile (or lower quartile). The portion between the top and bottom lines is shaded, which indicates where 50 percent of the distribution is concentrated.

Because a box plot is not available in Show Me, you must manually create the individual portions of the visualization. Consider the basic box plot illustrated in Figure 4-5. While there are several ways you can create this in Tableau, the box plot illustrated in this figure was created with the following steps:

1. The dimension desired to "slice" the box plot (Customer Segment) was placed on Columns (it could have been placed on Rows if a horizontal box plot was desired).

2. The measure to evaluate (Profit) was placed on Rows. This resulted in the default Tableau bar chart with the measure aggregated.

3. In order to evaluate the profitability over a distribution of individual orders, data was disaggregated by unchecking Analysis | Aggregate Measures from the drop-down menu. The result was individual data source profit values plotted as large open circles.

4. The Line mark type was chosen from the drop-down on the Marks card. While this created the desired line connecting the minimum and maximum values for each customer segment, the lines between customer segments were connected. This connection was eliminated by copying the measure used on the Rows shelf (using CTRL-drag) to Path on the Marks card. This broke the connection between customer segments, resulting in a single line for each segment connecting the maximum profit to the minimum profit, and all values in between.

5. A reference line was added by right-clicking on the axis and choosing Add Reference Line from the context menu. Distribution was chosen, scope was set to Per Cell, Value was set to Quartiles with the default number 4 chosen (which created quartiles), Label was set to None, a solid line color was chosen, and Symmetric was checked to display the same fill shade throughout the different portions of the reference distribution.

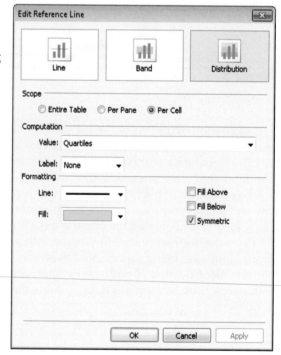

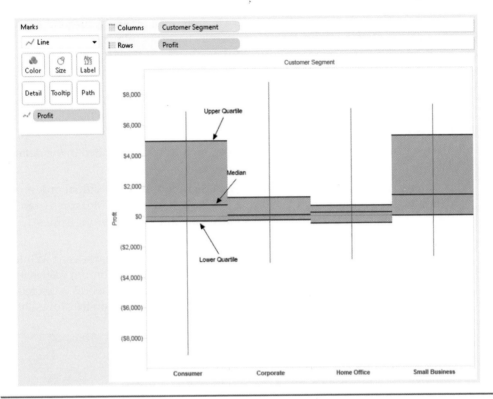

Figure 4-5   Basic box plot

A variation of the box plot adds *whiskers*, lines that denote some value at the top and bottom of the distribution. This use of whiskers allows a wider evaluation of distribution of data points beyond the box. In some cases, whiskers denote the minimum and maximum (which would have been a good application with the solid line box plot illustrated in Figure 4-5). However, other variations place the whiskers at low and high percentiles, but not the minimum and maximum. This type of whisker use is ideal if outliers that fall outside the whisker percentiles are to be identified.

Consider the box plot with whiskers illustrated in Figure 4-6. Here, individual profit values are being represented as small circles instead of a continuous line, which permits identification of outliers. Further, whiskers have been placed at the 2nd and 98th percentiles, leaving anything outside those percentiles to be clearly identified as outliers.

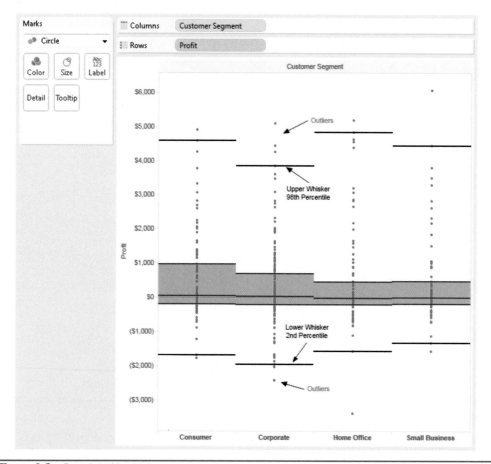

Figure 4-6   Box plot with whiskers

The steps described previously to create the basic box plot in Figure 4-5 apply to Figure 4-6, with the following differences:

- Instead of choosing a Line mark type after disaggregating data, Circle was chosen. This replaced the default open circles with solid circles. Size was clicked on the Marks card and the slider was used to greatly reduce the size of the circles.

- The whiskers were created by use of an additional reference line. Distribution was selected as this reference line type, Scope was set to Per Cell, Value was set to Percentiles (with the numbers 2 and 98 typed in manually separated by a comma), Label was set to None, a solid line color was chosen, and Fill was set to None.

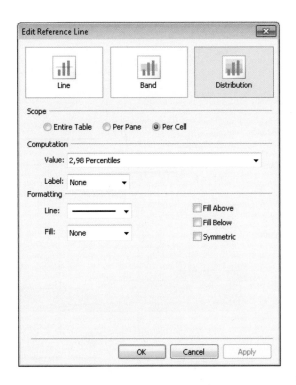

Tree Map

When faced with identifying the folders that resulted in a full hard disk in 1990, Ben Shneiderman of the University of Maryland began experimenting with a way of visualizing which folders were using up space. Rather than the typical folder/subfolder tree view that is still often used to decode hard disk contents, Shneiderman looked for a more compact way to evaluate hard disk space usage. The *tree map* was born. Despite its origin, it's useful for many other constrained-space visualization requirements. Tableau provides a Tree Map option on Show Me, and permits manual creation of tree maps as well.

A tree map is designed to display hierarchical data as rectangles within rectangles. For each rectangle, two measures can be coded—one will affect the size of a rectangle, and the other will affect color. If a single dimension is used, all dimension members will appear size- and color-encoded together. However, if more than one dimension is used (there should be a logical hierarchy between the dimensions, such as State and City), rectangles will be grouped together by the higher-level dimension, with the overall size of the higher-level group of rectangles encoded by a measure. The resulting tree map can display a large number of dimension members in a relatively small space. A particular rectangle whose color/size combination interests the viewer can be hovered over to show a more detailed tooltip.

If you want to modify a tree map created with Show Me, or create your own, the steps are straightforward:

1. Choose Square as the mark type from the Marks card drop-down.

2. Drag one or more dimensions whose members you want to create rectangles for to Label on the Marks card. Ensure that the higher-level dimension appears first (either drag it first or reorder dimensions on the Marks card).

3. Drag the measure you want to size-encode rectangles with to Size on the Marks card.

4. Optionally drag the dimension or measure you want to color-code rectangles with to Color on the Marks card.

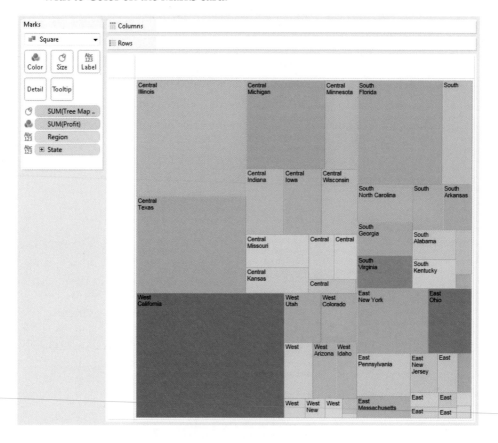

Note several traits of the resulting tree map:

• Member names for both dimensions appear on each rectangle.

• Rectangles for the higher-level dimension (Region) appear together. The overall size of the higher-level rectangles is based on the Size measure (in this example,

Central region has significantly higher sales overall than other regions, and East has significantly lower sales).

- Individual rectangles are color-coded (in this example, low-profit states display varying shades of red, while high-profit states display varying shades of green).

Word Cloud

The *word cloud* (sometimes also referred to as a tag cloud) displays members of a chosen dimension as text, but in varying sizes and colors, depending on one or two measures. A common example of word cloud usage is analyzing the effectiveness of search engine keywords in website visit metrics.

Although new, the word cloud visualization is not available in Show Me. To create manually, make use of the following Marks card settings:

- The mark type is set to Text from the drop-down.
- The dimension used to create the words is placed on Text.
- The measure used to vary the size of words is placed on Size.
- The dimension or measure used to vary the color of words is placed on Color.

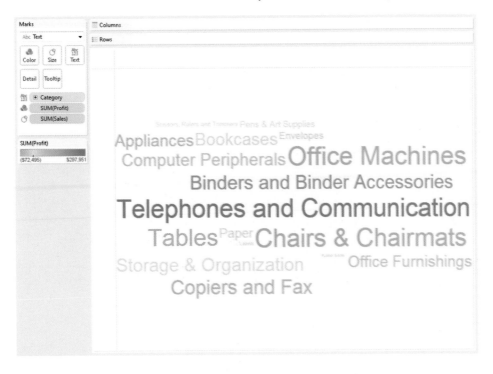

Interacting with the Viewer

Tableau provides a great deal of interactivity as you design visualizations. You can quickly modify visualizations by dragging and dropping different fields to different places on the workspace. Eventually, however, you may want to provide your charts and dashboards to viewers who don't have the full Tableau Desktop product, but who still want to fully interact with your visualizations. By adding interactive features such as quick filters, parameters, and actions, you can still provide an immense amount of flexibility and customizability for your audience without them having to understand the intricate details of Tableau design techniques.

Note *Most of the techniques described here require various Tableau interactive end-user environments, such as Tableau Reader, Tableau Online, or Tableau Server. Chapter 9 discusses these various distribution options in more detail.*

Note *Open the Chapter 5 - Interacting With The Viewer.twbx file in Tableau to see examples that relate to this chapter.*

Filtering Data

No matter what visualization or analytical tool you use, one of the first things you'll need to do is filter data. *Filtering* is simply the process of narrowing down your chart or graph to only the data that is relevant to your current need. For example, if you have an historical data warehouse that contains 10 years of data in millions (or more) of records, it's very unlikely that you'll want to include every row in your visualization—you'll almost certainly want to limit your view to a specific year, or few years. Other options for filtering are as numerous as are your choice of dimensions and measures; only certain regions, sales that are at least $1,000, and so forth.

Basic Filtering

While not necessarily an interactive feature of Tableau, basic filtering will often "lead to" interactive filtering. With the multiyear data warehouse example presented previously, you may choose to "hard code" a previous two-year filter in your worksheet. This will not be an interactive filter, as the ultimate viewer of your worksheet may not have the ability to change hard-coded filters. However, your viewer may later request the ability to be able to choose one or more years on the fly. Then, you will consider interactive filtering features discussed later in the chapter.

The focus point for filtering in Tableau is the *Filters shelf.* Like other shelves in Tableau, you may drag dimensions or measures to this shelf. Depending on the type of field (dimension or measure) and the field's data type (string, number, date, and so forth), various filter dialog boxes will result. For example, if you drag a string dimension to the Filters shelf, a filter dialog will appear showing all members of the dimension.

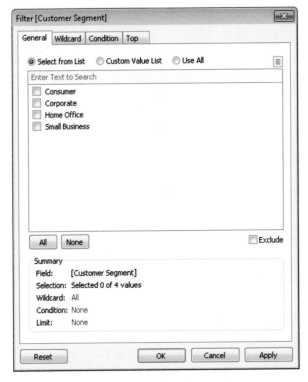

To only include certain values in your worksheet, check the values you wish to retain (the All and None buttons may be used to select all values if only some are checked and to clear all existing checkmarks, respectively). To exclude certain values in your worksheet, check the values you wish to exclude, as well as the Exclude checkbox in the lower right (the dimension values you select will appear with a line through them). When you click OK, the filter will be immediately applied; the field will be placed on the Filters shelf, and the chart will immediately update to reflect the new filter. Modify an existing filter by right-clicking the field indicator on the Filters shelf or by clicking the small arrow on the indicator, and choose Filter from the context menu. The filter dialog box will reappear where you may make desired modifications. To remove a filter, simply drag it off the Filters shelf.

A variation of the filter dialog box will appear if you drag a date or date/time field to the Filters shelf. First, you'll be prompted to choose the date level (year, month, and so forth) you wish to use for the filter. Clicking Next will display the standard filter dialog, presenting choices based on the initial date level you select:

- **Relative Date** This option will filter relative to some specified date (initially, today's date). Relative date filtering is helpful for "yesterday," "last week," "two previous years," and similar types of date ranges that will adjust automatically as your computer's date and time change.

- **Range of Dates** Allows selection of beginning and ending dates in a date range. Variations of this option allow specification of only a beginning or ending date to provide open-ended date range filters.

- **Date Level** Choose Year, Quarter, Month, and so forth to filter on one or more years, quarters, months, and the like. For example, if you choose Year, the filter dialog will show all years in the filter field. Conversely, choosing Month will display a choice of the 12 months of the year. Select one or more date values to include in the filter.

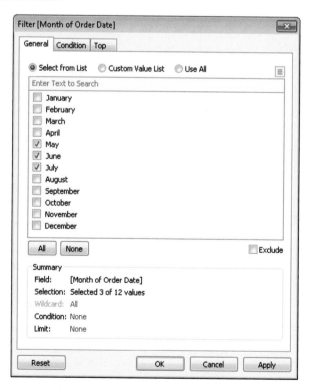

- **Count or Count (Distinct)** Evaluates the field as a numeric measure, presenting a numeric filter dialog (discussed later in this section).

Dimension and date filters also include additional options for more advanced filtering. In addition to the default General tab, the filter dialog box will display Wildcard, Condition, and Top tabs (date filters only include Condition and Top tabs). Click one of these tabs for more advanced filtering capabilities:

- **Wildcard**   Allows freeform filters using wildcard searches, such as "contains," "starts with," and "ends with" choices. Choose the desired radio button and type full or partial matching text in the Match Value text box.

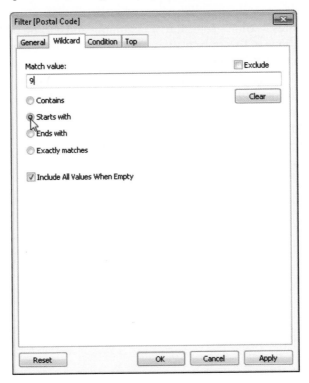

- **Condition**   Filters the chosen dimension, but not on the actual dimension members themselves. Instead, you may specify a condition based on an aggregated numeric value (the count of another dimension, or numeric aggregation of another measure). If, for example, you only wish to include customer segments that are unprofitable, click the Condition tab, click the By Field radio button, select Sum of Profit, and specify a less than (<) operator and zero comparison value. The By Formula option allows specification of a Tableau calculation formula (calculated fields are discussed in Chapter 7) for more advanced filter calculations.

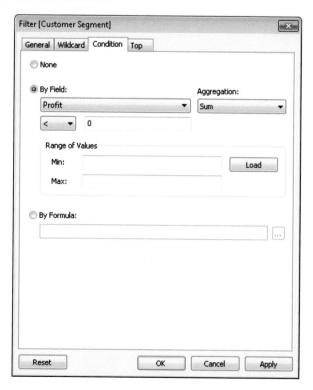

- **Top** Similar to the Condition tab, the Top tab will filter not on the actual dimension members, but on an aggregated numeric value. Rather than including all occurrences of dimensions that meet the filter, however, the Top tab will limit the filter to the top or bottom "N" occurrences of the dimension. For example, to see the top 10 selling products, select the Top tab, choose the By Field radio button, choose Top, type in a value of 10, and select Sum of Sales.

The By Formula option allows specification of a Tableau calculation formula (calculated fields are discussed in Chapter 7) for more advanced filter calculations.

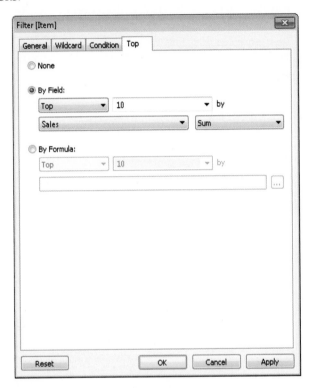

Filtering on a measure presents a different type of filter dialog that provides numeric options based on the range of values within the measure. First, you'll be prompted to choose the type of aggregation calculation you wish to use for the filter (sum, count, and so forth). Make this choice and click Next. The resulting filter dialog will allow a range of numeric values (minimum and maximum) to be specified or open-ended numeric ranges (at least/at most). Use the slider control to select beginning or ending range values, or type the desired values in directly.

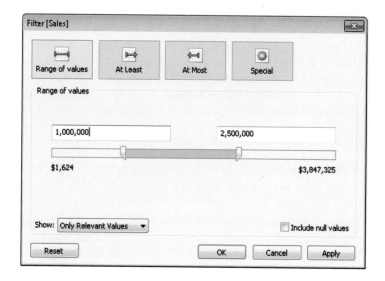

Interactive Filtering

While adding a field to the Filters shelf, as described previously, is the first approach to narrowing down your chart to a set of meaningful data, you may prefer a quicker, more intuitive way to perform repetitive filtering. More importantly, if your Tableau workbook is shared with your audience via some other method, such as Tableau Reader, Tableau Online, or Tableau Server, your audience may not be able to modify any shelves. However, they may still want to provide some of their own filtering to allow more interactive analysis.

The simplest approach to interactive filtering is to select one or more marks, or one or more dimension headers in a visualization, and then make choices from the tooltip or the context menu. Select one or more marks (bars, shapes, and so forth) by CTRL-clicking or drawing an elastic box around multiple marks with your mouse. Or, select one or more dimension headers with click or CTRL-click. Then, just hover your mouse over one of the selected items. A tooltip will appear that includes Keep Only and Exclude options. You may also right-click one of the items and choose Keep Only or Exclude from the context menu. Clicking Keep Only will create a filter to include only the highlighted dimension members. Others will be eliminated from the worksheet. Conversely, clicking Exclude will create a filter to exclude the selected dimension members, retaining all others. You'll notice the dimension now appears on

Sharing Filters Among Worksheets

By default, any filter you specify on the Filters shelf applies only to the worksheet where you add it. If you create another worksheet using the same data connection, any filters you specified elsewhere don't apply to the new worksheet. You may wish to share the filter with additional worksheets that use the same data connection.

To make this choice, right-click the desired field indicator on the Filters shelf, or click the drop-down arrow on the field indicator. Click Apply To Worksheets to display a sub-menu where you may choose the desired scope:

- **Only This Worksheet** This is the default. The filter will only apply to the worksheet where it has been placed on the Filters shelf. This was referred to as a "local" filter in previous versions of Tableau.

- **All Using This Data Source** The filter will apply to every worksheet in this workbook that's using the same data source as the worksheet where the filter is applied. You'll notice the filter appear on the Filters shelf on other worksheets with a small barrel icon next to it. This was referred to as a "global" filter in previous versions of Tableau.

- **Selected Worksheets** This option, only available when more than one worksheet exists in the workbook, will present a list of all worksheets in the workbook making use of the data connection the filter is based on. Select the worksheets you wish the filter to apply to. The filter will appear on the Filters shelf on these worksheets with a small two-page icon next to it.

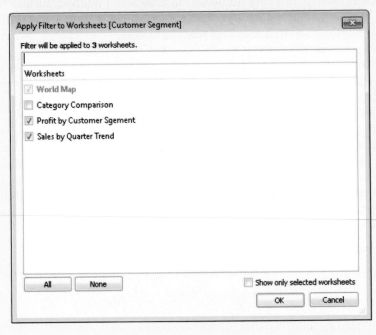

the Filters shelf. You may click the Undo toolbar button, type CTRL-Z, or drag the field off the Filters shelf to remove the just-created filter.

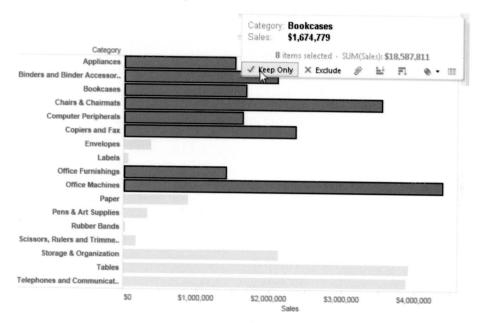

Quick Filters

 Video *Using Quick Filters*

The most intuitive filter interactivity in Tableau comes in the form of quick filters. *Quick filters* are customizable dialog boxes that prompt a viewer for filter values. When the viewer chooses values from the quick filter, the visualization is immediately updated to reflect those filter choices. There are two strong benefits of quick filters over filters specified directly on the Filters shelf or interactive filtering by mark/header selection:

- There are many flexible user interface choices for quick filter display, such as drop-down boxes, radio buttons, and so forth.
- They are fully supported in all other Tableau distribution environments, such as Tableau Reader, Tableau Server, and Tableau Online.

You may display a quick filter for existing filters already on the Filters shelf, or create one from scratch. Simply right-click either the field indicator on the Filters shelf, or a field in the Data Window (you may filter on dimensions or measures). Choose Show Quick Filter from the context menu. A quick filter dialog will appear on the right side of the worksheet and, if it wasn't already there, the field name will be added to the Filters shelf.

As with filters directly placed on the Filters shelf (discussed earlier in this chapter), you may remove a quick filter by dragging it off the Filters shelf. You may also remove the quick filter dialog box but leave the filter on the Filters shelf with its last-chosen value by right-clicking the quick filter title or clicking the small context arrow and choosing Hide Card from the context menu. And, as with filters added directly to the Filters shelf, you may choose the filter's scope (apply to just this worksheet, all worksheets using the data connection, or selected sheets) from the context menu, as discussed previously in this chapter.

Depending on the data type of the field the quick filter is based on, the quick filter dialog box will take on an initial default appearance and behavior. For example, if the quick filter is based on a dimension with a small number of members, the quick filter will default to a series of checkboxes, along with an (All) checkbox. If a dimension contains a large number of members, the default quick filter will be a search box. Date dimension quick filters behave in various ways, depending on the date level you choose when first creating the filter. If you create a quick filter directly from a date dimension in the Data Window, it will default to year level and will appear as checkboxes. However, if you first drag a date field to the Filters shelf and choose a different default date level, or choose relative dates or a range of dates, the resulting quick filter will display as either a drop-down list of options or a slider. Quick filters based on numeric measures will display a range slider—you may slide either side or type in values directly above the sliders to set minimum and maximum values.

You're hardly limited to this default behavior, though. Right-click the quick filter title or click the small context arrow in the upper right. The context menu will display a bevy of user interface options for your quick filter. Dimension quick filters will present many options for display, such as Single Value (List, Dropdown, Slider), Multiple Values (List, Dropdown, Custom List) and Wildcard Match. Here's the result of a Multiple Values (Dropdown) choice.

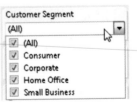

Date or date/time quick filters offer a different set of options. You may choose from sliders that present a date range or just a starting or ending date. The Relative Date option will display a rich dialog allowing most of the relative date choices found when initially adding a date field to the Filters shelf. And, Browse Periods presents a choice of pre-defined date ranges (1 day, 1 week, 1 month, and so forth) that may be selected. Here's an example using Range Of Dates.

Quick filters based on numeric measures have the fewest customization choices, but still offer sufficient options for most needs. Range Of Values will display a slider control with both starting and ending points, which may be moved to modify the starting and ending values of the range. At Least and At Most will present sliders to select just the beginning and ending values of an open-ended range. In all cases, you may also type values directly into the boxes above the sliders. This is the result of the default Range Of Values option.

Tip *You may notice two options on the quick filter context menu that pique interest: All Values In Database and Only Relevant Values. By selecting All Values In Database, the quick filter will always present all available values in the database for the matching field, even if choices from other filters would render some values invalid. However, choosing Only Relevant Values will apply other quick filters before showing available values in this quick filter. This feature (sometimes referred to as cascading filters) will permit, for example, a quick filter based on Sales Rep to only show sales reps within a selected region if another quick filter presents region choices.*

Parameters

 Video *Using Parameters*

While quick filters provide flexible interactivity for filtering data, there are other occasions when you may wish to prompt your audience for a value that's not based on an existing data field. In particular, you may wish to create customized calculated fields (discussed in detail in Chapter 7) that make use of a value supplied by a user. For this, Tableau provides parameters. A *parameter* is a prompt, similar to a quick filter, that returns a variable value that can be used in many parts of Tableau, such as calculated fields and portions of various dialog boxes, as well as being placed directly on a shelf. As with quick filters, parameters are usable with all Tableau distribution methods, such as Tableau Reader, Tableau Server, and Tableau Online. And, parameters are not limited to being used just on the worksheet where they are created—they can be used by any worksheet in your workbook. A value you supply to a parameter on the first worksheet can be used in any other worksheet in the workbook.

There are three general requirements to make use of parameters in your workbook:

- Create the parameter.
- Display the parameter.
- Use the parameter in a calculated field, in a dialog box, or on a shelf.

Creating a Parameter

There are three ways to create a parameter in Tableau. The first is from another dialog box where a fixed value can be provided, such as the value for a top filter or the value for a reference line. Consider the example of a top filter (discussed earlier in this chapter). Recall that a top filter permits you to choose whether to see the top or bottom values of a dimension based on a measure. You are also given a choice of how many top or bottom dimension members to see, with the default value of 10 appearing in the dialog box. However, if you wish to parameterize the input value rather than "hard coding" it, you may expand the value drop-down and choose Create A New Parameter.

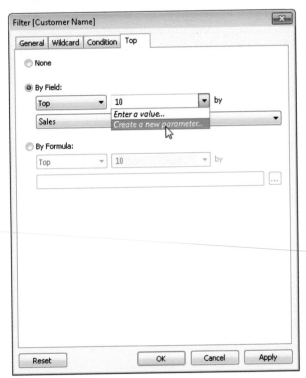

You may also create a parameter when creating or editing a calculated field (covered in Chapter 7). Click Create above the Parameters list within the Calculated Field dialog box.

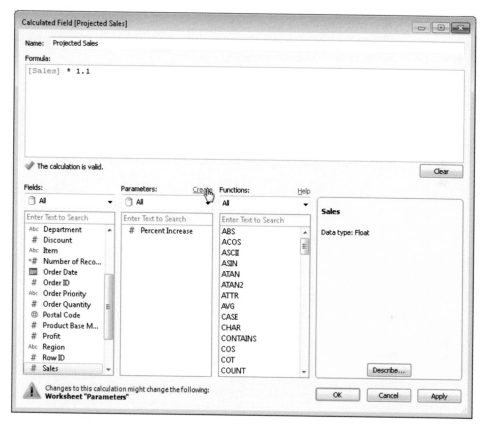

Finally, you may just right-click somewhere in the Data Window (either on a field or on a blank area). Choose Create Parameter from the pop-up context menu.

The Parameter dialog box will appear. Depending on where you created the parameter (from a dialog box, from the Data Window, and so forth), the dialog box may already have some values pre-specified. For example, if you create a parameter from the top filter dialog box (where the parameter will be used to replace the numeric *N* value), the parameter will already be defined with a data type of Integer. You must still give the parameter a meaningful name. You may optionally provide a comment. The remainder of the dialog box will change based on the data type of the parameter. Here, the default value of N is set to 10; formatting of the numeric parameter value will be automatic (if you wish, you may select from a variety of specific formats, depending on the parameter data type); and a range of values will be prompted for, with a minimum of 10, a maximum of 50, and a step size of 5. As such, this parameter will permit entry of integer values between 10 and 50 in increments of 5.

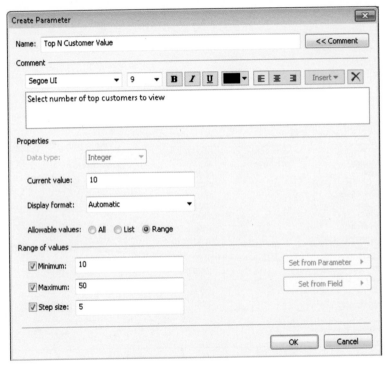

If you create a parameter from the Data Window, the Parameter dialog will be similar, but you must choose a data type as well. This is crucial, as it will determine how the parameter will appear on the worksheet, what properties you can set for the parameter, and how you can use the parameter. Consider your data type choice carefully. For example, you won't want to choose a string data type if you wish to use the parameter to ultimately affect the percent change in a numeric calculation. Also, if you want to create a dynamic reference line based off a date field to call out a reference date, string and numeric options will not even be available as selections from the date range axis.

In this example, a string parameter is being created to prompt for one of four string values. The values are being pre-defined in the parameter so that they will be the only available options when the parameter displays on the worksheet. A default value of "Profit" is being set, which will initially display when the workbook is opened. If an existing database field contains the desired values for a parameter, select it by clicking the Add From Field button. The parameter values will be read from the chosen field. You may also paste values from the clipboard by clicking the Paste From Clipboard button.

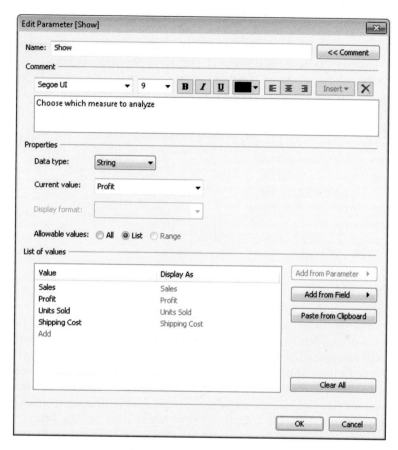

Caution *If you use the Add From Field button to populate a string parameter, new values added to the database later* will not *appear in the parameter (Tableau does not provide "dynamic" parameter lists). If you wish to add newly created values from the database to a parameter, you must edit the parameter and click the Add From Field button again after the database has changed.*

In all cases, once you create a parameter, it will appear in a new area of the Data Window dedicated to displaying parameters. Even if you add new worksheets to the workbook, the parameters will still display in the Data Window and will be usable in other worksheets.

Displaying a Parameter

Once a parameter is created, it must be displayed on the worksheet so that your audience can interact with it. If you created a parameter in a dialog box (the top filter parameter discussed earlier being an example), the parameter will automatically appear on the worksheet as soon as you close the dialog box where you created it. However, if you created a parameter in the Data Window, it will not automatically be displayed. You must explicitly right-click the desired parameter in the Data Window and choose Show Parameter Control from the context menu. The parameter will then appear on the right side of the worksheet, next to any existing parameters or quick filters.

Once a parameter appears on the worksheet, its user interface may be customized, much like a quick filter's can. As with a quick filter, right-click the title of the parameter or click the small context arrow to display the context menu. Depending on the parameter's data type and options you chose when you created the parameter, you'll find various choices for how the parameter is displayed (slider, single value list, and so forth). The previously discussed string parameter, for example, will display as radio buttons when the appropriate choice is made.

Using a Parameter in a Worksheet

Finally, the effort required to create and display a parameter won't be fully realized if the parameter is not used somewhere on your worksheet. If you created a parameter directly from a dialog box, such as the previously discussed top filter, then the parameter will automatically be placed in the dialog box and will immediately be reflected on your visualization. However, if you create a parameter in the Data Window, you must now choose where to make use of the parameter. You may wish to use it on a shelf (for example, to color some portion of your visualization), use it in a title or caption to annotate the visualization, or use it in a calculated field.

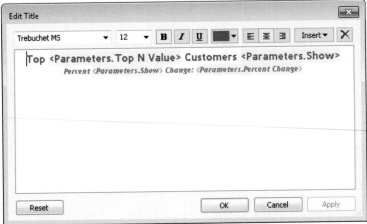

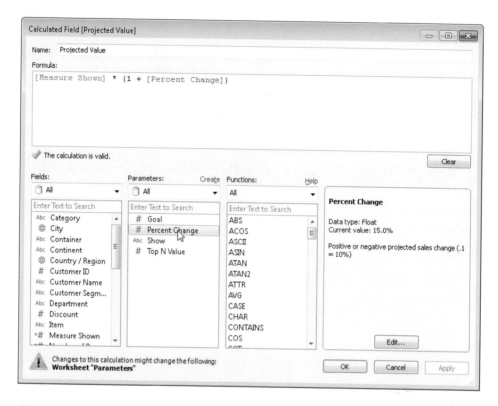

Don't forget that parameters may be used on any worksheet in your workbook. Even though you create them and use them in one particular worksheet, they are available everywhere else in your workbook—they will always appear in the Data Window no matter what worksheet you're currently editing. You may use them differently on different sheets. For example, you may supply a parameter to a top filter in one worksheet but use it in a calculated field on another. You'll soon find that parameters will take you to a whole new level of interactivity and flexibility with Tableau.

Tip *If you created a parameter but it doesn't appear in a variable portion of a dialog box, such as the N value in a top filter or the value to use for a reference line, it's because the parameter doesn't match the required data type for the dialog box. For example, the N value of a top filter will only expose numeric parameters. If a reference line is being created on an axis based on a date value, only date parameters will appear in the reference line value.*

Worksheet Actions

Another way of enabling interactivity is by using worksheet actions. *Worksheet actions* are an interactive feature to control behavior or appearance on either the current worksheet or other worksheets in the workbook, based on some action your viewer takes. There are three types of actions a viewer can initiate from a worksheet:

- **Filter Action**   This action filters other worksheets in the workbook based on marks selected on the current worksheet.
- **Highlight Action**   This action highlights marks on other worksheets in the workbook based on marks selected on the current worksheet.
- **URL Action**   This action launches a web page containing a specified URL based on marks selected on the current worksheet.

Furthermore, worksheet actions can be initiated in one of three ways:

- **Select**   This method initiates the action when a user selects a mark by clicking it, selects more than one mark by CTRL-clicking them, or selects multiple marks by drawing an elastic box around them.
- **Menu**   This method initiates the action when you hover your mouse over a mark and choose the action name from the tooltip. The action may also be initiated on the context menu that appears when you right-click selected marks.
- **Hover**   This method initiates the action when you hover your mouse over a mark.

Note *Hovering is generally used to initiate actions (typically, highlight actions) on dashboards and not worksheets. While hover works for single worksheets as well, you will want to only select the same worksheet that initiates the action as the target. You won't be able to see the results of the hover action on any other worksheets, unless they have been added to a dashboard.*

All worksheet actions are created from the Worksheet | Actions drop-down menu. The Actions dialog will appear, where you may create new actions or edit existing actions.

Filter Actions

A *filter action* adds a filter to one or more worksheets in your workbook. While there are many possible uses for a filter action, worksheet "drill-down" is one common popular use.

For example, you might create a text table/crosstab worksheet that contains detailed dimension/measure information that you wish to act as a drill-down target for a filter action. When you select one or more marks on a chart, the marks you selected can be used to filter the target text table.

Click the Add Action button in the Action dialog box, and choose Filter from the sub-menu. Complete the Filter Action dialog box:

- First, give the action a meaningful name (leaving the default name doesn't provide detail about what the action does, which makes it difficult to determine its purpose when you create multiple actions).

- In the Source Sheets box, choose the worksheet or worksheets you want to initiate the action from.

- Click the desired Hover, Select, or Menu button to determine what will initiate the action. If you click Select and want the action only initiated when a single mark is clicked, check the appropriate box (multiple mark selections with CTRL-click or drawing an elastic box around multiple marks won't initiate the action).

- In the Target Sheets box, choose the worksheet or worksheets you want the action to take place on. The sheets you select here will be filtered when the action is initiated.

- Select one of three radio buttons to indicate what you want to occur when the original marks that were used to initiate the action are cleared (the original mark is clicked again, or a blank space on the worksheet is clicked to clear previous selections). Leave The Filter will leave the filter in place even when you clear the selection. Show All Values will eliminate the filter and show all data in the target sheets. Exclude All Values will eliminate all data from the target sheets so they appear blank.

- Make choices in the Target Filters box, if necessary, to match fields between the source and target sheets. If, for example, the source sheet is based on one data connection and the target is based on a different connection, Tableau will not be able to determine how to match the field used for selection in the source worksheet to a field to filter in the target worksheet if the fields don't have the same name. In this case, click the Selected Fields radio button, and then click the Add Filter button to create one or more matching filters, choosing fields from the source sheet and target sheet that Tableau should match when creating the filter.

Click OK to create the filter action. In this example, a filter action has been created to filter a target crosstab worksheet when marks are selected on a map. Here, drawing an elastic box around five countries in South America filters the crosstab to the selected South American countries. When the action is initiated, the target sheet will be displayed and the filter applied.

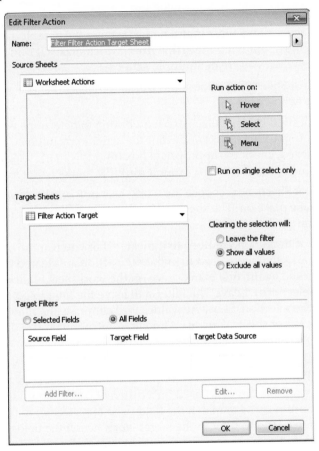

Country / Region	State	City	Order Quantity	Profit	Sales
Argentina	Province de Buenos Aires	Buenos Aires	14,789	$286,865	$1,037,812
Brazil	Bahia	Salvador	2,734	$126,331	$230,105
	Ceara	Fortaleza	2,397	$47,294	$209,041
	Distrito Federal	Brasilia	1,062	$14,658	$42,923
	Minas Gerais	Belo Horizonte	513	($1,422)	$38,882
	Parana	Curitiba	364	$367	$9,640
	Pernambuco	Recife	1,245	$14,710	$72,069
	Rio de Janeiro	Rio de Janeiro	10,355	$131,867	$666,902
	Rio Grande do Sul	Porto Alegre	1,108	$18,103	$101,600
	São Paulo	Sao Paulo	8,852	$156,017	$732,718
Chile	Santiago	Santiago	1,716	$22,551	$101,844
Colombia	Antioquia	Medellin	1,810	$97,324	$238,668
	Bogotá D.C.	BogotÃ¡	2,794	$70,570	$213,671
Peru	Provincia de Lima	Lima	2,592	$11,626	$112,767

Highlight Actions

A *highlight action* highlights particular marks on one or more worksheets in your workbook, based on marks you select on the source worksheet. When you select one or more marks on a chart, the other sheet will match the selection. When you select the other sheet in the workbook, you'll notice matching marks are highlighted.

Click the Add Action button in the Action dialog box and choose Highlight from the sub-menu. Complete the Highlight Action dialog box:

- First, give the action a meaningful name (leaving the default name doesn't provide detail about what the action does, which makes it difficult to determine its purpose when you create multiple actions).

- In the Source Sheets box, choose the worksheet or worksheets you want to initiate the action from.

- Click the desired Hover, Select, or Menu button to determine what will initiate the action.

- In the Target Sheets box, choose the worksheet or worksheets you want the action to take place on. The sheets you select here will be highlighted when the action is initiated.

- Make choices in the Target Highlighting box, if necessary, to match fields between the source and target sheets. All Fields will consider all combinations of dimensions in the source and target sheets when attempting to match what to highlight. Selected Fields will permit you to check specific dimensions in the source sheet that will be used to match marks in the target sheet to highlight. Dates And Times will match date and/or time fields in the target, based on what you select in the source sheet.

Click OK to create the highlight action. In this example, a highlight action has been created to highlight a target bar chart worksheet when marks are selected on a map. Here, selecting China on the map will highlight matching customers from China on the bar chart. After the selection, when the bar chart tab is selected in the workbook, matching customer bars are highlighted.

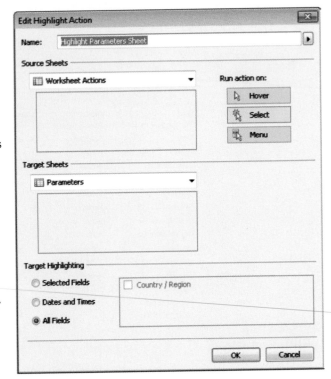

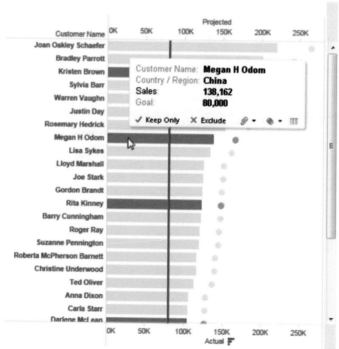

URL Actions

A *URL action* launches a web page based on marks you select on the source worksheet. The web page can contain a static web page URL. However, any field on your worksheet (the selected mark, in particular) can be used to customize the URL based on marks you select when the action is initiated. This provides for very powerful customized web pages to be delivered based on selections.

Click the Add Action button in the Action dialog box and choose URL from the sub-menu. Complete the URL Action dialog box:

- First, give the action a meaningful name (leaving the default name doesn't provide detail about what the action does, which makes it difficult to determine its purpose when you create multiple actions). If you wish to customize the action name by using a field from your data source, click the small arrow at the right of the Name text box. You may select a field to be included in the action name.

- In the Source Sheets box, choose the worksheet or worksheets you want to initiate the action from.

- Click the desired Hover, Select, or Menu button to determine what will initiate the action. Be very cautious if you choose Hover—understand that a web page will be launched whenever you just move your mouse over a mark!

- Specify the URL you wish to use when the web page is launched. To customize the URL with data from your worksheet, click the small arrow at the right of the URL text box. You may select a field to be used in the URL.

- If you wish to "URL encode" certain characters (spaces and so forth) in the URL, check the appropriate box. If you wish to allow selection of multiple marks to launch the URL (with CTRL-click or an elastic box), check Allow Multiple Values and type in the delimiter and escape character you wish to use to separate the resulting multiple values in the URL.

Click OK to create the URL action. In this example, a URL action has been created to display a Wikipedia web page when a mark is selected on a map. The URL has been customized with the Country/Region field to display a specific entry relating to the country that is selected. As this is a menu action, the option to run it appears on the tooltip when the mouse is hovered over a mark. By right-clicking the mark, the action can also be initiated from the context menu.

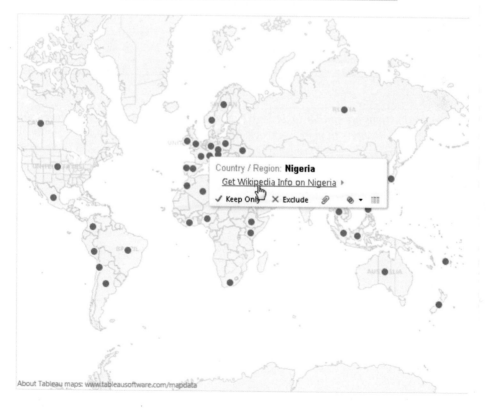

Note *Worksheet actions are similar to dashboard actions, with the exception that they only apply to other worksheets in your workbook. No dashboards need exist in your workbook for worksheet actions to be used. Dashboard actions are covered in more detail in Chapter 8.*

6
CHAPTER
Tableau Maps

If you've used other Business Intelligence or Data Discovery tools, you may have yearned for a comprehensive solution for analyzing geographic data via maps. While many "legacy" toolsets fall far short in this area, Tableau provides a rich mapping capability. By using a combination of geocoded data (data that Tableau interprets as containing a geographic location) and Internet-supplied background maps, you may perform detailed analysis geographically.

Consider this dimension portion of the Data Window from the Sample - Superstore - English (Extract) data source that's included with Tableau 8. Note, in particular, the Mapping Items hierarchy and the four dimensions within it. Although the underlying field type in the data source for these fields is String, they do not appear with the standard Abc icon that appears on other string fields. Instead, they are denoted with a small globe icon. And, if you glance at the Measures portion of the Data Window, you'll notice two "generated" fields that you may not have noticed before: Latitude and Longitude.

Double-clicking one of the geographic dimension fields (a field preceded by a globe icon) will create a map, displaying a blue circle on each occurrence of the underlying geographic field you double-clicked. This very quick default map gives you a basic idea of the power of Tableau mapping. Note that the actual geographic field has not been placed on the Rows or Columns shelf, but instead appears on the Marks card without any of the standard Marks card icons next to it. This denotes that the geographic field is on the Detail portion of the Marks card, which simply ensures that the members of the geographic dimension are included on the worksheet (but they are not used to denote color, size, shape, or any other mark property). The Rows and Columns shelves, instead, have been populated with the generated Latitude and Longitude measures.

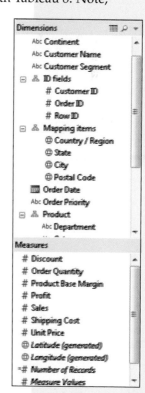

Tip *You may also create maps by selecting at least one geocoded field (with a globe icon) and clicking either of two map options in Show Me.*

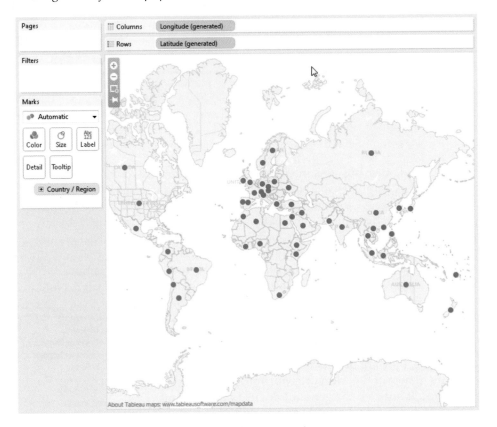

There are some basic concepts of mapping that this chapter will expand on:

- Tableau must evaluate a dimension as geographic to use it for maps. The globe icon indicates a geographic field.
- Tableau actually plots generated latitude and longitude derived from the geocoded dimension members as X and Y coordinates.
- Tableau displays a background map (by default, downloaded from the Internet) behind the X/Y coordinate map marks.

In particular, you will get an idea of basic Tableau mapping functionality from these two visualizations. The first is a map based on State when a filter has been applied limiting data to the United States. The second is the exact same map with "None" chosen from the Map | Background Maps drop-down menu. With no background map set, the chart looks like a standard scatter plot (discussed in Chapter 4), simply showing X and Y coordinates of the two numeric measures. A quick glance at the scatter plot, however, will still give you the general outline of U.S. geography.

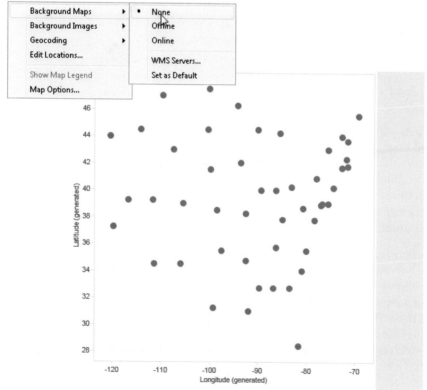

Note *Open the Chapter 6 - Tableau Maps.twbx file in Tableau to see examples that relate to this chapter.*

Geocoded Fields

 Video *Using Geocoded Fields*

The first requirement to use mapping is a proper dimension field or fields. *Geocoded fields* are fields that Tableau interprets as containing geographic data. Tableau automatically converts the string values of these fields to latitude and longitude that can be used as X/Y coordinates on the Rows and Columns shelves. These fields appear with a small globe icon instead of another data type icon—when they are double-clicked, a map will result. Tableau automatically assumes a field is geographic and will add the globe icon to it if its name includes some type of geographic keyword, such as Country, State, City, ZIP Code, and so forth. While this automatic geocoding assignment works well in standard situations, there are some situations where misinterpretation will occur:

- A field contains a name that Tableau interprets as a geographic field, but the field contains nongeographic data. A globe icon appears next to the field, but when the field is double-clicked, a map will result with no marks and a message indicating "*x* unknown" at the bottom right.

- A field contains geographic data, but the field name is not recognized by Tableau as such. No global icon will appear. If the field is double-clicked, a standard text table containing a row for each dimension member will appear instead of a map.

- A field will be interpreted as a geographic field based on field name. While the field does contain geographic data, Tableau will misinterpret the *type* of geographic data contained in the field. For example, a field named "Location State" may actually contain country data rather than state data. When the field is double-clicked, Tableau will create a map, but will be unable to interpret any of the fields as state fields. No marks will appear on the map, and a message indicating "*x* unknown" will appear at the bottom right.

While you may be tempted to return to your original data source to modify field names to accommodate Tableau's field-naming interpretation, there's a simple context menu that allows you to assign or unassign a geographic identification. Right-click the misinterpreted field in the Data window, choose Geographic Role from the context menu, and make the desired choice from the sub-menu. If a field has not been assigned a geographic role because of its field name, choose the role you wish to assign to the field. If a field has been mistakenly assigned a geographic role because of its field name but it doesn't contain geographic data, select None. If a field has been assigned the wrong role (for example, the field name contains the word "State," but actually contains country data), select the correct role.

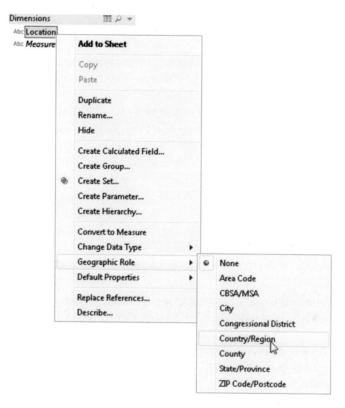

"Out of the box," Tableau includes geocoding interpretation for the following types of geographic data:

- **Area Code**   Standard U.S. three-digit telephone area codes. Other North American area codes, such as those in Canada, are not properly interpreted.

- **CBSA/MSA**   United States Core Based Statistical Area/Metropolitan Statistical Area. This will interpret both standard strings, such as "Denver-Aurora-Lakewood, CO," as well as many three-character codes (such as 216, which refers to Denver-Aurora-Lakewood, CO).

- **City**   Worldwide city names. In some cases, smaller towns may not be recognized. Note that because there can be more than one occurrence of a city name in the world, it may be beneficial to include country and state/province fields in the data source to narrow down to a unique country/state-province/city hierarchy (geographic hierarchies are discussed later in the chapter).

- **Congressional District**   U.S. congressional districts. This geographic role interprets variations of numbers, such as 1st, 4, 6th District, and 23rd. Note that because there can be more than one occurrence of a district in the United States, it may be beneficial to include a state field in the data source to narrow down to a unique state/district hierarchy (geographic hierarchies are discussed later in the chapter).

- **Country/Region**   International country and region names. This geographic role will interpret full spellings of countries/regions, as well as Federal Information Processing Standard (FIPS) 10-4 and International Organization for Standardization (ISO) two- and three-character abbreviations.

- **County**   U.S. county names. Note that because there can be more than one occurrence of a county name in the United States, it may be beneficial to include a state field in the data source to narrow down to a unique state/county hierarchy (geographic hierarchies are discussed later in the chapter).

- **State/Province**   States and provinces, interpreted worldwide. Both spelled and abbreviated values may be supplied. Note that because there can be more than one occurrence of a state/province name in the world, it may be beneficial to include a country field in the data source to narrow down to a unique country/state-province hierarchy (geographic hierarchies are discussed later in the chapter).

- **ZIP Code/Postal Code**   Standard U.S. ZIP codes. Postal codes are also interpreted from Canada, the United Kingdom, Australia, New Zealand, France, and Germany. Note that because there can be more than one occurrence of a ZIP/postal code in the recognized countries, it may be beneficial to include a country field in the data source to narrow down to a unique country/postal code (geographic hierarchies are discussed later in the chapter).

Dealing with Geocode Mismatches

While Tableau properly interprets and geocodes a fairly wide variety of standard geographic data, you may encounter situations where Tableau doesn't fully understand some (or all) of your geographic values. This may be due to data entry errors or variations on city or state names that Tableau doesn't understand. When Tableau doesn't find a latitude/longitude match in its internal geocoding tables for a value in a geographic field, a message will appear on the lower right of your map indicating how many values Tableau failed to resolve.

About Tableau maps: www.tableausoftware.com/map

In these cases, you'll probably want to choose some way to deal with the mismatched values (although you may choose to simply hide the message by right-clicking it and choosing Hide Indicator). Several choices exist when you left-click the message. A dialog box will appear providing three options:

- **Edit Locations**   Displays a dialog box that allows you to match the misinterpreted geographic values to a value that Tableau understands. The mismatched values will appear at the top of the list. On the Matching Location columns to the right, click to display a drop-down list of locations. Select that location you want Tableau to use for the misinterpreted location. Selecting the Map | Edit Locations drop-down menu option will also display this dialog box.

(continued)

- **Filter Data**   Filters out the mismatched values. The Latitude and Longitude fields will be added to the Filters shelf, set to exclude null values. If you later want to read the mismatched values and edit locations, you may remove Latitude and Longitude from the Filters shelf.

- **Show Data at Default Position**   This option will display a mark on the map for the mismatched values at the intersection of the equator and prime meridian (latitude/longitude 0, 0). Unless your mismatched geographic fields, in fact, *do* refer to the Gulf of Guinea in the Atlantic Ocean, this probably is the least desirable of these options.

Geographic Hierarchies and Ambiguity

Consider Tableau's challenge of determining an exact latitude and longitude for a city if there is more than one city with the same name in your country, much less in the entire world. In order for Tableau to properly narrow down ambiguous geographic locations, it employs a geographic hierarchy. This *geographic hierarchy* relies on a series of geographic dependencies to narrow down an ambiguous geographic location until it becomes unique. For example, Tableau employs a Country-to-State/Province-to-City hierarchy to determine the correct latitude and longitude for a particular city. Similar hierarchies are provided for Country-to-State/Province, Country-to-State-to-County (for U.S. counties), Country-to-ZIP/Postal Code, Country-to-Area Code, and Country-to-CBSA (Core Based Statistical Area).

If your data source contains a combination of these fields that Tableau interprets as containing geographic data (as mentioned previously, Tableau determines this based on field name), Tableau will automatically show the hierarchy in the Data window. The advantage of the pre-defined hierarchy comes when you use one of the lower-level geographic fields as the primary dimension for your map. For example, if your data source contains Country, State, and City fields, and you double-click City to generate a map for cities in your data source, Tableau will automatically add the hierarchical fields above city to Detail on the Marks card. This ensures that "city uniqueness" is employed to avoid ambiguous city names.

However, even if the set of geographic fields in your data source includes fields that would result in a hierarchy, a hierarchy *won't* appear if another geographic field that would break the hierarchy also exists in the data source. Consider a data source that contains Country, State, City, and ZIP Code. This would appear to present the opportunity for a geographic hierarchy. However, Tableau's built-in hierarchies start at the Country level, end at the City level, and don't include ZIP Code; or they start at Country and end at ZIP Code, but don't include City. As such, a data source that includes all four fields won't result in an automatic hierarchy. If you use a lower-level field that may be ambiguous, such as City, higher-level fields that would resolve the ambiguity are not automatically added to the Marks card. Results may be mixed, with some cities plotting properly but others being placed in the wrong country and/or state, or an "unknown" message appearing at the lower right of the map.

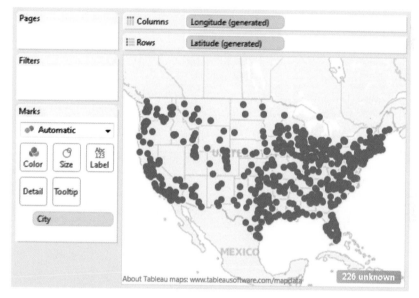

Several options exist to resolve this ambiguity:

- Before creating a map, manually create the necessary hierarchy by dragging and dropping geographic fields in the Data window (a discussion on how to create hierarchies in the Data window for all fields—not just geographic fields—appears in Chapter 3). Then, when you use a lower-level field to create a map, Tableau will automatically add higher-level fields to Detail.

- Drag higher-level geographic fields that will resolve the ambiguity on the Marks card. If you simply drag to the white area at the bottom of the Marks card (not on Color, Shape, and so forth), those fields will be placed on Detail. In particular, ensure that you drag these fields *above* the existing field in order of priority so that Tableau will understand the proper hierarchy to follow.

- If the set of geographic data in your data source is limited to certain countries or states/provinces, click the Unknown indicator at the lower right of the map and choose Edit Locations from the Special Values dialog box, or choose Map | Edit

Locations from the drop-down menus. The Edit Locations dialog box will
appear. Choose the desired dimensions at proper hierarchical levels to eliminate
the ambiguity.

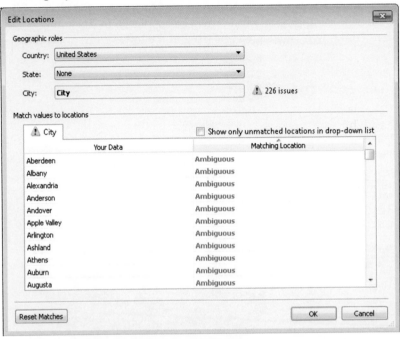

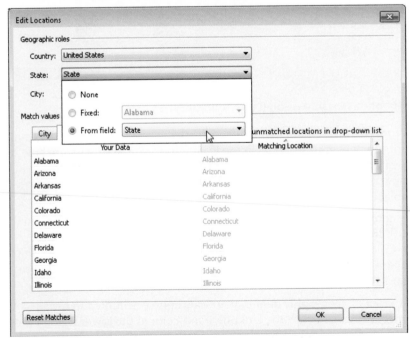

Custom Geocoding

While Tableau has a fairly extensive built-in set of geographic roles (as discussed earlier in the chapter), you may find more customized geographic roles are necessary for your particular needs. For example, you may need to map locations of smaller towns that aren't automatically included in Tableau's built-in geocoding. Or, you may have custom roles (such as airport codes or your own sales divisions/regions) that you wish to use for mapping. Tableau enables you to both extend its existing geographic roles by adding data (such as additional smaller cities) and add your own custom geographic roles and hierarchies.

Consider a data source that refers to a set of small towns in the author's home state of Wyoming. While the file contains the proper series of Country-State-City fields to adhere to Tableau's geographic hierarchy, double-clicking the City field only plots two cities in the state of Wyoming with relatively large populations. The remaining smaller towns are unrecognized, as indicated by the Unknown indicator at the lower right of the map. This is an opportunity to add to Tableau's existing Country-to-State/Province-to-City geographic hierarchy.

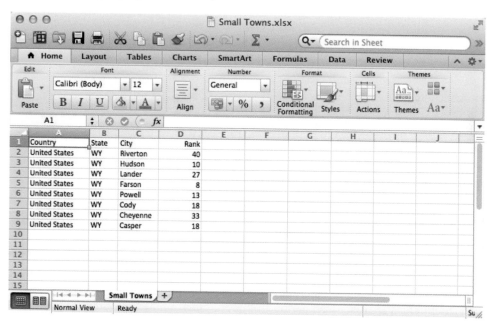

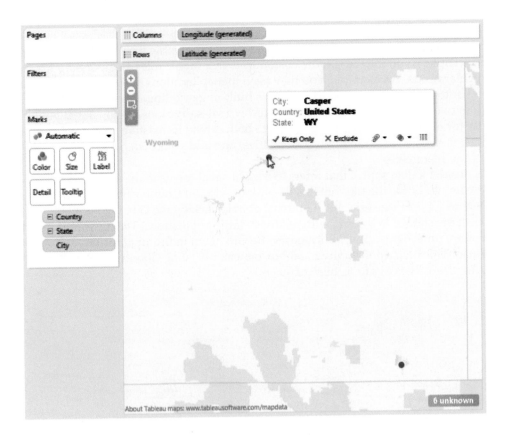

Regardless of whether you wish to extend exiting Tableau geographic roles or add your own custom roles, there are some basic requirements:

- You must create comma-separated value (.csv) text files. You may create these with Microsoft Excel, a text editor, or some other toolset that creates a CSV file. The file must be saved with a .csv file extension.

- If the file will extend an already existing Tableau geographic role, it must contain all fields that match a Tableau geographic field. Further, if the field you wish to add is part of a standard Tableau geographic hierarchy (existing hierarchies are discussed earlier in this chapter), a matching field for each member of the hierarchy must be included in the .csv file. For example, if you wish to add new cities to the existing Tableau City role, you must also include a Country (Role) field and a Province/State field for each new city to ensure that

Tableau won't confuse cities you're adding with other cities of the same name in other states or countries. Fields must be named the same as the geographic role already defined in Tableau (right-click a field in the Data Window and choose Geographic Role to see the sub-menu of existing geographic roles—fields must be named exactly the same in your .csv file).

- Latitude and longitude values must be the last two fields in the .csv file. Latitude must appear before longitude, fields must be specifically named "Latitude" and "Longitude," and they must contain "real" numeric values (at least one decimal place must be included—they cannot be integers).

For example, to add the small Wyoming cities exhibited earlier to Tableau's existing set of geocoded cities, this .csv file may be used. Note the geographic hierarchy of Country (Region)-to-State/Province-to-City is maintained, with fields appearing in that specific order. Following these fields, note the specifically named Latitude and Longitude fields (again, in that specific order), with real number values. The file is given a descriptive name and contains a .csv file extension.

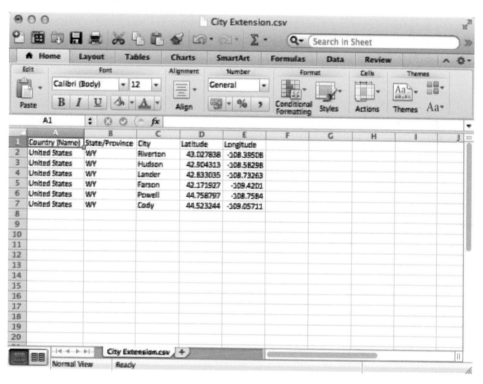

Furthermore, you may wish to add your own custom geocoded values, such as Sales Divisions, Plant Locations, and so forth. These can be independent of any existing Tableau geographic hierarchies, can depend on existing fields (such as Country or State/Province), or can establish their own hierarchies separate from any existing Tableau hierarchies. As with the previous example, field names in the .csv file need to be specific. In particular, any existing Tableau hierarchies must be accounted for with matching field names. New geographic fields should be properly named. And Latitude and Longitude fields should be the last two fields in the .csv file and should contain real number values. The file is given a descriptive name and contains a .csv file extension.

In this example, custom sales division locations need to be added to Tableau's geocoding. Because there are duplicate division names, they must be added to Tableau's existing Country (Name) hierarchy.

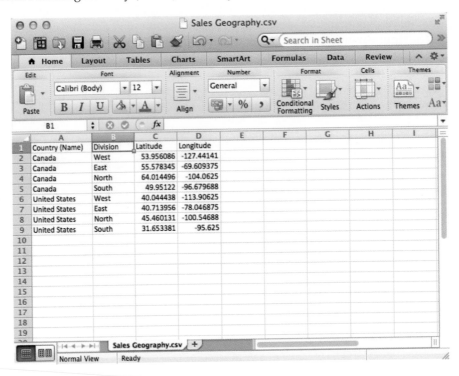

Once you have created one or more .csv files containing your custom geocoding, you may import them. Choose Map | Geocoding | Import Custom Geocoding from the pull-down menus. Because Tableau does not give you the opportunity to import individual .csv files, but imports all .csv files in a folder path, you'll be prompted to choose a folder. Choose the folder (or sub-folders) that contains the .csv files you wish to import. Click OK. Tableau will merge your custom geocoding with its existing geocoding (a large number of row counts will result, even if you are only importing a small number of new values).

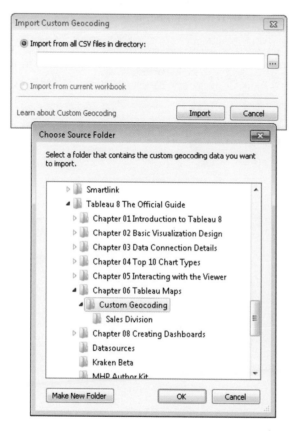

Once the import is complete, your custom geocoding values will be available to use for your own maps. After importing the small cities in Wyoming, as discussed previously, a map will now properly interpret the small town names in a data source.

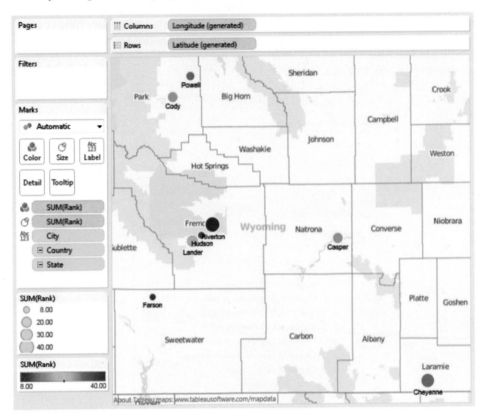

If you import your own custom role, it will now be available on the Geographic Role context menu when you right-click a field. Assign the custom role to a geographic field from your data source. Then, the new custom geocode will properly map your custom latitude and longitude values.

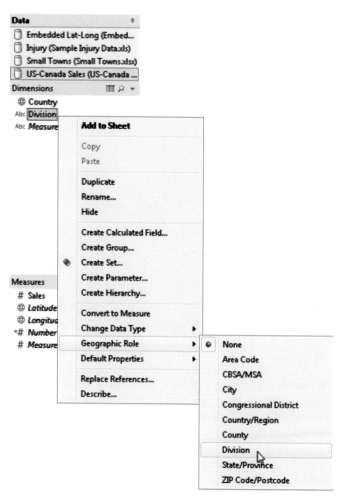

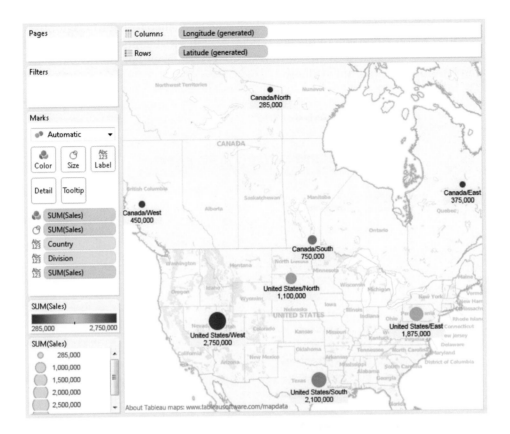

Note *To remove previously imported custom geocoding, select Maps | Custom Geocoding | Remove Custom Geocoding. Also, if you open a Tableau Packaged Workbook (a .twbx file), such as sample workbooks included with this book, any custom geocoding saved in the workbook will be retained for that workbook. You can even import custom geocoding saved with a workbook into your local repository to use for other workbooks. Just choose Maps | Custom Geocoding | Import Custom Geocoding and select the Import From Current Workbook radio button.*

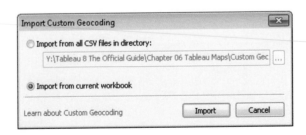

Mapping Latitude and Longitude Directly

Custom geocoding allows you to add custom latitude/longitude values to your own geographic dimensions. This is helpful when you need to create various maps on a regular basis using these custom values. However, if you have smaller "one-off" mapping requirements using custom latitude and longitude data, you may map directly using the latitude and longitude values contained in your data source. Custom geocoding will not be required.

Although not absolutely necessary, it's helpful if the latitude and longitude values in your data source are specifically named "Latitude" and "Longitude" and are numeric values. If so, Tableau will automatically assign them geographic roles (globe icons will precede them) and place them in the Measures portion of the Data Window. If latitude/longitude fields are named differently and Tableau doesn't automatically recognize them, simply right-click the fields and choose Geographic Role | Latitude Or Geographic Role | Longitude from the context menu. Tableau will then place the globe icon on the fields and treat them as latitude and longitude values. If latitude and longitude are stored in your data source as non-numeric values, or if you need to create customized latitudes and longitudes based on some sort of business rule, you may create calculated fields (covered in Chapter 7). The calculated fields should return "real" numeric values with at least one decimal place. They may then be assigned the latitude and longitude geographic role.

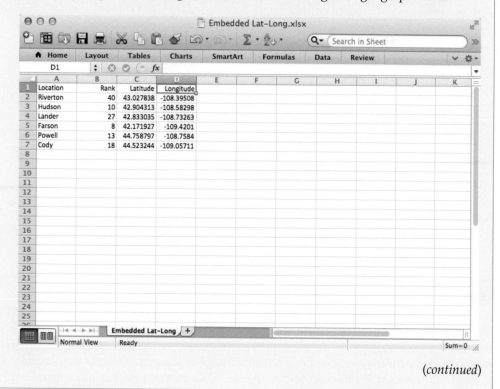

(continued)

Drag Longitude onto the Columns shelf and Latitude onto the Rows shelf. Tableau will automatically plot these fields to their geographic locations and display an appropriate background map. Depending on how your data is organized, you may only see a single point on the map consisting of the aggregated latitude and longitude values for all records in your underlying data source. In this eventuality, you may place a field that provides a breakdown of individual locations (a location, name, or customer field, and so forth) on Detail or Label on the Marks card. You may also choose to disaggregate your data so that Tableau plots each individual record in the data source rather than aggregating to a higher-level dimension. Uncheck Analysis | Aggregate Measures from the drop-down menus to do this.

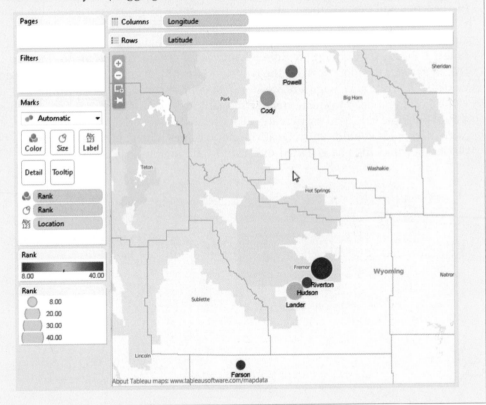

Background Maps and Layers

As has been discussed previously in this chapter, double-clicking a geographic field, using the map options in Show Me, or adding latitude and longitude fields to shelves will draw a Tableau map. While these provide extensive geocoding options, the other major necessity for mapping in Tableau is the image of the map itself (as demonstrated earlier in the chapter, if a background map image is turned off in Tableau, a map simply becomes a scatter plot).

Based on the geocoded fields used on the map, Tableau determines the portion of a background map to display. For example, if your map plots a mark in Seattle, Los Angeles, Miami, and Boston, Tableau will display a map of the United States, as it must show the entire country to plot the four marks in the four corners of the country. However, if the data your map encompasses only includes cities within a certain Canadian province, only that province will appear on the map. By default, Tableau uses *online maps*, which are downloaded via the Internet as needed. If you don't happen to have an Internet connection at the time of map generation, you'll receive an error indicating that the online map can't be loaded.

If your Internet connectivity is sporadic, or non-existent (for example, you're working on an airplane or similar location), you may choose to use *offline maps*, which are built into Tableau and are available regardless of Internet connectivity. However, they offer limited flexibility and features when compared to online maps. To use offline maps, choose Map | Background Map | Offline from the drop-down menus.

No matter the map source, you may need to zoom in or out of a map area, or move a previously zoomed map area left, right, up, or down. Zooming in or out on your map view is accomplished either using zoom controls that appear on the map or via keyboard shortcuts. By default, zoom controls appear at the upper-left corner of a map when you move your mouse over it. You may change zoom control appearance via sub-menu options on the Worksheet | Show Zoom Controls drop-down menu item:

- **Zoom In**   Click this control to zoom in on the map. If the zoom controls are hidden, double-click the map to zoom in. If you are using offline maps, you may be presented with a message indicating that additional map detail is only available with online maps.

- **Zoom Out**   Click this control to zoom out on the map. If the zoom controls are hidden, SHIFT-double-click the map to zoom out.

- **Area Zoom**   Click this control to turn on area zoom mode. The mouse cursor will change to a magnifying-glass-with-plus sign. Hold down the mouse button and draw an elastic box around the portion of the map you wish to zoom into. If the zoom controls are hidden, CTRL-SHIFT-click and draw an elastic box around the portion of the map you wish to zoom in to.

- **Reset**   Click this control to return the map to the default zoom level that appeared when the map was first created. This "pushpin" button is also duplicated on the Tableau toolbar.

If you have zoomed into a map and wish to move the map view left, right, up, or down, hold your mouse button down on the map for a second or two. The mouse cursor will change to a hand icon. Just drag the map in the desired direction.

Tip *If you often find the need to use offline maps or a particular custom WMS server (WMS servers are covered later in this chapter), you may change the default map source. First, choose the map source you wish to use by default (Online Maps, Offline Maps, None, or a previously added WMS server). Then, select Map | Background Maps | Set As Default from the drop-down menus.*

Map Options

Tableau online maps are very flexible, offering views based on worldwide geographic data. You may modify various visual characteristics, such as background style and washout level. Also, background maps have varying levels of detail known as map layers and data layers. *Map layers* are a variety of graphic overlays that can be turned on or off at will. For example, Tableau maps offer country name and boundary, state name and boundary, streets and highways, ZIP and area code boundaries and names, and similar overlays that will appear individually or in combination with each other on top of the initial map detail (some map layers are limited by the country being shown on the map). *Data layers* are colored shades that may be enabled on maps based on U.S. population data. Tableau map data layers include such various data breakdowns as population, age, race, occupation, and so forth.

Set map and data layer options by selecting Map | Map Options from the drop-down menus. The Data window will be replaced by the Map Options dialog. Here, you may change the map style (which changes the color and intensity of the map background), washout level (which changes the contrast of the map background), and the "Repeat Background" option, which will replace white space with repeated portions of the map, depending on screen size or zoom level.

Map layers may be checked on and off on this dialog box. Note that although some layers may be disabled, they may still be checked and will become active at an appropriate map zoom level. Check layer options you wish to enable. For example, checking street names, county borders, and place names will add elements on top of the existing map.

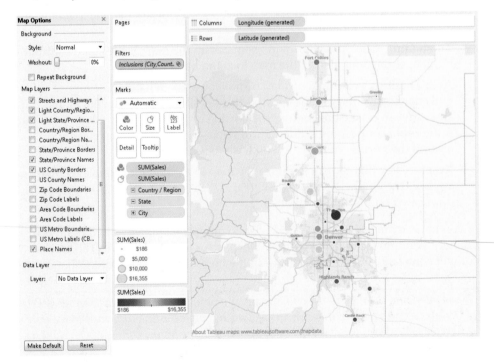

Data layers (which are only available on United States maps) may be enabled by clicking the drop-down in the Data Layer section of map options. Select the data layer you wish to display. You may also choose the geographic area (such as state, county, or ZIP code) that you wish to highlight for the chosen data layer, as well as the color palette you wish to use. The map will be shaded to match your choices, and a color legend will appear denoting the data layer.

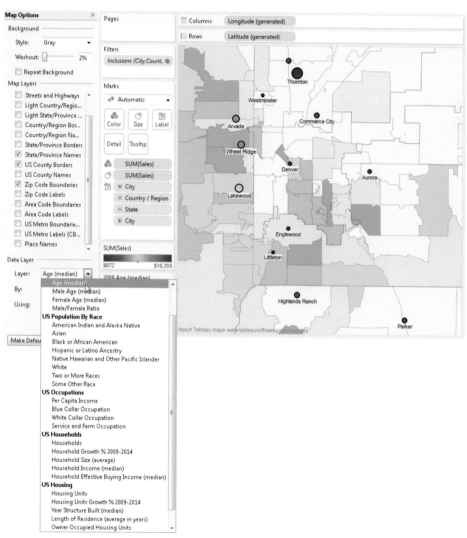

Web Map Services

While Tableau's built-in background maps are very flexible and provide a wide array of map and data layer options, you still may find occasion to use more customized, or industry-specific, map backgrounds. To expand these capabilities, Tableau supports external WMS servers. *Web Map Services* is a web-based standard that connects Tableau to a different set of custom background maps via the Internet. Various paid and open-source WMS servers exist (web searches will reveal a plethora of options) that may be added to Tableau for custom requirements.

To add a WMS server to Tableau, choose Map | Background Maps | WMS Servers from the drop-down menus. The WMS Server Connections dialog box will appear, showing any existing WMS servers that have already been added (if any). Click the Add button to specify a new WMS server to add. Type or paste the URL for the WMS server. If the selected WMS server supports tiled maps, checking the Use Tiled Maps option may improve performance. You may add as many WMS servers as you prefer—each will create an additional entry in the WMS Server Connections dialog box.

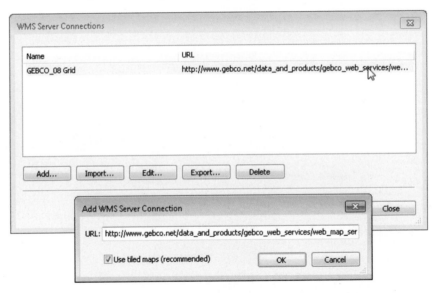

If you wish to edit or delete existing WMS servers in the WMS Server Connections dialog box, select the desired entry and select Edit or Delete. WMS servers will be available to all worksheets in the workbook. If you wish to share the WMS server URL with other Tableau users, you may select an entry in the dialog box and click Export. Tableau will display a Save As dialog box, prompting you for a filename. The file will contain a .tms (Tableau Map Source) extension. This file may be shared with other Tableau users, who can then add the WMS server to their copy of Tableau by clicking the Import button in the WMS Server Connections dialog box (all a .tms file contains is the URL—you may find that simply e-mailing the URL or providing it via some other interoffice communication method is preferable to creating a .tms file).

Once you have added one or more TMS servers and Tableau has validated their capabilities, a list of additional background map options (beyond None, Online, and Offline) will appear on the Map | Background Map sub-menu. Choose the desired

WMS-supplied map that you wish to use. In this example, a WMS is providing a custom background map displaying "bathymetry," the underwater counterpart to topography. Note that a separate set of map and data layers will exist in the Map Options dialog box, based on the particular WMS server's capabilities.

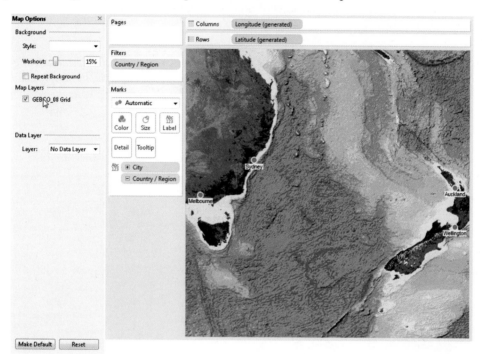

Mapping and Mark Types

When you first create a map via Show Me or by double-clicking a geocoded dimension (a globe icon will denote these), Tableau initially creates a map containing a mark for each occurrence of the field you used when creating the map. As discussed previously in the chapter, more fields may be added to the Marks card (Detail, in particular) to increase granularity of the map.

By default, Tableau suggests visualization best practices when creating a map by automatically choosing a blue circle as the mark type. However, you are free to choose a different mark type, as well as using all options at your disposal on the Marks card, as you would with any other chart type. For example, you may prefer to denote geographic areas on your map with a square instead of a circle. This is as simple as choosing Square from the Mark Type drop-down on the Marks card. The Shape mark type may even prove more appropriate, allowing you to not only choose a single shape from a variety of shapes and shape palettes, but to use variable shapes on the map based on another dimension (just drop the desired dimension on Shape on the Marks card). Color and Size on the Marks card may also be used either to change default size and color choices, or to control with other dimensions or measures. And, don't forget Label on the Marks card. By dropping various dimensions or measures here, marks on the map may be appropriately annotated.

Tip   *While you may think you need geocoded fields to take full advantage of Tableau mapping, you may use other nongeocoded fields to enhance your map. For example, by simply color-coding a map based on another nongeocoded dimension (such as region), your map exhibits various colors based on related geographic areas.*

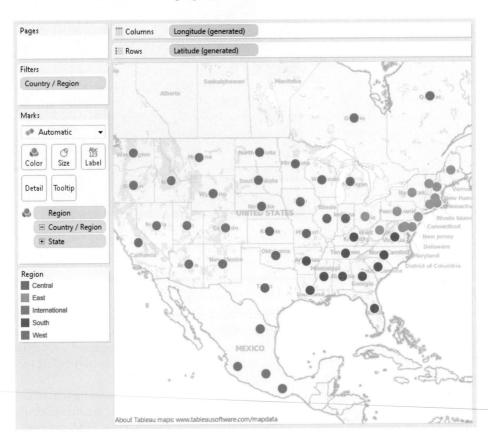

Two mark types have particular possibilities with maps. The first, Filled Map, is used automatically if you choose the Filled Map option in Show Me when first creating the map. However, if you initially created a map by just double-clicking a dimension, you may change the mark type on the Marks card to Filled Map to replace the default circle mark with a filled map. Filled maps benefit, in particular, from another dimension or measure added to Color.

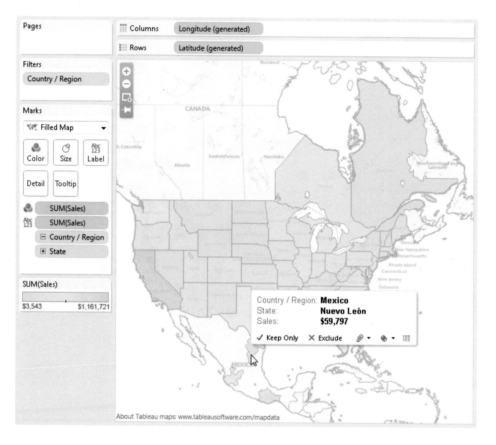

The second mark type that may not initially come to mind for map usage is Pie. Used judiciously, this mark can provide extra value to maps by breaking down geographic data by another dimension and measure. Once a map has been created, change the default mark type to Pie. Drop the dimension you wish to subdivide the pies by on Color (each dimension member will create a pie wedge)—be careful, as any dimension with more than four or five members will probably create too many wedges to be of use.

Then, drop the measure you wish to determine the size of pie wedges on Angle. Although you may find it diminishes the value of the map if overused, you may even consider dropping another dimension or measure on Size to vary the size of each pie.

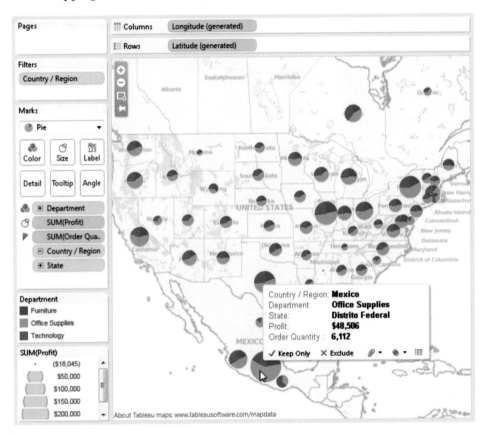

Custom Background Images

  Video *Custom Background Images*

With all the possibilities discussed earlier in this chapter, you may still find uses for geospatial data representation in Tableau that built-in geocoding, Tableau background maps, or custom WMS servers can't satisfy. Well, Tableau provides yet another way to plot data on your own custom background images. The possibilities are as rich as are the availability of pictures or drawings.

Consider the image illustrated in Figure 6-1. This type of visualization could be invaluable to an orthopedic surgical practice that is analyzing its case mix. Or, a company that evaluates employee injuries on a regular basis might find this of immense benefit.

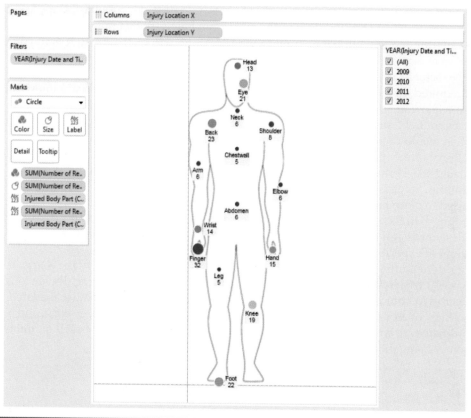

Figure 6-1   Custom background image

Much as with the two main components of Tableau mapping (geocoding data to derive latitude and longitude, and background maps), Figure 6-1 depends on two main components: (1) a consistent X/Y coordinate system to plot marks, and (2) a custom background image.

Generating Your Own Coordinate System

The first requirement for using a nonmap background image is to establish your own representation of X and Y coordinates, as opposed to latitude and longitude. As with a map, the underlying chart type for this equates to a scatter plot (scatter plots are discussed in Chapter 4). An individual mark is placed on the chart based on a combination of X and Y values. Measures or dimensions representing these X and Y values are placed on the Row and Columns shelves, which determine the specific location on the visualization where a particular mark will appear.

Determining the proper placement and relationship of these X/Y coordinates (the "coordinate system") will be dependent upon the background image the marks will appear on top of. Referring again to Figure 6-1, if the background image is 380 "units" wide and 400 "units" tall and the mark to indicate "Head" needs to appear at the top center of the image, the X coordinate should be 190 (halfway across the image) and the Y coordinate should be 365 (close to the maximum height of the image).

Determining the number of "units" wide and high will be the first decision you'll need to make. While the width and height of the background image in pixels is one way to achieve this (and the example in Figure 6-1 has been specified this way), this is not required. In fact, you may specify any beginning and ending X and Y values you wish when you add the background image. So, theoretically, the beginning X and Y values could be set to 0, with the ending X and Y values set to 1. Your coordinate system would then assume that all X and Y values used to plot marks would be fractional numbers between 0 and 1. The specified beginning and ending values could be 0 and 100, between –100 and 100, and so forth—you may set the minimum and maximum values to anything you choose, as long as the actual X and Y values that will be used to place marks on the visualization will fall between the minimum and maximum. In fact, you may often have to change the initial minimum and maximum values you assign to a background image to achieve proper placement of marks—a fair amount of experimentation may be required to get desired results.

Prior to adding a custom background image, you'll need to identify the X and Y fields you wish to use to place marks on the image. They can be existing dimensions or measures in your data source, or they can be calculated fields you create (calculated fields are covered in Chapter 7). In the example illustrated in Figure 6-1, the X and Y coordinates are created in calculated fields that assign specific values based on the type of injury being plotted.

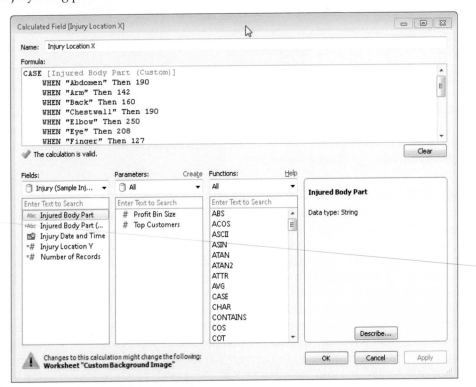

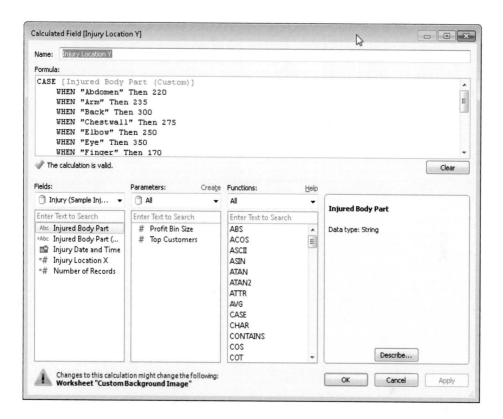

Adding a Custom Background Image

After establishing which fields you'll use for X and Y values, choose Maps | Background Images from the drop-down menus. You'll be presented with a list of data sources used in the workbook. Because a custom background image is matched to specific X/Y fields in a particular data source, you must initially choose the data source that will be used with your image. The Background Images dialog box will appear, showing any existing images that may have been added to the data source previously.

Click the Add Image button to add a new image. The Background Image dialog box will appear:

- Provide a descriptive name for the image. This name will appear in the list of images presented by the Background Images dialog box.

- Specify a filename or URL that points to the image. Tableau supports most standard Windows image formats, such as JPG, BMP, TIF, PNG, and so forth. Once you specify a filename, a thumbnail of the image will appear on the dialog box. Slide the Washout slider to change the contrast of the image.

- From the drop-down field list, specify the field in the data source to act as the X field. Only numeric fields will appear in the drop-down. Make the same field choice for the Y field.

- Specify left, right, bottom, and top values to establish the boundaries of your coordinate system. For example, the background image illustrated in Figure 6-1 is 380 pixels wide by 400 pixels tall, and the X and Y calculated fields have been designed to provide integer values between these limits. As such, left and right values are set to 0 and 380, with bottom and top values set to 0 and 400.

- On the Options tab, check Lock Aspect Ratio if you wish Tableau to maintain the same width-to-height ratio of the image as marks or zoom levels change. Otherwise, the image may be stretched horizontally or vertically when the worksheet resizes.

- On the Options tab, check Always Show Entire Image if you want Tableau to not zoom in past the edges of the image.

- On the Options tab, click the Add button if you wish to add filter conditions to determine when to show the images. For example, you may wish to choose from a variety of background images, depending on a Male/Female filter or a Child/Adult parameter.

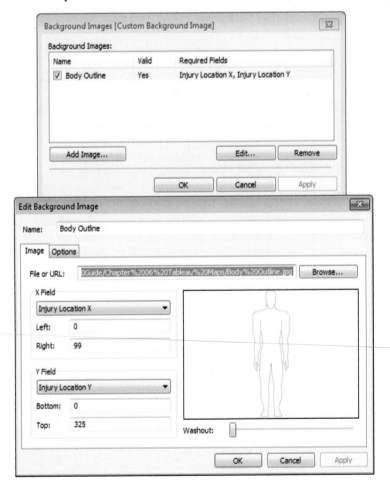

Once the image has been added, any time you drag the specified X and Y fields to the Rows and Columns shelves, the background image will automatically display behind the marks. Note that you won't want Tableau to aggregate the X and Y values when placing them on the worksheet, or the positions won't match to the desired values. For example, if the X/Y value for a particular dimension member should be 10-20, but there are five records in the underlying data source for that dimension member, Tableau will sum the X/Y values and place the mark on the chart at position 50-100. This may not display the background image at all, or may display it as a very small picture. In any event, marks won't be plotted at proper positions in front of the image.

To avoid this issue, either change the aggregation type for the X and Y values to something that returns the actual underlying value (such as Average, Minimum, or Maximum) or convert the numeric values to dimensions. Both of these approaches may be accomplished by right-clicking the field indicators on the Rows and Columns shelves and making the desired choice from the context menu.

Calculated Fields, Table Calculations, and Statistics

It won't be too long before you encounter a situation where the data in your underlying data source or database won't fit your analysis needs exactly. For example, you may need to calculate the result of one or more numeric measures in your data source to determine a desired number you wish to analyze. Or, a dimension in the data source may not be organized precisely in the way you wish to use it.

For these types of situations, Tableau provides calculated fields. A *calculated field* is a custom calculation (often simply referred to as a formula) that can use combinations of existing dimensions and measures from the underlying data source, combined with built-in operators and functions, to create a custom result. The resulting calculated field will appear in the Dimensions or Measures area of the Data Window, along with existing dimensions and measures, ready to be dragged and dropped just like any other field.

Standard *operators* available in a calculated field include arithmetical operators, such as addition, subtraction, multiplication, and division. Logical operators are also available, such as equals to, less than, greater than, and not equal to.

Built-in *functions* provide various capabilities for manipulating and converting data. For example, there are functions to convert string values to all uppercase or all lowercase characters, or to strip off characters from the beginning, end, or middle of a string. Data-type conversion functions exist to, for example, convert numbers to strings or strings to dates. Arithmetical functions exist to return cosine, absolute value, and other standard mathematical results. Aggregating data is possible with functions such as SUM, AVG, and COUNT. And, manipulating date or date/time values is possible with functions to extract just the month, day, or year from a date, and so forth. Functions are different from operators in that they typically require one or more *arguments*—data source fields or specific values that are supplied to determine what the function will use to perform its calculation or manipulation.

Note *Open the Chapter 7 - Calculated Fields-Table Calculations-Statistics.twbx file in Tableau to see examples that relate to this chapter.*

Creating Calculated Fields

There are two ways to create a calculated field:

- In the Data window, right-click an existing dimension or measure that you wish to use in a calculated field and choose Create Calculated Field from the context menu. The Calculated Field dialog box will appear with the selected field appearing in the Formula section of the box.

- Choose Analysis | Create Calculated Field from the drop-down menus. The Calculated Field dialog box will appear with no fields pre-added.

The Calculated Field dialog box, illustrated in Figure 7-1, contains several sections you'll soon be familiar with. You may type portions of your calculated field in the Formula box directly. However, you may find that placing the cursor in the Formula box where you want a field, function, or parameter to appear and then double-clicking the desired field, function, or parameter is the best way to create the calculated field.

Video *Creating Calculated Fields*

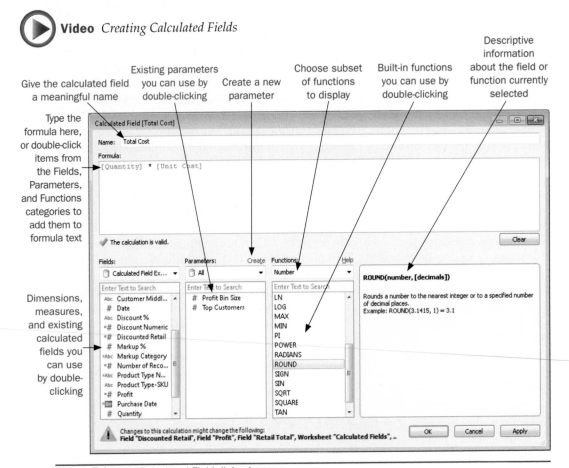

Figure 7-1   The Calculated Field dialog box

There are some general tips and techniques you'll want to keep in mind as you create calculated fields:

- Give the calculated field a meaningful name. The default "Calculation1" won't be helpful when you are evaluating fields in the Data Window to add to your chart.

- Tableau will check the *syntax* (the field/function/operator organization) of your calculated field when you stop typing for approximately one second. If Tableau understands the formula syntax, a green checkbox, followed by "The calculation is valid" will appear below the formula text. However, if the formula text results in a syntax error, a red X will appear, followed by "The calculation contains errors" text and a small drop-down arrow. Click the drop-down arrow for a more descriptive (but not always definitive) error message. Also, the offending portion of the formula text will be underlined with a small red squiggle.

- If you double-click fieldnames from the Fields box, Tableau will always surround them with square brackets when they are added to the Formula box. If you type fieldnames in manually, you may leave the square brackets off, provided the fieldname doesn't contain any spaces. If the fieldname does contain spaces, you'll receive a syntax error if you fail to surround the fieldname with square brackets. If the fieldname itself includes square brackets, type two additional matching square brackets before or after the fieldname's bracket to ensure proper syntax.

- By default, the Fields list will show all dimensions and measures from the currently selected data source. If you wish, you may narrow the Fields list to just numbers, strings, and so forth by clicking the drop-down at the top of the Fields list. If you wish to refer to fields in another data source open in your workbook, you may choose that data source in the same drop-down. The same data-type choices also exist in the drop-down above the Parameters list.

- To see a hint describing the purpose of a built-in function, as well as what arguments it requires, select it in the Functions list. The yellow box to the right of the Functions list will display the hint.

- Once you've saved a calculated field, it will appear in the Data window with a small equal sign to the left of the data-type icon. To edit the calculated field, right-click the field in the Data Window and choose Edit from the context menu.

Tip *The appendix contains a complete reference for all built-in Tableau functions.*

Numeric Calculations

If your data source contains various numeric measures that you wish to use in a calculated field, add them to the Formula box. Use standard numeric operators, such as * (multiplication), / (division), + (addition), and – (subtraction). For example, you could create a calculated field called Total Cost that multiplies Quantity by Unit Cost.

```
[Quantity] * [Unit Cost]
```

Since this calculated field includes two existing numbers and a numeric operator, the result of the calculated field will be numeric. As such, the calculated field will be placed in the Measures box of the Data window.

If you wish to use a percentage value in the data source to mark up the Total Cost formula, you may use this:

```
[Total Cost] + [Total Cost] * [Markup %]
```

Two items are of note here. First, a previously created calculated field can be used in another calculated field. Second, the order in which the operations are performed will affect the final result. For this calculated field to return the correct result, multiplication must be done first. However, it's the second operator in the formula. The result is still correct, however, because the standard *order of precedence* you may remember from school math applies. Multiplication will occur before addition, moving from left to right, in a formula. If you want to change the order of precedence, parentheses may be added where needed.

String Manipulation

Often, you may find a need to modify or expand on the way dimension data is presented. For example, you may have string data that is provided in a separate field that needs to be combined in a single field (often referred to as *concatenation*). Or, you may exhibit an opposite situation, where string data residing in a single field needs to be split apart (or *parsed*).

Concatenation is accomplished by using a plus sign to "add" strings together. String fields, as well as string *literals* (values surrounded by apostrophes or quotation marks), may be concatenated into one combined string. For example, if a customer contact's name is contained in three database fields (first name, last name, and middle initial), you may create one combined name with a calculated field:

```
[Customer First Name] + " " + [Customer Middle Initial] + ". " + [Customer Last Name]
```

The first name field from the database will be followed by a space, followed by the middle initial, followed by a period and space, followed by the last name. Since all portions of this calculated field are strings, the result of the calculated field will be a string. As such, it will be placed in the Dimensions portion of the Data Window.

Caution *Note that a plus sign can be used both for addition with numeric fields and concatenation with string fields. If your calculated field mixes both strings and numbers in the same formula, Tableau won't know whether to add or concatenate. A syntax error will result. In this instance, you'll need to either convert the string to a number (with FLOAT or INT functions) for addition, or convert the number to a string (with the STR function) for concatenation.*

One situation that often confounds analysts when dealing with database systems is inconsistent case within string data. Depending on the data entry application that populates your data source, you may find string data appearing in all caps, in all lowercase, or in a (potentially inconsistent) mixed case. General best practices dictate that you display string data in a case that is easy for your audience to read. For example, if the customer names described in the previous example are entered in the database in inconsistent case, you may want to add functions to a calculated field to convert them to the desired case:

```
UPPER([Customer First Name])
```

This formula text will convert all occurrences of the Customer First Name database field to uppercase, whereas the following will convert all characters of the last name to lowercase:

```
LOWER([Customer Last Name])
```

However, you may wish to use mixed case (sometimes referred to as *proper case*) for inconsistent database fields. This presents more of a challenge, as Tableau doesn't include a built-in function to convert string data to proper case. Performing this in Tableau requires more complex parsing (picking apart) of a string in combination with UPPER and LOWER functions.

To capitalize the first letter of an inconsistent string and display the remainder of the string in lowercase requires both determining the number of characters in the string (using the LEN function) and extracting certain characters from the left (using the LEFT function), right (using the RIGHT function), or middle (using the MID function) of the string. Here's an example of a calculated field named First Name Proper Case:

```
UPPER(LEFT([Customer First Name],1)) +
LOWER(RIGHT([Customer First Name], LEN([Customer First Name])-1))
```

You may find undesirable results if any database field you add to your calculated field contains a *null* (an empty value in the data source, where no data has been added for a particular field in the underlying data source). Depending on the underlying data source, a calculated field that contains any underlying data field that contains a null may itself return a null. For example, if any records in the database don't contain a middle initial for a customer, the entire value returned by the Combined Name calculated field for that customer will return a null, even though the first and last names contain values.

Tableau features built-in functions (ISNULL and IFNULL) to detect null values and change your calculated field accordingly. Once calculated fields to create proper case versions of a customer first name and customer last name field have been created, another calculated field can test for a potential null value for middle initial and return just first and last names in this instance. Here's the formula text for a calculated field named Customer Full Name (IF/THEN/ELSE/END logic is covered later in the chapter under "Logic Constructs"):

```
IF ISNULL([Customer Middle Initial]) THEN
      [Customer Last Name ProperCase] + ", " + [Customer First Name ProperCase]
ELSE
      [Customer Last Name ProperCase] + ", " +
      [Customer First Name ProperCase] + " " +
      UPPER([Customer Middle Initial]) + "."
END
```

Date Calculations

Tableau provides a great deal of analytical power when using date or date/time fields from the underlying data source. Automatic date hierarchy drill-down (Year to Quarter to Month, and so forth), built-in date level flexibility, and discrete-versus-continuous date treatment are all benefits of using date or date/time fields.

It's possible, however, that the underlying data source contains date or date/time data that's not presented in a true date or date/time data type. In particular, older database systems (perhaps converted from mainframes) or proprietary vendor-based systems may present dates in a number or string field. In some cases, these are presented in "yyyymmdd" format, which facilitates proper date sorting, or in some form of numeric value, whereby a number indicates the number of days since a particular "start" date, such as a Julian date. Until these types of dates are converted to actual date or date/time data types, none of Tableau's rich date capabilities will be available.

Depending on the original data type and layout of these fields, different approaches are required to convert them to date or date/time fields. For example, if an underlying data source contains a numeric field with a date in "yyyymmdd" numeric format, this calculated field will convert it to an actual date field:

```
DATE(MID(STR([Date]),5,2) + '/' + RIGHT(STR([Date]),2) + '/' +
LEFT(STR([Date]),4))
```

In this example, the DATE function converts a string, organized in "mm/dd/yyyy" format, into an actual date value. Because the underlying data source presents the date as a number, the STR function is used to convert it to a string value. Then, MID, RIGHT, and LEFT functions are used to parse the string into individual month, day, and year values, which are concatenated together with "/" literal characters, and finally supplied to the DATE function.

Another common use of date-oriented calculated fields is determining the difference between two dates (in days, weeks, months, or otherwise), as well as adding or subtracting a number of periods (days, weeks, and so forth) to an existing date. If, for example, a shipping goal exists to ship a product within one week of its order date, the following calculated field will return the expected ship date:

```
DATE(DATEADD('week',1,[Purchase Date]))
```

The DATEADD function accepts three arguments: a "period" value, expressed as a string literal, indicating what type of date interval to add to the existing date; the number of intervals to add, expressed as a positive or negative number; and the existing date field/date calculated field to add the intervals to. Because the DATEADD function returns a date/time data type, the DATE function is used to strip the time value away from DATEADD and return just the date portion of the field.

Creating Custom Dates Without Calculated Fields

When you initially drag a date field to a shelf, Tableau will display the date at the year level. If you wish to change the date level to quarter, month, or some other level in addition to determining whether the date appears as a discrete or continuous value, you may right-click the date field indicator and make choices from the context menu. If you prefer to always show a particular date at a particular date level, you may consider creating a calculated field. You would then use the DATETRUNC or DATEPART functions to specify the date level to use.

Tip *Any date or date/time field—whether a calculated field or database field—may be immediately set to a specified date level when dropping it onto the workspace. Just right-click and drag the field to a shelf. You'll immediately see a Drop Field dialog box prompting for the date level you wish to use.*

(continued)

However, Tableau permits you to create a duplicate date field at a desired date level right in the Data window without needing to create a calculated field. Just right-click the desired date or date/time field in the Data window and choose Create Custom Date from the context menu. Give the new custom date a meaningful name, and choose the date level you wish to use from the drop-down list. Finally, click the Date Part radio button to assign the custom date a discrete designation (individual values for only actual occurrences of dates), or click the Date Value radio button to assign the custom date a continuous designation (a range of date values from the first date to the last date). The new custom date will now appear directly in the Data window where it may be dragged to the workspace.

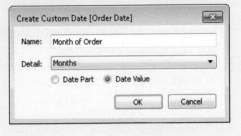

Logic Constructs

More involved calculated field logic may require you to perform one or more tests on various database values or values returned by other calculated fields. These tests will typically use a logical comparison operator, such as an equal sign, less-than sign, greater-than sign, and so forth. Based on the results of these tests, the calculated field will return a particular result.

The most common type of logical test capability comes in the form of If-Then-Else logic, typically found in most standard software programs. Tableau calculated fields require, at minimum, use of IF, THEN, and END keywords. ELSE and ELSEIF keywords are only required for multi-condition tests. Consider a requirement to create categories based on a numeric measure (another way to do this is discussed later in this chapter, in the section "Creating Binned Fields"). A Markup % measure contains percent markup numbers. However, you wish to categorize orders into High, Medium, and Low values, with these three values appearing in a dimension created by a calculated field. This example of IF/THEN/ELSEIF/ELSE/END logic will meet the requirement:

```
If [Markup %] >= .35 Then
    "High"
ElseIf [Markup %] >= .20 Then
    "Medium"
Else
    "Low"
End
```

Tip *You may notice that this formula displays mixed-case text for the IF/THEN/ELSEIF/ELSE/ END keywords, as well as line breaks and tabs between parts of the formula. This is perfectly acceptable. The Tableau formula language is not case-sensitive (although string literals within quotation marks or apostrophes* are *case-sensitive). And, pressing* ENTER *to break your formula up into multiple lines, as well as pressing* TAB *to indent parts of the formula, will not affect the outcome of the formula and may make the formula easier to read.*

A modified form of test logic uses the CASE/WHEN/THEN/END construct (the ELSE keyword is only required if a "catch all" result is desired). Similar to IF/THEN/ END logic, CASE logic tests a single field or expression and returns different results for each condition. In some cases, IF/THEN/ELSEIF/END will be required if multiple tests are needed. However, for a single test with many results, CASE logic may be easier to read and modify.

In this example, a combined Product Type-Part Number database field is being tested to determine the type of product the combined field refers to. The calculated field will evaluate the product-type portion of the combined field (which is separated from the part number by a dash) and return one of three descriptive words indicating the type of product. If an unanticipated product-type value is encountered, the calculated field will return "Unknown."

```
CASE LEFT([Product Type-SKU], FIND([Product Type-SKU],"-")-1)
    WHEN "SFT" THEN "Software"
    WHEN "HD" THEN "Hardware"
    WHEN "ACC" THEN "Accessory"
    ELSE "Unknown"
END
```

Because the number of characters indicating the product type is variable (in some cases, two characters; in other cases, three), the FIND function is used to determine the position of the hyphen, which separates the product type from the part number. Subtracting one from the location of the hyphen permits the LEFT function to be used to retrieve only the abbreviated product type. CASE logic is then used to assign a value to each abbreviated product type. If an unanticipated product type is encountered, the optional ELSE keyword will return the word "Unknown." If ELSE was not used and an unanticipated product type was encountered, the calculated field would return a NULL value.

Aggregation Within Calculated Fields

Tableau, by its nature, makes heavy use of data aggregation. From the simplest of basic charts to more complex visualization requirements, Tableau is typically dealing with "rolled up" rows from the data source that include aggregated numeric measures for each occurrence of a dimension member (by default, using a SUM aggregation). Because of this, you may need to consider aggregation when creating calculated fields in Tableau more than you would in other data analysis products.

(continued)

Consider a simple requirement to determine profitability. In an individual data record, a Profit measure will contain a positive value if the product was sold for more than it cost. If the product was sold at a loss, the Profit measure will contain a negative value. Thus, the following IF/THEN/ELSE calculated field will return a "Yes" or "No" value, depending on whether the record indicates a profit or loss:

```
If [Profit] > 0 Then
    "Yes"
Else
    "No"
End
```

If this calculated field is then placed on Color on the Marks card to indicate profitability of a series of product categories, the following will result.

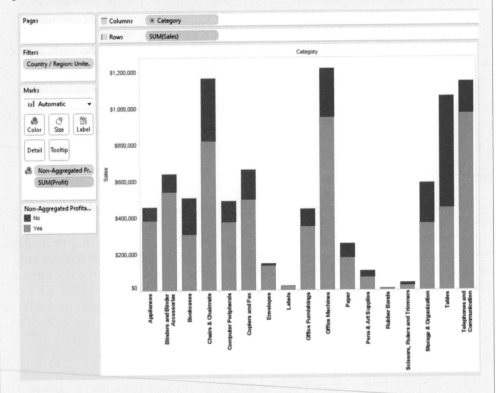

In this instance, the calculated field is evaluated at the underlying data source row level, with each individual row returning a "Yes" or "No" value. Tableau then aggregates the Yes and No values itself, breaking down each bar color based on the number of Yes and No values. The result is a visualization of the portion of each product category that is profitable or not.

But what if you want to analyze the entire product category to determine if the category, in its entirety, is profitable or not? Consider the following slight change to the calculated field:

```
If SUM([Profit]) > 0 Then
    "Yes"
Else
    "No"
End
```

Here, the calculated field is making use of a built-in Tableau aggregation function. In this case, the calculated field itself is evaluating the rolled-up aggregate profit value, determining whether the SUM of profit is positive or negative. When this is placed on Color on the Marks card, a different chart results.

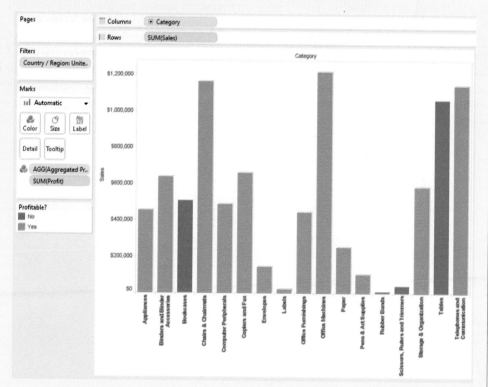

Tip *If you perform aggregation within a calculated field (by using SUM, MAX, or other aggregation functions), Tableau will always place the calculated field in the Measures portion of the Data Window, even if the calculated field returns a non-numeric result. Also, when placed on a shelf, the calculated field will show an AGG aggregation type. This indicates that the calculated field itself is performing internal aggregation and that Tableau will not attempt to aggregate the field again using a SUM.*

Creating Binned Fields

As demonstrated earlier in the chapter, it's possible to create a calculated field that evaluates a numeric measure and returns a series of categorical results (such as "High," "Medium," and "Low") based on a range of measure values. This measure-categorized-into-dimension capability doesn't always require a calculated field, however. By creating a binned field, Tableau provides the capability directly in the Data window. A *binned field* is a measure that is broken into a consistent set of "buckets" or bins, with each bin consisting of a range of values. For example, if your data source contains an Age measure, you may prefer to analyze data for people aged 0–10, 10–20, 20–30, 30–40, and so forth. Each of these age ranges would become a member of a new dimension, allowing you to analyze sales, website hits, or a similar measure for each of the age ranges.

Consider the following bar chart (this type of chart is often referred to as a *histogram*). This chart consists of a large number of dimension members, each consisting of a $50 range of profitability. The dimension members start at the minimum profit in the data source and end at the maximum profit in the data source, with $50 bins appearing in between. The measure being charted is the Count of Row ID, indicating the number of line items falling in each profit range. Notice the large concentration of line items near minimal loss or profit. While there are a few extreme loss and profit line items on each end of the range, the largest concentration is at the little loss/little profit portion of the range. This is not at the center of the range, however, indicating that, overall, more line items are profitable than not profitable.

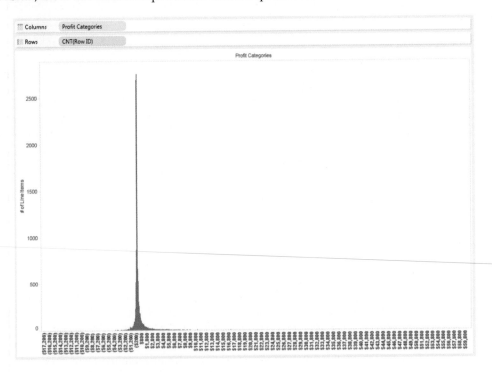

The key to this histogram is the $50 profit "buckets" or bins. While it might be possible to create a calculated field that broke down the Profit measure into this huge number of bins, Tableau's built-in bin capability makes this very simple. By just right-clicking the Profit measure and choosing Create Bins from the context menu, a new dimension is created. In this case, the new dimension is given a meaningful name (by default,

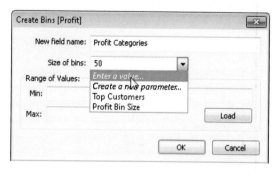

Tableau will give the dimension the same name as the measure, followed by "bin"), and the bin size is specified. If you so choose, you may use an existing parameter or create a new parameter to set the bin size "on the fly." Once created, the new bin field will appear in the Dimensions portion of the Data Window. As with any other dimension, it may be dragged to the desired location on the workspace.

Table Calculations

So far, this book has presented myriad scenarios for displaying data in any number of ways via various chart types, as well as using text tables (also referred to as crosstabs). For the most part, these various visualization types have displayed numeric measures aggregated for each dimension member included on the chart. By design, Tableau takes maximum benefit of your underlying data source or database and requests that *it* perform aggregation, only returning summarized rows to your visualization (the exception to this rule comes into play if you uncheck Aggregate Measures from the Analysis drop-down menu). For example, even if your underlying database contains many (perhaps millions) of underlying rows and you build a visualization that simply displays one measure for a dimension that exposes only 10 members, the database itself will "roll up" the dimensions to 10 levels, calculating the aggregated value for the measure for each level. The database will actually only return 10 rows to Tableau.

 Video *Using Table Calculations*

Consider the simple crosstab illustrated in Figure 7-2, which only displays Sum of Sales by Year and Region. Notice that both row and column grand totals have been enabled from the Analysis | Totals drop-down menu. In this case, regardless of the number of underlying records in the data source, the data source itself has calculated all summed values and only returned 25 aggregated values to Tableau—all Tableau has done is formatted and displayed them without performing any calculations whatsoever.

But what if you wanted to perform some other kind of analysis on this data instead of, or in addition to, just looking at total sales by year and region? Perhaps, for example, you would like to analyze how much sales has changed from year to year, either in dollars or percent. Or, maybe you would prefer to visualize these numbers as a running total that gets larger and larger as it "runs" across the crosstab by year, or down the

Region	Year of Order Date				
	2010	2011	2012	2013	Grand Total
Central	$448,285	$602,849	$619,324	$869,885	$2,540,342
East	$592,166	$510,539	$518,147	$801,953	$2,422,805
South	$357,105	$304,837	$433,216	$502,188	$1,597,346
West	$526,777	$526,283	$660,045	$678,335	$2,391,439
Grand Total	$1,924,333	$1,944,507	$2,230,731	$2,852,360	$8,951,931

Figure 7-2   Simple crosstab

crosstab by region. In these types of cases, an additional calculation will need to be done once the aggregated values have already been returned by the database.

As a general rule, standard industry databases don't have the capability to carry out these "secondary" calculations, performing multiple "passes" over the data to calculate a secondary result based on the values from a primary result. Well, Tableau provides the ability to perform these additional calculation passes by way of *Table calculations*, additional calculations that Tableau performs *after* aggregated values have been returned from the underlying data source.

To create a table calculation, you must first design a visualization using standard dimensions and measures, as discussed previously in this book. Once a measure has been added to the workspace and assigned an aggregation type (Sum, by default), you may then create a table calculation. There are several ways of creating table calculations:

- Select one of the sub-menu options from the Analysis | Percentage Of drop-down menu.
- Right-click the measure on the workspace and choose one of the sub-menu options from the Quick Table Calculation context menu item.
- Right-click the measure on the workspace, choose Add Table Calculation from the context menu, and complete the resulting dialog box.

Revisiting the "percent change from year to year" requirement discussed earlier, Figure 7-3 shows the crosstab originally displayed in Figure 7-2 after Percentage Of | Table has been selected from the drop-down menus.

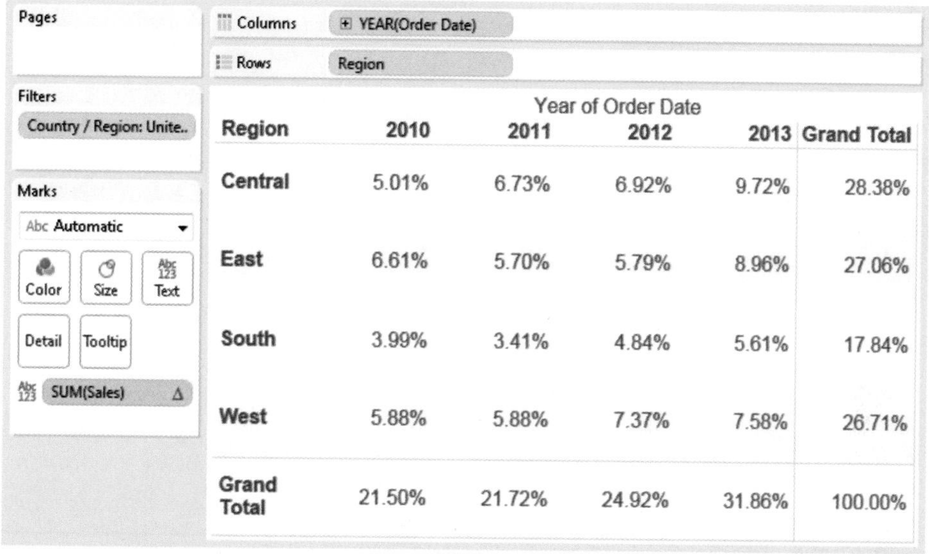

Pages							

Columns	YEAR(Order Date)
Rows	Region

Filters

Country / Region: Unite..

	Year of Order Date				
Region	**2010**	**2011**	**2012**	**2013**	**Grand Total**
Central	5.01%	6.73%	6.92%	9.72%	28.38%
East	6.61%	5.70%	5.79%	8.96%	27.06%
South	3.99%	3.41%	4.84%	5.61%	17.84%
West	5.88%	5.88%	7.37%	7.58%	26.71%
Grand Total	21.50%	21.72%	24.92%	31.86%	100.00%

Marks

Abc **Automatic**

Color   Size   Text

Detail   Tooltip

SUM(Sales)   Δ

Figure 7-3   Percentage Of | Table menu option

One change is blatantly obvious. Rather than displaying dollar values indicating aggregated sales for each combination of year and region, the crosstab now displays percentages, with each individual year/region value showing as a percentage of overall sales. Row and column dollar totals have also been replaced with percentages of the overall total they are responsible for. And, the "grand-grand total" at the lower right indicates that it is, in fact, 100 percent of the total amount. What may not be so obvious is the change to the SUM(Sales) field indicator on the Marks card. Looking closely, you'll notice that a small delta (triangle) icon now appears on the field indicator. This confirms that this measure has been converted to a table calculation.

SUM(Sales)   Δ

If you undo the previous Percentage Of option (or choose Percentage Of | None) to return the measure to its original aggregation and then right-click the measure and choose Quick Table Calculation | Percent Of Total from the context menu, you'll see a slightly different result, as illustrated in Figure 7-4. Here, the percentages are still displayed, but are calculated across each region row rather than the entire crosstab.

One of the immediate questions you may ask after creating a table calculation is, "How do I see the original measure, as well as the table calculation, to help me analyze further?" Especially when you first start working with table calculations, you'll probably want to see the original measure along with the table calculation to begin to understand how table calculations behave. This is a fairly simple process.

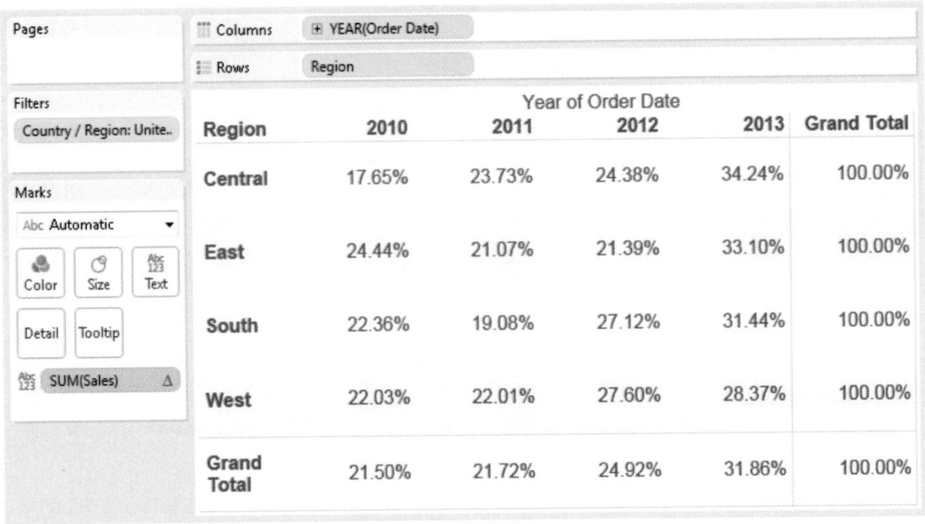

Figure 7-4   Quick table calculation – percent of total

Just re-add the original measure to the visualization again. In the case of a crosstab, you may drag the original measure to Text on the Marks card, or just double-click the original measure to invoke Measure Names and Measure Values on the crosstab. The original measure won't display the delta icon, while the table calculation will.

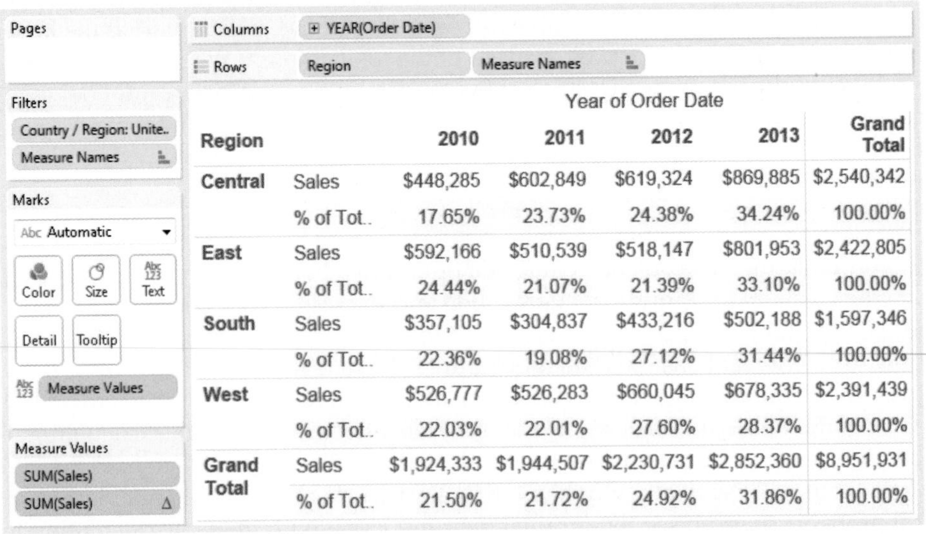

Caution *Using the Percentage Of drop-down menu option prohibits the original measure from being added to the visualization alongside the table calculation. If you wish to display both the original measure and a percentage table calculation, use right-click context menu options to create the table calculation instead of the drop-down menus.*

Even though the table calculation illustrated in both Figures 7-3 and 7-4 was created with a percent of total option, you'll notice a difference. When using the pull-down menu Percentage Of | Table option, the table calculation evaluated for the entire table—each combination of year and region was calculated as a percent of the overall total. However, when the Percentage Of Total quick table calculation was used, each region row was calculated individually, with the total for each region row indicating 100 percent and the yearly values for each region contributing to the region total, rather than the overall total for the entire crosstab. You may wish to modify the second table calculation to behave like the first—calculating each year/region combination as a percentage of the overall total. Or, perhaps you prefer to have the percentages calculated down the yearly columns with each region total contributing to a 100 percent yearly total.

What determines the end result is a table calculation's direction and scope. A table calculation's *direction* refers to the order in which individual table "cells" are calculated—left to right (referred to as *across*), top to bottom (referred to as *down*), left to right and then top to bottom (referred to as *across then down*), or top to bottom and then left to right (referred to as *down then across*). A table calculation's *scope* determines when the table calculation will reset to a beginning value.

Sometimes, it's difficult to separate the two properties. For example, the direction used in the table calculation illustrated in Figure 7-3 is "across then down." The scope used is "table," as the percentage never resets within the entire table. Conversely, the direction used in the table calculation illustrated in Figure 7-4 is simply "across," as the percentage is always reset before any "down" calculation takes place. And the scope used is "table (across)," indicating that the table calculation value will be reset when it reaches the end of a row.

Note *Tableau table calculation documentation also refers to the terms "addressing" and "partitioning." Addressing can be considered similar to direction, while partitioning can be considered similar to scope.*

Direction and scope choices are set automatically for quick table calculations and for Percentage Of pull-down menu choices. However, you may edit direction and scope after a quick table calculation has been created by right-clicking the table calculation field indicator (it will display a delta icon) and choosing either the Compute Using or Edit Table Calculation context menu option. If you wish to customize direction and scope options when initially creating a table calculation, you may right-click the desired measure and choose Add Table Calculation from the context menu. The Table Calculation dialog box will provide a choice of calculation type (Running Sum, Percent Of Total, Moving Calculation, and so forth), as well as direction and scope options in the Running Along drop-down list. You can even select "Advanced" from the Running

Along drop-down list to display another dialog box providing precise options for direction and scope options.

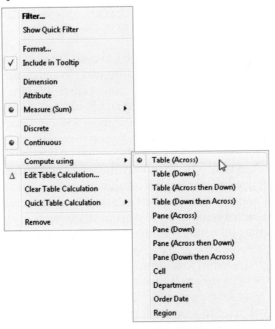

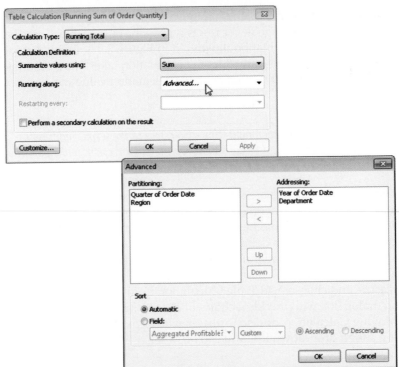

Consider another crosstab that analyzes order quantity by year and quarter on columns and product type and region on rows. Grand totals are shown to help evaluate table calculation behavior.

		Order Date								Grand Total
		2012				2013				
Department	Region	Q1	Q2	Q3	Q4	Q1	Q2	Q3	Q4	
Furniture	Central	305	517	512	801	258	487	988	919	4,787
	East	197	344	488	646	304	322	564	1,101	3,966
	South	122	243	353	520	227	267	542	382	2,656
	West	218	498	282	1,013	380	424	645	729	4,189
Office Supplies	Central	777	1,328	1,183	1,616	1,055	1,174	2,342	2,584	12,059
	East	881	1,270	1,013	1,963	770	1,449	2,032	1,701	11,079
	South	536	986	713	1,045	611	794	1,142	1,501	7,328
	West	905	901	935	1,686	957	1,308	1,737	2,207	10,636
Grand Total		3,941	6,087	5,479	9,290	4,562	6,225	9,992	11,124	56,700

Now look at various direction and scope behavior when a Running Sum table calculation is added:

- **Table (Across)**   Notice that the value increments across each row, with the last value in the row equaling the row total. The table calculation resets at the beginning of each row.

		Order Date								Grand Total
		2012				2013				
Department	Region	Q1	Q2	Q3	Q4	Q1	Q2	Q3	Q4	
Furniture	Central	305	822	1,334	2,135	2,393	2,880	3,868	4,787	4,787
	East	197	541	1,029	1,675	1,979	2,301	2,865	3,966	3,966
	South	122	365	718	1,238	1,465	1,732	2,274	2,656	2,656
	West	218	716	998	2,011	2,391	2,815	3,460	4,189	4,189
Office Supplies	Central	777	2,105	3,288	4,904	5,959	7,133	9,475	12,059	12,059
	East	881	2,151	3,164	5,127	5,897	7,346	9,378	11,079	11,079
	South	536	1,522	2,235	3,280	3,891	4,685	5,827	7,328	7,328
	West	905	1,806	2,741	4,427	5,384	6,692	8,429	10,636	10,636
Grand Total		3,941	10,028	15,507	24,797	29,359	35,584	45,576	56,700	56,700

- **Table (Down)** Notice that the value increments down each column, with the last value in the column equaling the column total. The table calculation resets at the beginning of each column.

		Order Date								
		2012				2013				Grand Total
Department	**Region**	Q1	Q2	Q3	Q4	Q1	Q2	Q3	Q4	
Furniture	Central	305	517	512	801	258	487	988	919	4,787
	East	502	861	1,000	1,447	562	809	1,552	2,020	8,753
	South	624	1,104	1,353	1,967	789	1,076	2,094	2,402	11,409
	West	842	1,602	1,635	2,980	1,169	1,500	2,739	3,131	15,598
Office Supplies	Central	1,619	2,930	2,818	4,596	2,224	2,674	5,081	5,715	27,657
	East	2,500	4,200	3,831	6,559	2,994	4,123	7,113	7,416	38,736
	South	3,036	5,186	4,544	7,604	3,605	4,917	8,255	8,917	46,064
	West	3,941	6,087	5,479	9,290	4,562	6,225	9,992	11,124	56,700
Grand Total		3,941	6,087	5,479	9,290	4,562	6,225	9,992	11,124	56,700

- **Table (Across then Down)** Notice that the value increments across each row, with the last value in the row equaling the accumulated value as of that row. The table calculation then continues to increment starting at the next row. The value is never reset and accumulates all the way across, then down, until reaching the overall grand total at the lower right.

		Order Date								
		2012				2013				Grand Total
Department	**Region**	Q1	Q2	Q3	Q4	Q1	Q2	Q3	Q4	
Furniture	Central	305	822	1,334	2,135	2,393	2,880	3,868	4,787	4,787
	East	4,984	5,328	5,816	6,462	6,766	7,088	7,652	8,753	8,753
	South	8,875	9,118	9,471	9,991	10,218	10,485	11,027	11,409	11,409
	West	11,627	12,125	12,407	13,420	13,800	14,224	14,869	15,598	15,598
Office Supplies	Central	16,375	17,703	18,886	20,502	21,557	22,731	25,073	27,657	27,657
	East	28,538	29,808	30,821	32,784	33,554	35,003	37,035	38,736	38,736
	South	39,272	40,258	40,971	42,016	42,627	43,421	44,563	46,064	46,064
	West	46,969	47,870	48,805	50,491	51,448	52,756	54,493	56,700	56,700
Grand Total		3,941	10,028	15,507	24,797	29,359	35,584	45,576	56,700	56,700

- **Pane (Across)**   Notice that the value increments across each row until it reaches the last quarter in a year (the partition for each year is referred to as a *pane*). It then resets at the beginning of the next year pane. The row grand total consists of the pane accumulated totals.

| | | Order Date | | | | | | | | Grand Total |
| | | 2012 | | | | 2013 | | | | |
Department	Region	Q1	Q2	Q3	Q4	Q1	Q2	Q3	Q4	
Furniture	Central	305	822	1,334	2,135	258	745	1,733	2,652	4,787
	East	197	541	1,029	1,675	304	626	1,190	2,291	3,966
	South	122	365	718	1,238	227	494	1,036	1,418	2,656
	West	218	716	998	2,011	380	804	1,449	2,178	4,189
Office Supplies	Central	777	2,105	3,288	4,904	1,055	2,229	4,571	7,155	12,059
	East	881	2,151	3,164	5,127	770	2,219	4,251	5,952	11,079
	South	536	1,522	2,235	3,280	611	1,405	2,547	4,048	7,328
	West	905	1,806	2,741	4,427	957	2,265	4,002	6,209	10,636
Grand Total		3,941	10,028	15,507	24,797	4,562	10,787	20,779	31,903	56,700

- **Pane (Down)**   Notice that the value increments down each column until it reaches the last region in a department (the partition for each department is referred to as a *pane*). It then resets at the beginning of the next department pane. The column grand total consists of the pane accumulated totals.

| | | Order Date | | | | | | | | Grand Total |
| | | 2012 | | | | 2013 | | | | |
Department	Region	Q1	Q2	Q3	Q4	Q1	Q2	Q3	Q4	
Furniture	Central	305	517	512	801	258	487	988	919	4,787
	East	502	861	1,000	1,447	562	809	1,552	2,020	8,753
	South	624	1,104	1,353	1,967	789	1,076	2,094	2,402	11,409
	West	842	1,602	1,635	2,980	1,169	1,500	2,739	3,131	15,598
Office Supplies	Central	777	1,328	1,183	1,616	1,055	1,174	2,342	2,584	12,059
	East	1,658	2,598	2,196	3,579	1,825	2,623	4,374	4,285	23,138
	South	2,194	3,584	2,909	4,624	2,436	3,417	5,516	5,786	30,466
	West	3,099	4,485	3,844	6,310	3,393	4,725	7,253	7,993	41,102
Grand Total		3,941	6,087	5,479	9,290	4,562	6,225	9,992	11,124	56,700

While this is not a complete overview of all possible direction and scope options, you should now have a good idea of the general approach to using table calculations. You'll want to experiment with various table calculation options—you may always "undo" or make another choice—until you arrive at the correct result.

Tip *While their name may imply that table calculations are only appropriate for "tables," such as text tables or crosstabs, they perform equal functions with any chart type. As with text tables, simpler single dimension/single measure charts will provide fewer scope and direction options than charts that use multiple dimensions/measures on rows and columns.*

Using Table Calculation Functions in Calculated Fields

When creating a new table calculation with the Add Table Calculation option or editing an existing table calculation, there are many choices in the dialog box, such as the type of calculation (Running Sum, Difference From, and so forth), the type of aggregation to use in the calculation (Sum, Average, and others), and direction and scope options. While this dialog box makes specifying table calculations straightforward, there are yet more ways to customize a table calculation. For every table calculation you create with the dialog box, an option to view and customize becomes available which will result in a new calculated field in the Data window.

Consider this table calculation, created to act as the right axis line chart value of a Pareto chart.

This particular table calculation actually performs two calculations (this is sometimes referred to as a *two-pass* table calculation). The first is a running sum to accumulate sales totals across the bars that make up the left axis of the Pareto chart. Then, a second calculation is selected (again, calculating across the "table," or bars of the left axis) to determine the percent of total based on first the running sum. The ultimate purpose of this table calculation is to determine when 80 percent of product sales have occurred.

Note the Customize button at the bottom left of the dialog box. Clicking this button will display a formula editor, similar to that illustrated earlier in the chapter when creating a calculated field. You'll see special Tableau table calculation functions (in the Table Calculation category of the Functions list) that perform table calculation logic after the aggregated set of data has been returned from the database.

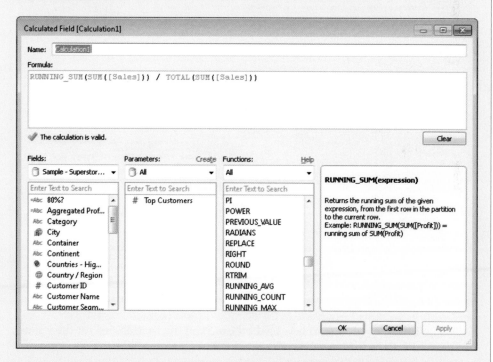

If you wish to modify the Tableau-generated table calculation formula, make any desired changes. Make sure to give the calculation a meaningful name, as a new calculated field with that name will be created and placed in the Data Window. When you click OK, a modified table calculation dialog box will appear

(continued)

where you may choose direction/scope options. Make the desired choice and click OK. The original table calculation will then be replaced with the new calculated field you just created.

You may also copy the logic from the original table calculation in another calculated field, while leaving the original table calculation as-is. For example, to apply a color value to the left axis bars on the Pareto chart, indicating which categories make up the 80 percent of sales illustrated on the right axis line chart, the logic from the table calculation can be copied to the Clipboard and used in another calculated field.

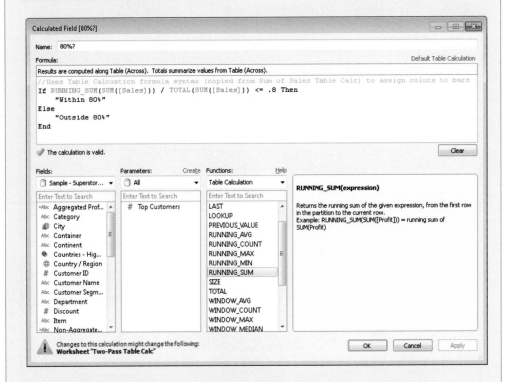

When this calculated field is placed on Color on the Marks card for the left axis bar chart, the same logic used to calculated the percent of total running sum will color bars based on the 80 percent "Pareto Principle."

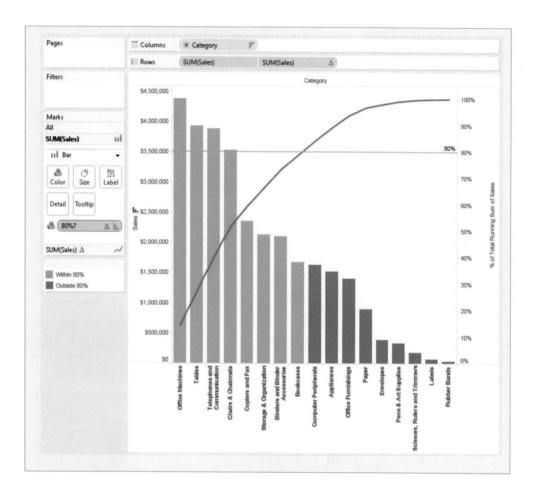

Reference Lines, Bands, and Distribution

Although not strictly tied to statistical analysis, reference lines are often helpful in highlighting a desired portion of a visual chart. A *reference line,* as the name implies, is a line that is drawn across the numeric axis of a chart denoting a particular desired value, such as the average, maximum, median, or some other constant value (such as a sales goal). Variations of reference lines include a *reference band,* a shaded portion of a numeric axis beginning and ending at specified values. Another variation, a *reference distribution,* results in several gradient shaded bands at various intervals across the numeric axis.

No matter which option you prefer, begin by right-clicking in the numeric axis on your chart and selecting Add Reference Line from the context menu. If reference lines already exist on your chart, you may also edit or remove them via context menu choices. You may also select an existing reference line on the chart itself, right-click, and choose appropriate options from the context menu.

Single Reference Line

A single reference line denotes one particular point on the numeric axis. It may be based on a variety of calculations, using existing measures in your chart. You may also base the value on a constant number that you "hard code" into the dialog box, or the value of a parameter.

In this case, one line will appear across the entire "table" (the entire chart, regardless of how many nested dimensions have been used). The average of the sales measure is being displayed by the reference line. A custom label has been specified, which enables a freeform text box where literal text and a combination of existing values from the chart may be used to label the reference line. The line has been formatted as a bold red line with no fill options.

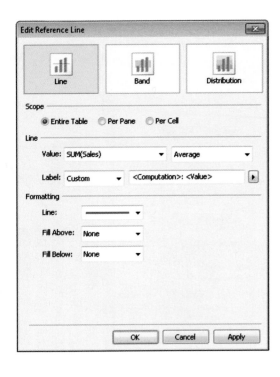

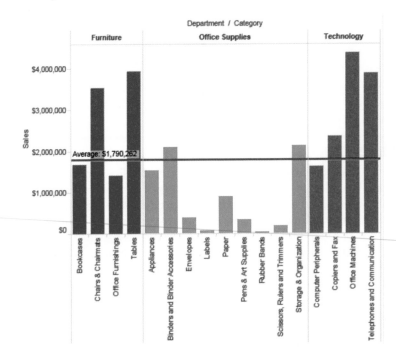

Tip *A measure must be "in use" somewhere on your chart in order to base a reference line on it. If you want to base a reference line on a measure other than the one actually being displayed on the chart, drag the desired measure to Detail on the Marks card. Then, when you create or edit a reference line, the additional measure will be available in the Reference Line dialog box.*

Reference Band

A reference band highlights a range on the numeric axis. The beginning and ending values may be based on a variety of calculations, using existing measures in your chart. You may also base the beginning and ending values on a constant number that you "hard code" into the dialog box, or the value of a parameter.

In this case, a separate band will appear for each "pane" (in this particular example, a pane exists for each department). The lower portion of the band is based on the median of the sales measure, with the upper band based on the maximum of the same measure. Custom labels have been specified, which enables a freeform text box where literal text and a combination of existing values from the chart may be used to label the upper and lower boundaries of the band. No line is specified to denote the upper and lower boundaries of the band, but the band is shaded with a medium gray color.

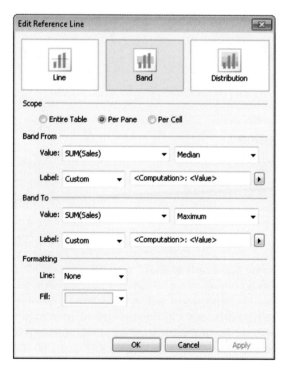

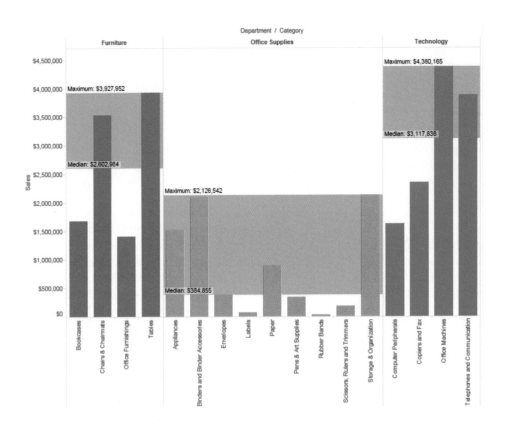

Reference Distribution

Like a reference band, a reference distribution shades a defined area on the numeric axis. However, rather than just specifying a beginning and ending point for a distribution, you may specify several points, which are shaded with various gradients. Variations may be based on a number of statistical values, including confidence interval, percentages, percentiles, quantiles (four quartiles, five quintiles, and so forth), or standard deviation. Reference bands are particularly helpful for certain chart types, such as bullet charts and box plots (both are covered in Chapter 4).

In this case, a separate band will appear "per call" (for each bar in the chart). The distribution is based on 60 percent and 80 percent of the average of the sales goal measure. No label or line is being specified. A graduated gray/light palette has been chosen, and options to fill both above and below the 60 and 80 percent levels have been selected. Used in combination with another single reference line, the reference distribution allows comparison of the actual sales bar to the 60/80 percent range of the goal on a bullet chart.

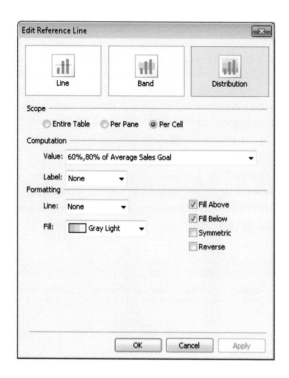

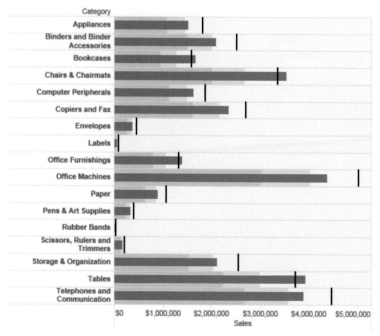

Trend Lines

As the name indicates, a *trend line* is a line (or series of lines) that appears on a chart indicating the general trend the underlying marks on the chart are exhibiting. A trend line uses various built-in statistical models (which are selectable) to determine appearance and behavior. To create a trend line, choose Analysis | Trend Lines | Show Trend Lines from the drop-down menus, or right-click the chart (not an axis or headers) and select Trend Lines | Show Trend Lines from the context menu.

Tip *Trend lines require that both the Column and Row shelves contain a numeric measure (typically, this results in a scatter plot, covered in Chapter 4). A trend line is also permitted if a chart is based on a date or date/time dimension (unless they are set to month/day/year or month/year date levels) and a measure. If you attempt to display trend lines otherwise, an error message will result.*

A default trend line will appear. You may immediately hover your mouse over a trend line, or select it, to display a tooltip. The tooltip will display basic statistical information about the makeup of the trend line. If you wish to examine or modify the statistical model that creates the trend line, right-click a selected trend line or the chart itself. From the context menu, choose Edit Trend Lines. Or, select Analysis | Trend Lines | Edit Trend Lines from the drop-down menus. A dialog box will appear, permitting you to change trend line behavior.

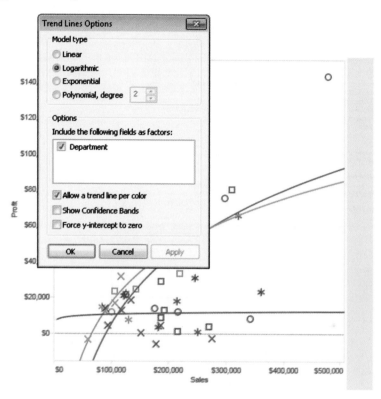

A more detailed discussion of the statistical model making up the trend line may be displayed by choosing Describe Trend Model from the same right-click context menu or by choosing the Analysis | Trend Line drop-down menu.

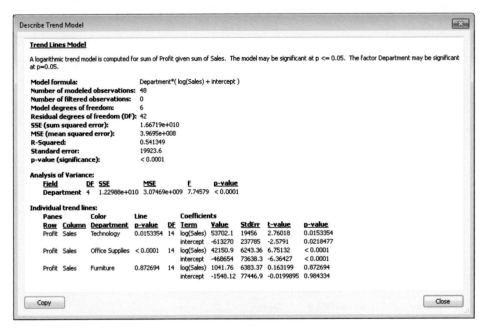

8
CHAPTER

Creating Dashboards

In many cases, the finished product in a business intelligence project consists of one or more dashboards. A Google search on "dashboard" probably will return more computer-related definitions than descriptions of the portion of a car that displays the speedometer, fuel gauge, and other key performance indicators. Still, a BI *dashboard* serves a similar purpose: to combine, in one viewable space, more than one key performance indicator, chart, or diagram to present a unified view to your audience.

While some other BI products allow starting with a blank dashboard and adding components to it, Tableau presents a different dashboard paradigm. In Tableau, individual worksheets, each with a single visualization, are first created within a workbook. After desired sheets have been created, one or more sheets are combined on one or more dashboards in the same workbook. Depending on how the workbook is finally distributed or viewed (in a copy of Tableau Desktop or Tableau Reader, exported to a PDF file, or posted to Tableau Server or Tableau Public), the end user may view the combined dashboard, individual sheets, or both.

Note *A complete discussion of Tableau distribution options is presented in Chapter 9.*

Note *Open the Chapter 8 - Dashboards.twbx file in Tableau to see examples that relate to this chapter.*

Creating a Simple Dashboard

As mentioned previously, Tableau's basic dashboard paradigm revolves around existing worksheets. As such, you'll want to think about your ultimate dashboard requirement as you create individual worksheets. Probably the most basic, but sometimes ignored, consideration is the names given to worksheets. Not only will meaningful worksheet names help you keep track of desired views when designing the dashboard, but worksheet names will automatically appear on the dashboard as individual titles.

Other dashboard considerations include additional visual elements in each worksheet beyond the basic visualization. For example, visible color legends, size legends, and quick filters will be included on the dashboard when you initially add the worksheet. While you can move or remove any extra element that you don't want on a dashboard, you may choose to hide any extraneous legends or quick filters on the worksheet itself before you even begin dashboard design.

 Video *Creating a Dashboard*

When you're ready to create a dashboard in an existing workbook, right-click on the tab list or filmstrip view and choose New Dashboard from the context menu, click the New Dashboard tab along the bottom of the workspace, or choose Dashboard | New Dashboard from the drop-down menus. A blank dashboard will appear with the Data window replaced by four sections: a list of existing worksheets in the workbook, a selection of additional dashboard elements (covered in the next section of this chapter), a layout section containing the organization of items added to the dashboard, and a sizing section for customizing dashboard element sizes.

If you've used Tableau versions prior to 8, one dashboard change will be of particular interest. Notice the Tiled/Floating choice just below the list of dashboard elements about midscreen. By default this is set to Tiled, which will result in behavior you are familiar with from previous Tableau versions. The Floating option, new in Tableau 8, allows far more free-form placement of objects on the dashboard.

This selection can be changed at any time, and applies to any worksheets you add to the dashboard moving forward. If the default Tiled setting is retained, worksheets will be placed on the dashboard in a logical side-by-side, top-and-bottom fashion, with no worksheet, legend, title, caption, or quick filter permitted to overlap any other dashboard element. If Floating is chosen, any worksheet added to the dashboard from that point forward (even if there are already tiled worksheet elements on the dashboard) can be freely placed in any location.

Add new sheets and objects as:

Tiled	Floating

Best Practice *Especially if you've used earlier versions of Tableau, you may be immediately tempted to add all dashboard elements with the Floating option for maximum flexibility. You'll soon discover, however, that perfectly aligning dashboard elements may prove difficult. It may be preferable to use the Tiled option to facilitate good element alignment. You can then select individual dashboard elements that you want to move freely (such as legends), and choose the Floating option for them only. This is discussed later in the chapter under "Floating Placement."*

Tiled Placement

This default setting uses the same dashboard design approach as previous versions of Tableau, placing worksheets and their associated elements (captions, quick filters, and so forth) in a strict "no-overlap" order on the dashboard. The most basic way to use tiled placement is to simply double-click on worksheet names in the order you want to add them to the dashboard. Tableau will add each worksheet to the dashboard in a side-by-side, then top-and-bottom order.

For example, if you double-click two worksheets, the second will be placed to the right of the first, with the dashboard divided in half vertically. If you double-click a third sheet, the dashboard will split vertically on the left, with the third worksheet appearing below the first. A fourth double-click will divide the dashboard into four even quarters, one worksheet being placed in each. All related worksheet elements (such as quick filters and legends) will be placed on the right side of the dashboard. Figure 8-1 illustrates a simple dashboard containing four worksheets that were double-clicked in order of appearance in the worksheet list.

You can also drag and drop worksheets from the worksheet list onto the dashboard. While resulting placement of new views can seem confusing if you're just getting used

Figure 8-1   Basic tiled dashboard created using double-click

to dragging and dropping sheets, there are a few tips that will help you master exactly where the sheet you are dragging will appear in relation to existing sheets.

- A large gray box indicates that the sheet will split the dashboard in half vertically or horizontally.

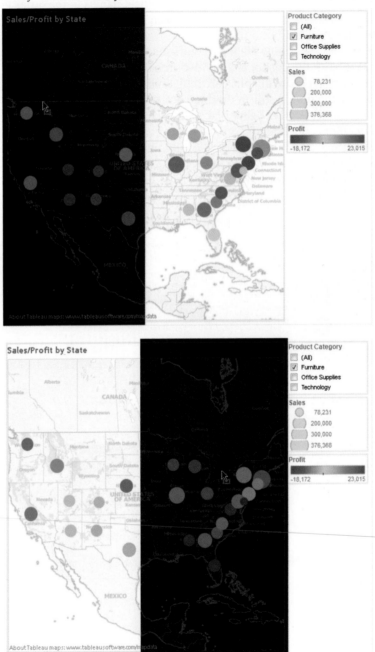

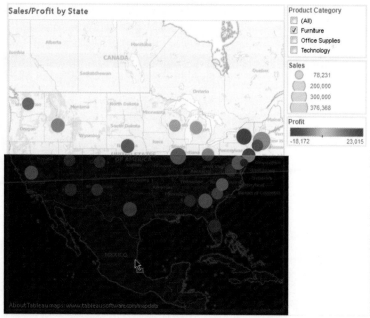

- A thin gray box (typically at the very edge of the dashboard, but also between legends and worksheets) indicates that the sheet will take up that entire portion of the dashboard, resizing all other dashboard elements to accommodate it.

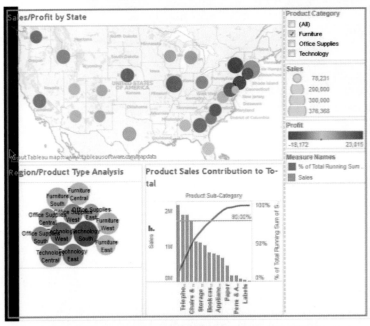

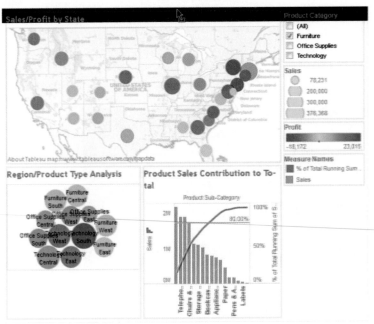

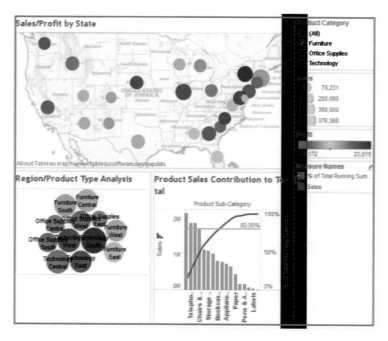

- A medium gray box indicates that the sheet will be placed in between the two elements on either side, resizing the other two elements to accommodate it.

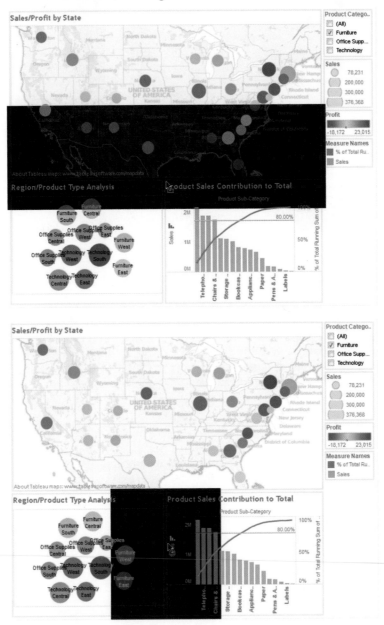

Once you've placed a worksheet on the dashboard, you can move it to a different location. When you select the desired sheet on the dashboard, you'll notice the small series of white dots at the top of the title bar (known as a "move handle"). Hold your mouse down on the move handle and drag the sheet to the desired location, keeping in mind the tips just discussed.

You can also resize a worksheet or legend once it has been placed on the dashboard. Point to the top, bottom, left, or right edge of the element you want to resize until you see a double-arrow cursor. Drag to resize the selected element, and resize adjoining elements accordingly. Tableau makes experimenting easy. If you don't like the result of a worksheet placement or resize, simply click the undo button in the toolbar, or press CTRL-Z, and try again.

Tip *After you add a worksheet to the dashboard, you may find that the visualization in the worksheet is not properly sized. There may be scrollbars that you don't want to see, or an object may be too small or too large for the space it's been allotted on the dashboard. Similar to the fit option available in the toolbar when you're creating a worksheet, you can size the object separately within the dashboard. Select the desired sheet on the dashboard and click the context arrow in the upper right of the title bar. Make the desired choice from the Fit option on the context menu.*

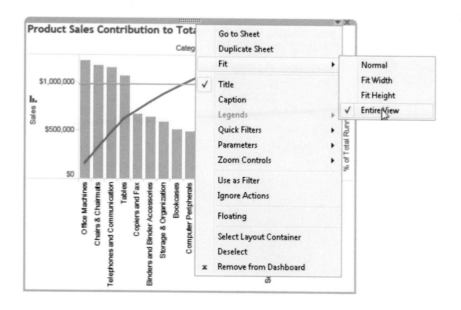

Floating Placement

While tiled dashboards guarantee perfect alignment, they also present a certain amount of rigidity that has sometimes proven frustrating in previous Tableau versions. Tableau 8 introduces *floating placement* that permits worksheets and associated dashboard elements to be placed freely anywhere on a dashboard.

After clicking the Floating button under "Add new sheets and objects as," worksheets can be freely placed anywhere on the dashboard. If the worksheet includes legends, quick filters, or a caption, these items will also be placed on the dashboard as free-form elements. Once they have been dropped, worksheets and their associated elements can be freely moved and resized without limitation. An immediate benefit of floating placement is the ability to move legends on top of existing worksheets that may have blank areas, such as maps. Figure 8-2 illustrates this.

If you already have existing tiled worksheets on the dashboard, floating worksheets will always appear on top of them. If you have multiple floating worksheets, you can choose the floating order, placing one object on top of or behind other floating objects.

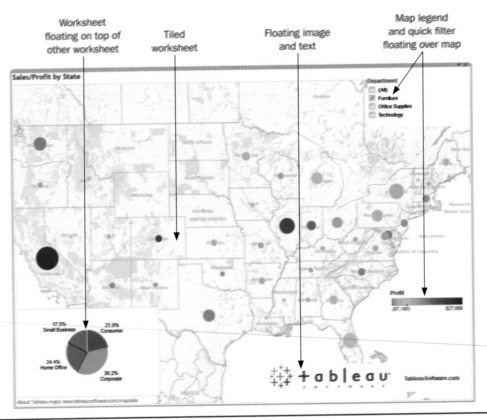

Figure 8-2 Floating worksheets and legends

Select the desired floating sheet on the dashboard and click the context arrow in the upper right of the title bar on the object, and make the desired floating-order choice from the context menu.

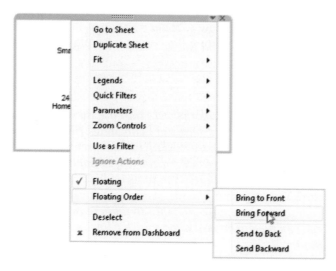

Tip *You may find that a combination of tiled and floating dashboard elements gives you the best of both worlds. For example, you may prefer the perfect alignment of several tiled worksheets. However, you then may want to place map legends over unused areas of a map (such as open water). Simply select the legend you want to float, click the context arrow in the title bar, and check Floating from the context menu. The legend can then be moved to any place on the dashboard.*

Associated Dashboard Elements

Any legends, titles, quick filters, and parameters originally belonging to a worksheet will appear on the dashboard when you add the worksheet. If you add a worksheet in tiled mode, the associated elements will be tiled. If you use floating mode, associated elements will be free-floating on the dashboard. If the worksheets that make up your dashboard contain even a moderate number of these associated elements, the dashboard can quickly become cluttered with multiple legends, filters, and parameters.

Consider removing extraneous elements that don't add to overall dashboard effectiveness. For example, if a worksheet mark is size encoded, and the actual values of the size aren't necessary for effective use of the dashboard, a size legend may unnecessarily take up valuable dashboard space. The same consideration may apply to a color legend if general color encoding can be deduced by simply looking at the worksheet. In these cases, simply select the legend and click the small × in the upper-right corner to remove the legend. If you later want to redisplay a dashboard element, just select the associated sheet on the dashboard. Then make the desired choice from the Analysis drop-down menu, or context menu (displayed by clicking the context arrow in the title bar).

You can also move elements away from their default location (the right side of the dashboard for tiled worksheets, and next to the associated worksheet in floating mode). For example, a tiled legend on the right side of the dashboard may be more effective if it appears next to its associated worksheet that may have been placed in the lower left of the dashboard. Don't forget the new Tableau 8 option to float legends, even if the associated worksheet is tiled, permitting the legend to be placed partially or fully on top of the associated worksheet.

Best Practice *If you have several worksheets that use the same quick filter, consider one of several approaches to eliminate duplicate quick filters appearing on a dashboard. Tableau 8 provides more flexibility than previous versions with options on the quick filter context menu. Look for choices to apply the quick filter to the entire data source (previously referred to as Global), or one or more sheets on the dashboard. You may also consider using a parameter instead of a quick filter. The parameter can be applied flexibly to more than one worksheet, but need only be displayed on the dashboard once. Quick filters and parameters are covered in detail in Chapter 5.*

Advanced Dashboard Elements

So far, this chapter has discussed adding worksheets, and their associated elements, to a dashboard. Tableau includes additional elements you can add from the left side of the screen when creating a dashboard. These additional elements permit text and images to be placed on the dashboard, as well as additional items to support web pages within dashboards, blank objects for spacing, and containers to help further refine the way a dashboard is organized. In addition, the Layout and Size sections provide various ways of interacting with and customizing your dashboard.

Layout Container

A *layout container* is an outline or box that contains other objects, such as worksheets, legends, and quick filters. The main benefit of a layout container is automatic resizing of objects within it. If, for example, a quick filter changes the size of a worksheet in a container (perhaps a crosstab shows fewer rows), the other objects in the container will automatically resize to accommodate the smaller worksheet.

With tiled worksheets (when using tiled mode in version 8, and with Tableau versions before 8), layout containers are an integral part of a dashboard. In fact, even though you don't explicitly choose them, layout containers are added in quantity when you add worksheets in tiled mode. Consider the dashboard illustrated in Figure 8-3, which was created by simply dragging three worksheets to a new dashboard with tiled mode selected. Because one worksheet includes two legends and a quick filter, and another worksheet includes another legend, several layout containers are automatically created to accommodate the combination of worksheets and associated dashboard elements.

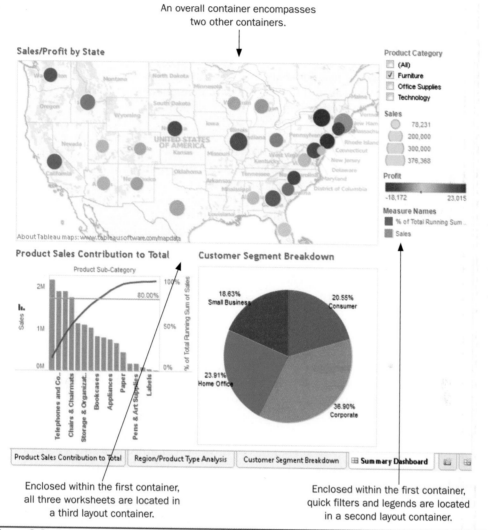

Figure 8-3 Layout containers automatically added to a dashboard

Note *If you are using floating mode, you will probably find layout containers to be of little benefit. They are generally only applicable to tiled dashboards.*

There are two general ways to familiarize yourself with automatic layout container creation:

- From a worksheet's context menu (click the context arrow in a worksheet's title bar), choose Select Layout Container. This will highlight the layout container that the worksheet is contained within.

- Examine the Layout section of the dashboard window on the left side of the screen (covered in more detail later in the chapter). This section outlines the layout container hierarchy of the dashboard, indicating how many layout containers there are, whether they are horizontal or vertical, and what dashboard elements are contained within them.

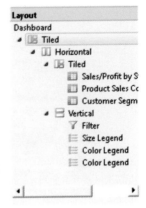

You can add your own layout containers to your dashboard by dragging them from the left side of the screen to the dashboard. Choose a horizontal or vertical container, depending on whether you want worksheet widths or heights to automatically resize, respectively. Then drag worksheets into the just-added containers. Look carefully—a thin blue outline around an existing container indicates that a worksheet will be dropped in that container.

You can add a border to layout containers with the Format option. Select the desired layout container and click the context arrow in the title bar, choosing Format from the context menu. You can also right-click on the container name in Layout and choose Format Container. The dashboard section on the left will be replaced by a Format Container drop-down. Choose the type of border you would like the container to display.

Blank

Another dashboard element that's primarily intended for tiled dashboards is the *blank*. When dragged to a dashboard and sized to a desired width or height, this element simply inserts white space that can be used to separate dashboard elements from each other.

Text

In addition to individual worksheet titles (which appear automatically when a worksheet is added to a dashboard), as well as an overall dashboard title that can be displayed by way of the Dashboard | Show Title drop-down menu item, you can add additional text by dragging this item from the left side of the dashboard window. When you drop the text element, an Edit Text dialog box will appear allowing you to type and format text, including adding predefined dashboard fields from the Insert drop-down menu. Text can be added in either tiled or floating mode. In tiled mode, text will exhibit the same "gray box" behavior as other dashboard elements when being placed or moved on the dashboard.

Image

Also usable in tiled or floating mode, a bitmap graphic can be added to your dashboard by dragging Image from the left of the dashboard window. Once dropped on the dashboard, a dialog box will appear prompting for the choice of an image file from a local or network drive. Navigate to the desired folder and select an image file. You can also type in a full URL to an image on a web server. Once an image has been added, you can change or format the image by right-clicking on the image on the dashboard or right-clicking on the image item in Layout.

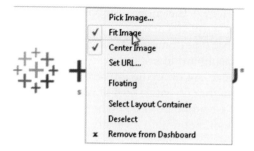

Best Practice *Many a dashboard includes a large company logo, often in the upper left of the dashboard. Reconsider this approach. As the human eye generally processes information from left to right and top to bottom, the upper left of a dashboard is often the first thing seen. A key metric is probably better suited for upper-left placement in a dashboard.*

Web Page

A web page can be embedded in a dashboard by dragging Web Page from the left side of the screen. A URL prompt accepts any standard web page address. All typical web page interactivity, such as hyperlinks, is available on the web page in the dashboard. While this allows you to include a static web page in your dashboard, exceptional flexibility to customize web page interactivity exists with dashboard actions, which are discussed later in the chapter.

Setting Dashboard and Element Sizes

As a general rule, placing worksheets on dashboards is a simple drag-and-drop process. And sizing elements once they appear on a dashboard is simple—just point to the element and resize when the sizing handles appear. However, Tableau 8 introduces the Size section in the lower left of the dashboard window, which provides precise control over the position and size of individual dashboard elements (provided they are in floating mode). Either on the dashboard itself or in the Layout section above the Size section, select the worksheet, legend, or other element that you want to change. Then make desired entries in the Size section.

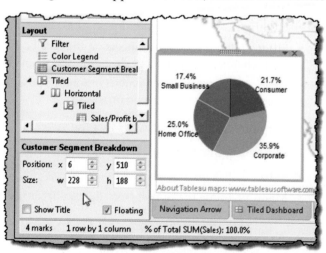

There is also an option to size the entire dashboard. You may, for example, find that scrollbars appear on the right or bottom of the dashboard that you don't want to see. Or you may prefer to match the dashboard to a standard web page size or computer desktop size. Again in the Layout section, select Dashboard (or ensure that no worksheet or other elements are selected on the dashboard itself). The Size section presents a drop-down menu with a variety of dashboard size options.

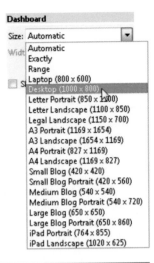

Dashboard Actions

Tableau provides flexible interactivity in your dashboards beyond the default tooltips that appear when you hover your mouse over worksheet marks. This interactivity is supplied via *dashboard actions*, interactive settings that allow you to highlight, filter, and navigate from any mark on any worksheet on your dashboard.

Note *Some of the interactivity discussed in this section also applies to individual worksheets. When editing a worksheet, choose Worksheet | Actions from the drop-down menus to create and edit actions.*

Video *Using Dashboard Actions*

There are three types of dashboard actions:

- **Highlight**   Highlight matching marks on one or more sheets in the dashboard.
- **Filter**   Filter one or more sheets on the dashboard based on a chosen mark, or navigate to another sheet or dashboard in the workbook.
- **URL**   Navigate to a web page. Optionally, pass selected information from the worksheet to the URL to personalize it.

Furthermore, there are three ways that the viewer can initiate a dashboard action:

- **Hover**   Simply hover your mouse over a mark.
- **Select**   Click on a mark.
- **Menu**   Choose the option from the tooltip or right-click context menu.

Caution *Be judicious with use of dashboard actions initiated by hovers. Typically, only highlight actions are appropriate for this method. Otherwise, simple mouse movement may initiate time-intensive or undesired actions.*

Highlight Action

The purpose of a highlight action is to highlight related marks on other sheets in your dashboard based on a chosen mark in a source sheet. A basic example of highlighting that Tableau provides by default is exhibited when you click on an individual entry in a color legend. You'll typically see marks on the related sheet highlighted based on the legend entry you click. When you deselect the color legend entry, marks are un-highlighted on the sheet. A highlight action takes this capability a step further and allows selections on the actual worksheet itself to highlight other related marks on other sheets.

To create a highlight action, select Dashboard | Actions from the drop-down menus. The Actions dialog box will appear. Click the Add Action button and choose Highlight from the pop-up menu. From the Edit Highlight Action dialog box, select the method of initiating the action (hover, select, or menu). In the Source Sheets section of the dialog box, choose one or more worksheets that you want the action to occur on. In the Target Sheets section, choose one or more worksheets that you want to be highlighted based on the selected mark in the source sheet or sheets. There should be a common dimension in source and target sheets, or highlighting won't have the desired effect.

In this example, when the mouse is hovered over a section of a Region % Breakdown pie chart, corresponding regions will be highlighted in the Customer Count by State sheet.

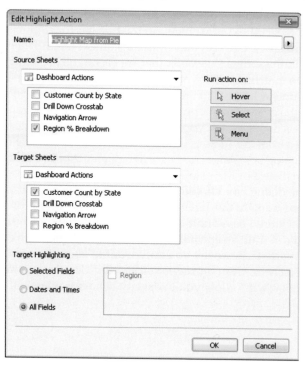

Filter Action

While quick filters and parameters are options for filtering interactivity on a dashboard, a filter action permits additional interactivity, where one or more worksheets on the dashboard are filtered based on a chosen mark on the source sheet. For example, when a certain mark is clicked on one sheet, other sheets will refresh, only showing marks that match the item that was clicked on the source sheet.

Filter actions can be created directly from a worksheet's context menu, or from the Dashboard | Actions dialog box discussed earlier. Decide which sheet you want to act as the filter source. Select the context menu in the title bar (or right-click on the desired sheet in Layout) and check Use As Filter from the context menu. Thereafter, when you click on any mark in the source sheet, all other sheets on the dashboard will be filtered to only show values matching what you clicked on the source sheet. Choose the same context menu and uncheck Use As Filter if you want to turn this option off.

When you use the context menu option, a "generated" filter action will appear in the Dashboard | Actions dialog box. If you want to remove or customize the generated filter action, make choices from the Actions dialog box. You can also create new filter actions directly from this dialog box. After creating a new filter action, select the method of initiating the action (Select or Menu are probably the best two choices). In the Source Sheets section of the dialog box, choose one or more worksheets that you want the action to be executed from. In the Target Sheets section, choose one or more worksheets that you want to be filtered based on the selected mark in the source sheet or sheets.

By default, you can multiselect marks on the source sheets with CTRL-click to filter on more than one mark. If, however, you only want to allow a single mark to be highlighted to filter, check "Run on single select only." The three options under "Clearing the selection will" allow you to specify behavior when a filter action is cleared (for example, if the viewer clicks the same mark that was initially filtered, or clicks on a blank area of the source sheet). "Leave the filter" will leave the filter active on other sheets. "Show all values" will return all values to target sheets as though no filter was applied. And "Exclude all values" will display no data at all on the target sheets. While the "Exclude all values" option may initially seem of little use, it comes in handy for drill-down types of actions, where you only want target sheets to appear when a filter has been selected, and to display nothing when no filter is selected. Finally, the Target Filters section allows you to choose a limited set of fields to apply the filter action to, and to map source and target fields if different sheets are not using the same field names.

In this example, a click on a mark in the Customer Count by State sheet will filter a Drill Down Crosstab on the dashboard. When the filter is cleared on the source sheet, the Drill Down Crosstab will show no data.

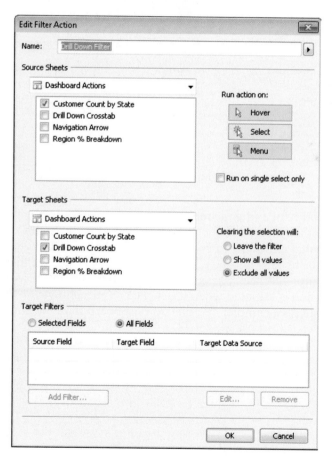

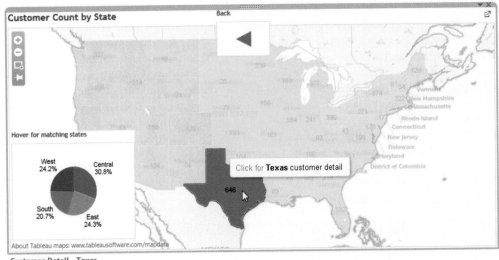

Customer Detail - Texas

Region	State	Customer Name	Count of Order ID	Sales	Profit	Shipping Cost
Central	Texas	Aaron Dillon	4	$258	$33	$14
		Adam Barton	6	$2,595	$1,046	$36
		Alex Harrell	2	$268	$160	$4
		Alexander O'Brien	8	$16,978	$2,542	$40
		Allison Kirby	7	$31,574	$217	$83
		Alvin B Winstead	3	$2,598	($898)	$88
		Amanda Huang	2	$73	($65)	$6
		Anne Bland	7	$516	($351)	$58
		Annie Booth	4	$12,531	$413	$131

Another capability of a filter action that may not be initially obvious is the ability to navigate to another sheet or dashboard in your workbook. In this case, a standard filter action is created as described previously, but a dashboard or worksheet other than the current dashboard is selected in the Target Sheets area. In this example, an "arrow" visualization has been placed on the dashboard to appear as a navigation button. A filter action is initiated when it's clicked. Notice, however, that the Target Sheets section displays a completely different dashboard than the Source Sheets section.

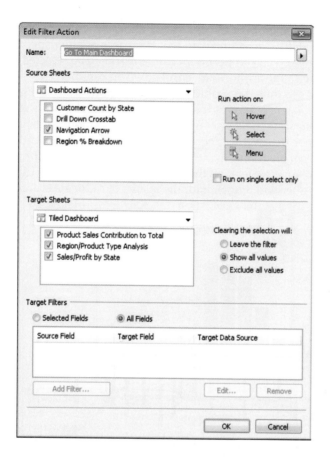

URL Action

A URL action allows a web page to be launched from within your dashboard. Furthermore, any field in use on the source worksheet can be used to customize the URL. This permits Tableau to display custom web pages from the Internet or to integrate with other web-based systems in your organization.

After creating a new URL action, select the method of initiating the action (Select or Menu are probably the best two choices). In the Source Sheets section of the dialog box, choose one or more worksheets that you want the action to occur on. Then type or paste the desired URL into the URL box. To customize the URL depending on which mark is selected to initiate the action, click the small right-arrow at the end of the URL to display fields that are used in the source sheets. When you select one of the fields, a placeholder will be added to the current cursor position in the URL. When the URL is executed, the current value from that field will be placed in the URL.

URL options at the bottom of the dialog box allow you to URL-encode custom field values added to the URL (for example, to replace spaces or other special characters with % encoded characters). You can permit multiple marks to be selected when the URL action is initiated with the appropriate checkbox. You can then specify the item and escape delimiter to separate the multiple values and end of the value list in the URL.

In this example, if a user hovers their mouse over or right-clicks on the Drill Down Crosstab sheet, they'll be presented a hyperlink option to Google the currently highlighted customer. When this is clicked, a URL action will display the Google web page with the current customer name added to the URL at an appropriate point (as a value to a "q=" parameter). As there is no Web Page element in the dashboard, a separate web browser will launch with the results of a Google search on the current customer's name.

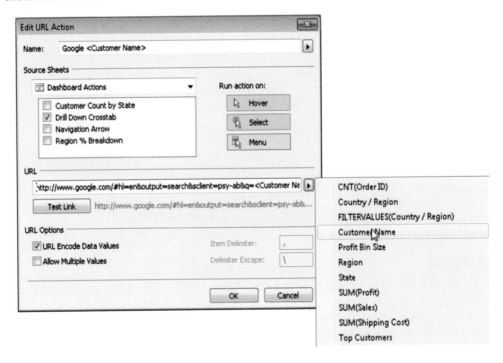

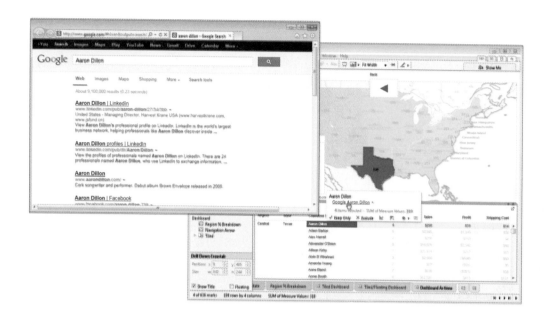

Note *If your dashboard contains a Web Page element added from the dashboard menu, it will be updated in-place when a URL action takes place. If there is no such element in your dashboard, Tableau will launch a separate web browser window as the target for the URL action.*

Distributing and Sharing Your Visualizations

So far, this book has presented a great deal of information on how you, as a visualization designer, can use Tableau Desktop to its fullest. But what happens when you want to share the results of your work with others? Perhaps you wish to export the underlying data from one or more of your worksheets for use in Microsoft Excel, Microsoft Access, or other data tools. Or, you may want to include the chart or graph from one or more worksheets in a presentation or word-processing document. Perhaps you want to make an entire dashboard, including all the interactivity you have built into it, available to multiple analysts/viewers just using a web browser. Tableau allows all of these options, and more.

Exporting Worksheets and Dashboards

Tableau facilitates exporting information from individual worksheets in your workbooks, as well as combined dashboards, in a variety of ways:

- Create a .pdf version of one or more worksheets or dashboards.
- Export the data that makes up individual worksheet charts or graphs. You may copy data to the Clipboard for pasting into another application, pass data to an Excel worksheet, or export the data to Microsoft Access format.
- Export an individual worksheet image, either from the worksheet tab itself, or when an individual worksheet is selected in a dashboard. You may copy it to the Clipboard for pasting into other documents, or export it to a variety of standard graphic file formats.

Printing to PDF Format

It's easy to create a Portable Document Format (PDF) version of one or more worksheets or dashboards in your workbook. Choose File | Print To PDF from the drop-down menus. The Print To PDF dialog box will appear. If you wish to print a separate page in the PDF file for every sheet and dashboard in your workbook, click the Entire Workbook radio button. Active Sheet will print just the currently selected sheet or dashboard. If you are displaying your worksheets in Filmstrip View and you have CTRL-clicked more than one worksheet or dashboard in the filmstrip, each will appear in a separate page in the PDF. Select the desired paper size and orientation. If you check Show Selections, any selected marks in a worksheet will be highlighted in the resulting PDF as they are on the worksheet. Otherwise, all marks will appear unselected in the resulting PDF. Click OK.

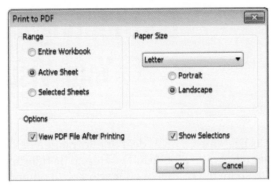

A standard Windows dialog will appear, prompting for a filename. Specify the desired file and click OK to save the .pdf file. If you checked the View PDF File After Printing checkbox, the .pdf file will appear in Adobe Acrobat or Adobe Reader for your review.

Exporting Worksheet Data

With the exception of text tables (also known as crosstabs), Tableau worksheets are typically graphical in nature. However, the data that's used to make up bar charts, maps, and other visual elements in your worksheets may be helpful when shared with other applications or shared with colleagues. There are several ways of exporting the data that make up a chart or graph:

- **Copy as Crosstab**   Copies the underlying data that makes up your worksheet to the Clipboard as a row/column matrix of data. This may be pasted into a spreadsheet, word processor, or other application. Right-click in a blank area of the worksheet, or choose the Worksheet drop-down menu, and select Copy | Crosstab.

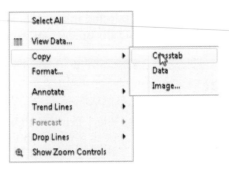

- **Copy Data**   Similar to Copy as Crosstab, but may not organize in the same row/column format, depending on the data that the worksheet is based on. Right-click in a blank area of the worksheet, or choose the Worksheet drop-down menu and select Copy | Data.

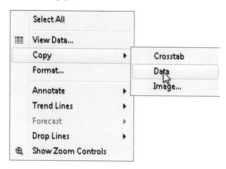

- **Export Crosstab to Microsoft Excel**   Organizes the underlying data that makes up your worksheet as a row/column matrix of data and places it in a new Microsoft Excel worksheet. The worksheet may be modified as you prefer and then saved as an Excel file. From the Worksheet drop-down menu, choose Export | Crosstab To Excel.

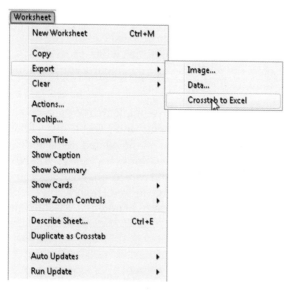

- **Export Data to Microsoft Access .MDB File**   Creates a Microsoft Access .mdb database file containing one table that includes the data that makes up the selected worksheet. From the Worksheet drop-down menu, choose Export | Data. A standard Windows file dialog will appear. Specify the location and name of the file you wish to create and click Save. The Export Data To Access dialog box will appear. Specify the name of the table you wish Tableau to create in the database. If you wish to immediately have Tableau create a data connection to the resulting table so that it may be used in another worksheet, check "Connect after export" and specify the connection name. If you had selected a set of marks prior to choosing the menu option, you'll have the choice of exporting data from the entire worksheet or just the selected items. Click OK. An Access database will be created containing the table.

Exporting Worksheet Images

The visualization in each worksheet or dashboard can also be exported for use in other applications, such as PowerPoint presentations, word-processing documents, or graphics programs. Select the worksheet or dashboard you wish to export and then choose one of two options:

- **Copy to Clipboard**   Right-click in a blank area of the worksheet or dashboard, or click the Worksheet drop-down menu, and select Copy | Image. The Copy Image dialog box will appear. Depending on the related items appearing in the selected worksheet (legends and so forth), various checkboxes will be enabled, allowing you to choose what to include in the copied image. Also, you have several choices of where to place legends. Make the desired choices and click Copy. The image will be copied to the Clipboard. You may now paste it into another application.

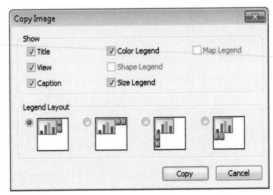

- **Export to Image File**   From the Worksheet drop-down menu, choose Export | Image. The same dialog box described for copying an image to the Clipboard will display. Choose which portions of the visualization to include, as well as preferred legend placement, and click Save. A standard Windows Save dialog box will appear prompting for a file location and name. You may also choose a JPEG, PNG, BMP, or EMF file format. Click Save to export the image to the specified filename and format.

Exporting Dashboard Images

If you have combined worksheets into one or more dashboards, you may export the entire dashboard as a single image. Select the dashboard you wish to export and choose Dashboard | Copy Image, or Dashboard | Export Image, from the drop-down menus.

If you choose Copy Image, the entire dashboard will be copied to the Clipboard. Navigate to an alternate application and paste the copied image in the appropriate location. If you choose Export Image, a standard Windows Save dialog box will appear prompting for a file location and name. You may also choose a JPEG, PNG, BMP, or EMF file format. Click Save to export the dashboard image to the specified filename and format.

Tip *If you have a dashboard selected, only the selected view in the dashboard will be exported with the Worksheet drop-down menu options. Use the Dashboard drop-down menu options to export the entire dashboard image.*

Using Tableau Reader

A read-only version of Tableau Desktop, *Tableau Reader,* is available as a free download from the Tableau Software website. Tableau Reader is a "fat client" product, requiring installation on your Windows computer. Once installed, Tableau Reader will open Tableau Packaged Workbooks (.twbx files).

In Tableau Desktop, you may save a workbook for distribution to Tableau Reader by saving your workbook in .twbx format. Simply choose the .twbx format within the Save dialog box when saving your workbook. The resulting .twbx file may be distributed to Tableau Reader users to open and interact with.

Tableau Packaged Workbooks require that all data sources be embedded in the .twbx file. Desktop data sources (Excel, Access, Tableau Data Extracts, and so forth) will automatically be included in the workbook. However, if your workbook makes use of some external data source, such as a standard corporate SQL server, you'll receive a message when you attempt to save the workbook in .twbx format. Once you have created Tableau Data Extracts from these data sources (Extracts are covered in Chapter 3), resave the .twbx file.

Warning dialog box reading: "This workbook connects to remote data sources that Tableau Reader cannot open. To create a packaged workbook compatible with Tableau Reader, create a Tableau Data Extract and re-save. Continue saving with remote connections?" with Yes and No buttons and a "Do not show again" checkbox.

Caution *Because of the core requirement for .twbx files to embed all data sources, Tableau Reader will be unable to make real-time connections to standard corporate SQL databases. If you require that your distributed Tableau workbooks make real-time connections to SQL data sources, your audience will require their own copy of Tableau Desktop, or will need connectivity to Tableau Server.*

Publishing to the Web

While Tableau Reader is an economical method for distributing finished workbooks to your audience, it requires that every user maintain a "fat client" installation on their Windows computer. Users of Apple OS X, Linux, or other operating systems will be unable to use Tableau Reader. Also, as previously discussed, Tableau Reader cannot make real-time connections to corporate databases, which reduces the ability to analyze with the latest data available. To solve these issues, Tableau workbooks can be published to a number of web-based server systems for distribution to any user with a standard web browser.

There are three options for web-based publication:

- **Tableau Public**   A free hosted version of Tableau Server, permitting workbooks based on Tableau Data Extracts to be posted on the Web. There are limitations on the amount of data that may be included, no connection to internal corporate SQL databases is supported, and all data and worksheets posted are fully viewable by the public—there is no security available.

- **Tableau Online**   A paid hosted version of Tableau Server, permitting workbooks based on Tableau Data Extracts to be posted on the Web. There are limited capabilities to updated extracts with fresh data. Workbooks posted are not publicly viewable. And there is a limited user/group security system permitting granular viewing capabilities and rights assignments.

- **Tableau Server**   A server-based system, installed inside your organization, permitting workbooks based on any data source (including live connections to internal or external standard corporate SQL databases) to be posted. Based on your firewall configuration, viewers may be inside or outside your organization. Although not required, data extracts published to your local Tableau Server may be automatically updated from their original data sources on a regular schedule. Tableau Server features a robust security system, permitting various users and groups to be defined for granular viewing and access rights, as well as user-based filtering to provide different views of the same workbook, based on Tableau Server security settings. Tableau Server also allows (with proper permissions) web-based modification of existing worksheets or creation of new simple worksheets, all in a web browser.

Sharing on Tableau Public

Once you have created a Tableau Public account (visit the Tableau Software web site to create an account), make sure your workbook meets Tableau Public requirements before attempting to save it to the Tableau Public server:

- Data sources must be Tableau Data Extracts (Chapter 3 discusses how to create Extracts).

- Data sources cannot contain more than 100,000 rows of data.

Choose Server | Tableau Public | Save To Web. If prompted, supply your user ID and password. Specify a name for the workbook on the server and click OK. A confirmation dialog will display illustrating the workbook you just saved. You may now share or view the workbook on the Web via your Tableau Public account.

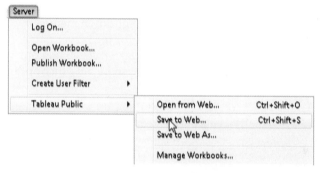

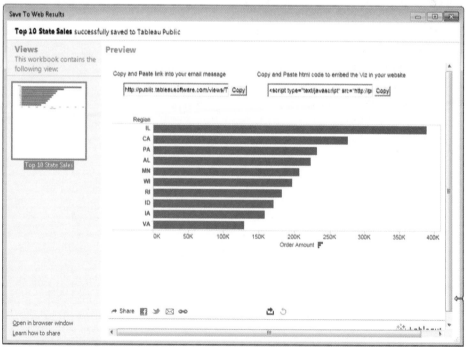

Publishing to Tableau Server and Tableau Online

Similar to Tableau Public, Tableau Online and Tableau Server provide web-based access to Tableau workbooks. Tableau Online, hosted by Tableau Software and offered as a "Software as a Service" product, provides a reduced set of capabilities when compared to the full Tableau Server product, which customers install on their own servers within their own network infrastructure.

Publishing a finished workbook to Tableau Online requires that all data sources be converted to Tableau Data Extracts before the workbook can be published (creating Extracts is covered in Chapter 3). And the set of users and rights available in Tableau Online is reduced when compared to the full version of Tableau Server. The full version of Tableau Server will permit publication of workbooks connecting to any data source, provided the server has been configured to support the data source used when creating a workbook. And a full set of user rights may be specified when publishing. Otherwise, publishing to both platforms follows the same steps.

Select Server | Publish Workbook from the pull-down menus. If you have not already logged into a server, you'll be prompted for the server name, user ID, and password. Then, the Publish Workbook To Tableau Server dialog box will appear. In addition to supplying the name of the workbook, there are other options to complete on this dialog box:

- **Project** Like a folder, a *project* is a category that you may assign your workbook to. Then, when looking for available workbooks on Tableau Server, you may select a specific project to narrow down your search. Choose an existing project from the drop-down list (projects are created using administration tools on Tableau Server).

- **Add Tags** Optionally add one or more keywords, separated by spaces or commas (if the keyword itself contains a space, surround it with quotation marks). Keywords may be used to search for workbooks on the server.

- **Views to Share** Select the worksheets/dashboards you want to be visible within the workbook on the server. You may wish to only include dashboards in this list, unchecking the worksheets that make up the dashboard. This will prevent viewers from navigating to the individual worksheets that make up the dashboard (these worksheets, however, will be available if a user downloads the workbook from the server).

- **View Permissions** By default, all users will be given a set of default rights (determined by the "All Users" group), while you (as the owner) will have full rights to the workbook. If you wish to set more granular permissions for your workbook, click the Add button below the View Permissions list. The Add/Edit Permissions dialog box will appear.

Select a user or group on the left side of the dialog box and set permissions for the user or group on the right. You may choose from a pre-defined set of rights by choosing an entry in the Role drop-down list, or select individual rights with radio buttons. When finished, click OK. The users and groups you added rights for will appear in the View Permissions list.

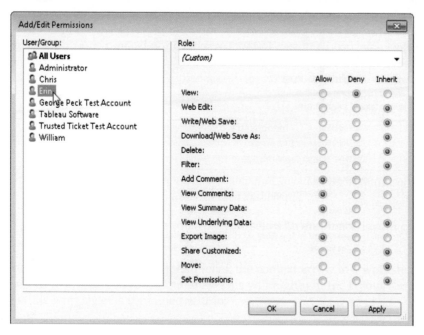

- **Show Sheets as Tabs**   Much as with Filmstrip View in Tableau Desktop, checking this option will show tabs for worksheets in the view on Tableau Server.

Caution *If you are using filter actions in your worksheets (covered in Chapter 5) or dashboards (covered in Chapter 8) to navigate from one dashboard or worksheet to another, you* must *select this option to enable navigation on the server.*

- **Show Selections**   If you've pre-selected any marks on a worksheet, these marks will be pre-selected on your server workbook when initially viewed on the Web.
- **Include External Files**   Upload any desktop data sources (Excel, Access, Tableau Data Extracts, and so forth) and background images to the server with the workbook. This will prevent the server from not being able to locate data sources (perhaps on your local hard disk) that were used to create the workbook. If you don't select this option, ensure that your data sources are accessible by the server, either via standard corporate SQL database connection methods or via a Universal Naming Convention (UNC) name used to connect to network-based desktop data sources.

If your workbook contains data sources that have been extracted to a Tableau Data Extract (.tde) file or connections to standard corporate SQL databases that require permission to access, additional options are available by clicking the Scheduling & Authentication button.

You may choose to automatically refresh data extracts that will be published to the server with your workbook via the drop-down list. Schedules, such as "End of Month," "Saturday Night," and "Weekday Early Mornings," are configured on the server in advance and will be available for you to choose for automatic extract refresh.

External databases (such as standard corporate SQL databases) may require authentication when processing queries from your on-premise version of Tableau Server. Select any such databases in the Authentication list and choose how you wish to supply a user ID and password to the database when the workbook is refreshed. Click OK to return to the Publish Workbook dialog box.

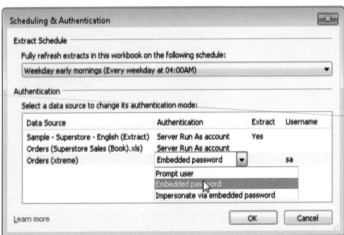

When all options have been selected, click Publish to publish the workbook to the server. After the workbook and any associated data files are published, a confirmation dialog box will appear. You may interact with the workbook in the confirmation dialog box, click Open In Browser Window to open the workbook in your browser, or just close the confirmation dialog box.

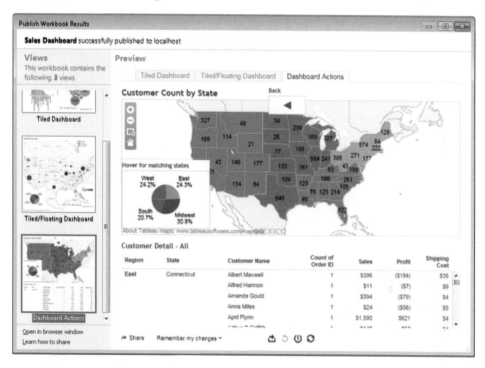

Using Tableau with iPad, Android, and Other Smartphones and Tablets

Not only can Tableau web-based options (Tableau Public, Tableau Online, and Tableau Server) provide complete interactivity in a web browser; they can support various mobile devices as well. If your audience will want to interact with a worksheet or dashboard on their smartphone or tablet, several options are available.

Creating Tableau Server User Filters

One of the benefits of using Tableau Server is its built-in security system. Not only does this determine various rights and privileges granted or denied to users, it can also be used to provide a different view of data to the viewer based on their user ID. This is accomplished with *user filters*: a series of filter settings that are applied based on a Tableau Server user ID.

Using the drop-down menus, choose Server | Create User Filter, and then select the dimension you wish to filter based on user ID. If you're not already logged on to a Tableau Server, you'll be prompted for logon credentials. The User Filter dialog box will appear, displaying a list of Tableau Server users and groups on the left and the members of the selected dimension on the right. Select each user or group on the left, and then check the members of the dimension that the selected user or group should be able to see in the worksheet.

The All and None buttons under the Members list will select all or no members as a starting point. If you have many users and you wish to copy settings from one user to another, click the Copy From button and select an existing user to copy to the currently selected user. When finished setting user/member combinations, click OK to save the filter. It will initially appear in the Data window in the Sets category (with a slightly different icon than traditional sets). The user filter will not take effect until dragged to the Filters shelf.

Server
Log On...
Open Workbook...
Publish Workbook...
Create User Filter ▸
Tableau Public ▸

Category...
City...
Container...
Continent...
Country / Region...
Customer ID...
Customer Name...
Customer Segment...
Department...
Item...
Order Date...
Order ID...
Order Priority...
Postal Code...
Region...
Row ID...
Ship Date...
Ship Mode...
State...
Supplier...

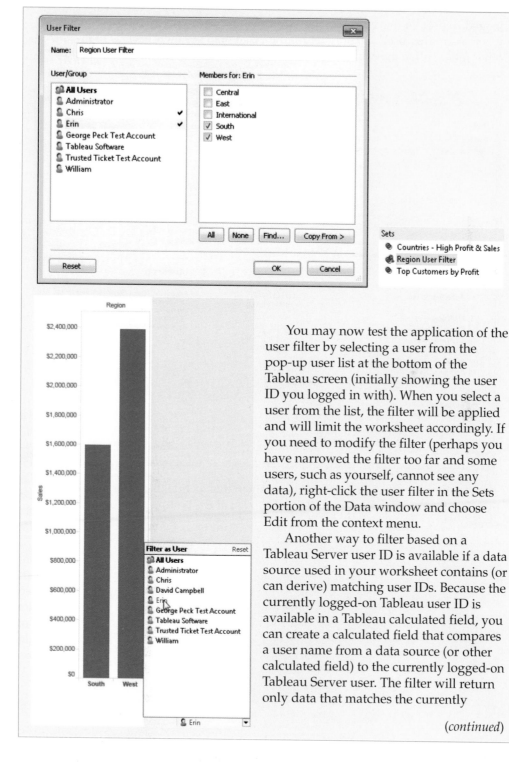

You may now test the application of the user filter by selecting a user from the pop-up user list at the bottom of the Tableau screen (initially showing the user ID you logged in with). When you select a user from the list, the filter will be applied and will limit the worksheet accordingly. If you need to modify the filter (perhaps you have narrowed the filter too far and some users, such as yourself, cannot see any data), right-click the user filter in the Sets portion of the Data window and choose Edit from the context menu.

Another way to filter based on a Tableau Server user ID is available if a data source used in your worksheet contains (or can derive) matching user IDs. Because the currently logged-on Tableau user ID is available in a Tableau calculated field, you can create a calculated field that compares a user name from a data source (or other calculated field) to the currently logged-on Tableau Server user. The filter will return only data that matches the currently

(continued)

logged-in user. In this example, the Administrator account will return all data, whereas another user will only return data that matches their user ID. As with other filters, place the calculated field on the Filters shelf and choose the True value.

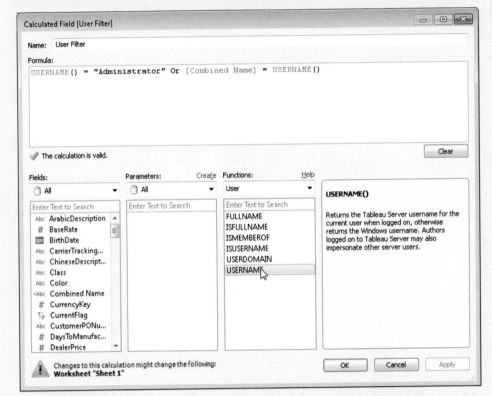

As with user filters described previously in this section, the filter may be tested by selecting different users from the pop-up list at the bottom right of the Tableau screen.

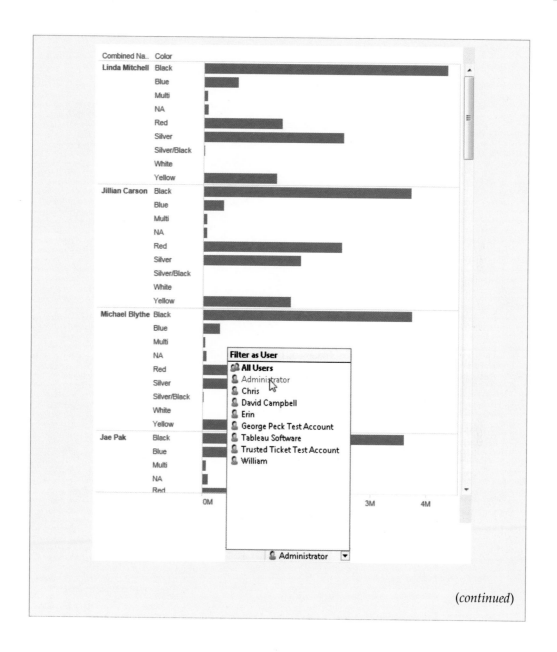

(continued)

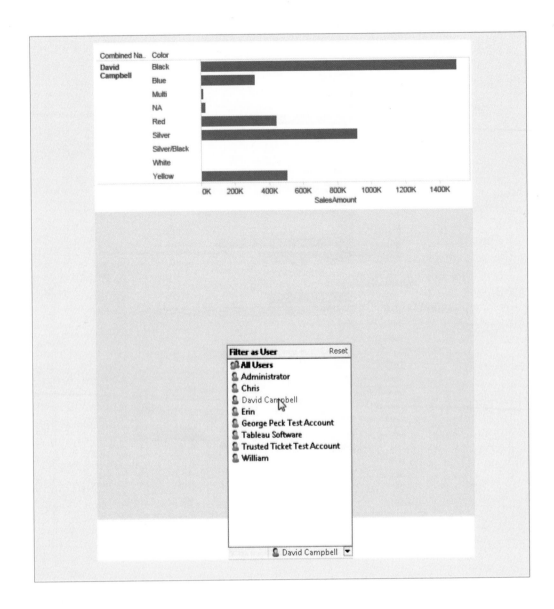

Tableau App for iPad

If you search the Apple App Store for "Tableau," you'll find the Tableau Mobile app. This free app (for iPad only) will connect to a Tableau Server and present a highly interactive interface to workbooks and dashboards on the server. Full interactivity is available when displaying worksheets or dashboards in the app.

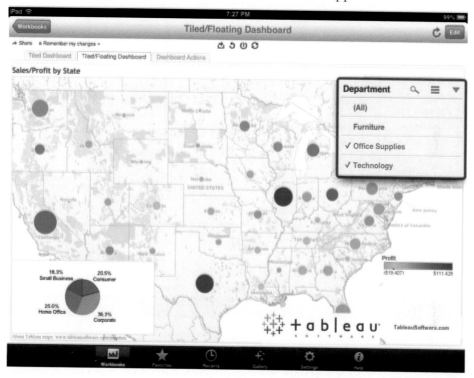

Tableau 8 now features the ability to modify existing worksheets, as well as create new basic worksheets, using the Tableau Mobile app. This powerful feature opens an entirely new set of possibilities by allowing rich design capabilities on an iPad.

Dimensions and measures can be dragged to and from shelves, options can be set from the Marks card, and Show Me can be used.

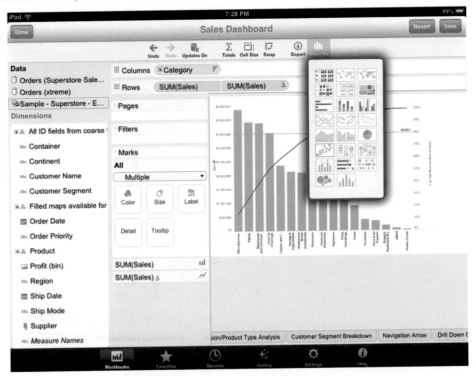

Web Access via HTML5 Mobile Browsers

While the Tableau Mobile app only works with iPad, other mobile devices are fully capable of interacting with Tableau Server. If your mobile device includes a web browser that supports HTML5 (most Windows mobile, Apple, and Android devices do), then complete interactivity with Tableau Server is available as well. Just connect to a Tableau Server via the mobile device browser as you would on a desktop computer. Tableau Server will automatically detect the mobile browser and present an appropriately sized presentation of dashboards and worksheets.

Full interactivity is available, including quick filters, actions, and tooltips.

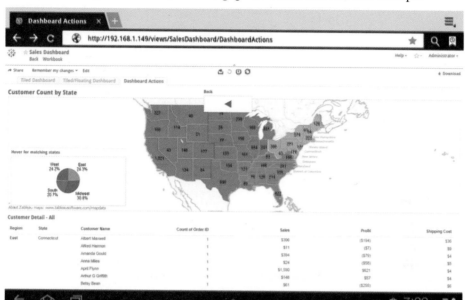

A very powerful addition to Tableau 8 Server is the ability to edit existing worksheets and create new simple worksheets right in a web browser (either on a desktop computer or on a mobile device). Dimensions and measures can be dragged to and from shelves, options can be set from the Marks card, and Show Me can be used.

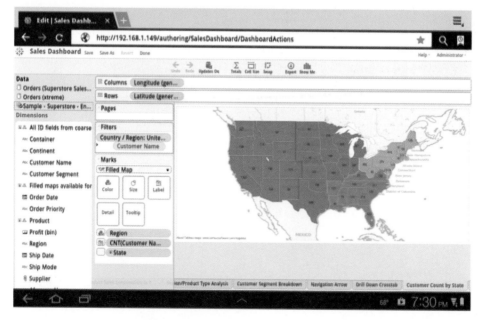

Function Reference

This appendix documents functions available in the Tableau calculated field language. Add these functions to a calculated field by double-clicking the desired function in the list on the lower right of the Calculated Field dialog box. The function list displays all available functions in alphabetical order, or a subset of related functions in alphabetical order if a category is chosen in the drop-down list above the function list. Most functions accept one or more *arguments,* or values that are supplied to the function inside parentheses and separated by commas.

Number Functions

These functions perform numeric operations and return numeric results. They also accept numeric arguments.

ABS

Returns the absolute value of a number.

ABS(number)

```
ABS([Profit])
```

returns the numeric value 74.25 if the [Profit] database field contains –74.25.

ACOS

Returns the arc cosine (inverse cosine), in radians, of the supplied number.

ACOS(number)

```
ACOS(-.5)
```

returns the numeric value 2.094395102.

ASIN

Returns the arc sine (inverse sine), in radians, of the supplied number.

ASIN(number)

```
ASIN(.5)
```

returns the numeric value .523598776.

ATAN

Returns the arc tangent (inverse tangent), in radians, of the supplied number.

ATAN(number)

```
ATAN(45)
```

returns the numeric value 1.548577785.

ATAN2

Returns the arc tangent (inverse tangent), in radians, of the two supplied numbers.

ATAN2(y number, x number)

```
ATAN2(45, 10)
```

returns the numeric value 1.352127433.

COS

Returns the cosine, in radians, of the supplied number.

COS(number)

```
COS(45)
```

returns the numeric value .525321960.

COT

Returns the cotangent, in radians, of the supplied number.

COT(number)

```
COT(45)
```

returns the numeric value .617369592.

DEGREES

Returns a value, in degrees, of the supplied radian number.

DEGREES(number)

```
DEGREES(.7865)
```

returns the numeric value 45.063130587.

EXP

Raises *e* (the base of the natural logarithm) to the specified power.

EXP(number)

```
EXP(10)
```

returns the numeric value 22,026.46484375.

LN

Returns the natural logarithm of the supplied number (or a null value if the specified number is ≤ 0).

LN(number)

```
LN(10)
```

returns the numeric value 2.302585125.

LOG

Returns the logarithm of the supplied number. An optional second argument, base, is used to supply a numeric base. If the second argument is not supplied, base 10 is used.

LOG(number, [base])

```
LOG(100)
```

returns the numeric value 2.

```
LOG(100, 5)
```

returns the numeric value 2.861353159.

MAX

Returns either the largest aggregate value of a supplied database field if used with one argument, or the larger of two supplied values if used with two arguments.

MAX(expression)
MAX(expression1, expression2)

```
MAX([Discount])
```

returns the numeric value .25 if the highest discount value in the underlying set of data records is .25 (25 percent).

```
MAX([January Sales], [February Sales])
```

returns the numeric value 24,103.00 if January Sales is 24,103 and February Sales is 18,109.25.

MIN

Returns either the smallest aggregate value of a supplied database field if used with one argument, or the smaller of two supplied values if used with two arguments.

MIN(expression)
MIN(expression1, expression2)

```
MIN([Discount])
```

returns the numeric value .25 if the lowest discount value in the underlying set of data records is .25 (25 percent).

```
MIN([January Sales], [February Sales])
```

returns the numeric value 18,109.25 if January Sales is 24,103 and February Sales is 18,109.25.

PI

Returns the numeric constant of pi. This function takes no arguments, but still requires parentheses.

PI()

```
PI()
```

returns the numeric value 3.141592654.

POWER

Raises the supplied numeric value by the power specified in the second numeric argument. The ^ operator may be used for the same purpose.

POWER(number, power)

```
POWER([Rating], 3)
```

returns the numeric value 125 for a Rating field value of 5.

```
[Rating] ^ 3
```

will return the same result.

RADIANS

Returns a value, in radians, of the supplied degree number.

RADIANS(number)

```
RADIANS(45)
```

returns the numeric value .785398163.

ROUND

Rounds the supplied numeric value. If the second numeric argument is supplied, ROUND rounds to that number of significant digits. Otherwise, ROUND rounds to a whole number.

ROUND(number, [decimals])

```
ROUND([Weight])
```

returns 185 for a Weight database field value of 185.724.

```
ROUND([Weight], 1)
```

returns 185.7 for a Weight database field value of 185.724.

SIGN

Returns a numeric value indicating whether the supplied numeric value is positive, negative, or zero. SIGN returns a numeric value of –1 for negative numbers, +1 for positive numbers, and 0 for zero.

SIGN(number)

```
CASE SIGN([Profit])
      WHEN 1 THEN "Profit"
      WHEN -1 THEN "Loss"
      ELSE "At Cost"
END
```

returns the string value "Profit" if the Profit database field is greater than zero, "Loss" if the field is less than zero, and "At Cost" if the field is exactly zero.

SIN

Returns the sine, in radians, of the supplied number, also in radians.

SIN(number)

```
SIN(5)
```

returns the numeric value –0.958924294.

SQRT

Returns the square root of the supplied number.

SQRT(number)

```
SQRT(64)
```

returns the numeric value 8.

SQUARE

Returns the square (raised to the power of two) of the supplied number. The POWER function and ^ operator may also be used.

SQUARE(number)

```
SQUARE(8)
```

returns the numeric value 64.

Equivalents are

```
POWER(8, 2)
8 ^ 2
```

TAN

Returns the tangent, in radians, of the supplied number.

TAN(number)

```
TAN(1.25)
```

returns the numeric value 3.009569674.

ZN

Returns the numeric value of the supplied number if it is not null. Otherwise, returns 0.

ZN(expression)

```
ZN([Salary])
```

returns 125,000 if the Salary database field contains the value 125,000. If the Salary database field contains a null value, the result will be 0 instead of a null.

String Functions

These functions perform string operations and return various results (either strings or numbers). Depending on the function, they accept a combination of string and/or numeric arguments.

ASCII

Returns the American Standard Code for Information Interchange (ASCII) numeric value for the first character in the supplied string.

ASCII(string)

```
ASCII([Middle Initial])
```

returns the numeric value 69 if the Middle Initial database field contains a capital E.

CHAR

Converts the supplied integer numeric value into a single string character, based on the American Standard Code for Information Interchange (ASCII) value of the supplied number.

CHAR(integer)

```
[Company Name] + CHAR(10) + [City] + ", " + [State]
```

returns

```
Tableau Software
Seattle, WA
```

for a Company Name of "Tableau Software," City of "Seattle," and State of "WA." The ASCII number 10 equates to a line feed character.

CONTAINS

Determines whether the value in the first string argument contains the value in the second string argument. If so, the function returns True. Otherwise, it returns False.

CONTAINS(string, substring)

```
IF CONTAINS([Product Name], "BD") THEN
      "BluRay Media"
ELSE
      "DVD Media"
END
```

returns the string "BluRay Media" if the characters "BD" are contained anywhere within the Product Name database field. Otherwise, the result is "DVD Media".

ENDSWITH

Determines whether the value in the first string argument ends with the value in the second string argument. If so, the function returns True. Otherwise, it returns False.

ENDSWITH(string, substring)

```
IF ENDSWITH([Product Name], "-BD") THEN
      "BluRay Media"
ELSE
      "DVD Media"
END
```

returns the string "BluRay Media" if the characters "-BD" appear at the end of the Product Name database field. Otherwise, the result is "DVD Media".

FIND

Searches the first value in the first string argument for the value in the second substring argument, returning a numeric value indicating the position where the second argument exists. If the optional third numeric argument is provided, FIND starts the search at that position. If the search fails, FIND returns 0.

FIND(string, substring, *[start]*)

```
FIND([Product Type-SKU], "-")
```

returns 5 for a Product Type-SKU value of "SOFT-A103881".

```
FIND([Product Type-SKU], "-", 10)
```

returns 0 for a Product Type-SKU value of "SOFT-A103881".

ISDATE

Tests the supplied string argument and returns True if it can be converted to a date value with the DATE function. Otherwise, returns False.

ISDATE(string)

```
IF ISDATE([DateOrderedString]) THEN
      DATE([DateOrderedString])
ELSE
      DATE("01/01/1900")
END
```

will return the string database field DateOrderedString as a date value if it contains a string value that the DATE function can properly interpret. Otherwise, it will return the date value January 1, 1900.

Simply using

```
DATE([DateOrderedString])
```

will return a null if the supplied string argument does not contain a properly formatted date. By using ISDATE, null values may be avoided.

LEFT

Returns a string value consisting of the number of characters specified in the second argument from the beginning (or left) of the string specified in the first argument.

LEFT(string, num_chars)

```
IF LEFT([Type-Part#], 3) = "BLU" THEN
      "BluRay Media"
ELSE
      "Other Media"
END
```

will test the first three characters of the Type-Part# database field and return "BluRay Media" if those characters = "BLU." If the first three characters are anything else, the result will be "Other Media".

LEN

Returns a numeric value indicating the number of characters contained in the supplied string argument.

LEN(string)

```
IF LEN([Phone]) = 10 THEN
        LEFT([Phone], 3)
ELSE
        "No Area Code"
END
```

returns the first three characters from the Phone database field if the Phone database field contains 10 characters. Otherwise, returns "No Area Code".

LOWER

Converts the supplied string to lowercase letters.

LOWER(string)

```
LOWER("GeOrgE")
```

returns "george".

LTRIM

Trims away leading spaces (any spaces on the left side) from the supplied string.

LTRIM(string)

```
LTRIM(" George ")
```

returns "George " (the trailing space remains).

MAX

Returns either the last alphabetic string value of a supplied database field within the underlying set of data records if used with one argument, or the last alphabetic value of two supplied values if used with two arguments.

MAX(string)
MAX(string1, string2)

```
MAX([CustomerLastName])
```

returns "Williams" if the highest alphabetical value in the CustomerLastName database field within the underlying set of records is Williams.

```
MAX([City1], [City2])
```

returns "Yuba City" if the City1 database field contains Denver and the City2 database field contains Yuba City.

MID

Returns a subset of the characters from the string argument, starting at the position supplied by the numeric start argument. If the optional length numeric argument is supplied, only the number of characters specified in length is returned.

MID(string, start, [length])

```
MID("Tableau Software", 4)
```

returns "leau Software".

```
MID("Tableau Software", 6, 5)
```

returns "au So".

MIN

Returns either the first alphabetic string value of a supplied database field within the underlying set of data records if used with one argument, or the first alphabetic value of two supplied values if used with two arguments.

MIN(expression)
MIN(expression1, expression2)

```
MIN([CustomerLastName])
```

returns "Butler" if the lowest alphabetical value in the CustomerLastName database field within the underlying set of records is Butler.

```
MIN([City1], [City2])
```

returns "Denver" if the City1 database field contains Denver and the City2 database field contains Yuba City.

RIGHT

Returns a string value consisting of the number of characters specified in the second argument from the end (or right) of the string specified in the first argument.

RIGHT(string, num_chars)

```
RIGHT([Type-Part#], 5)
```

will return "81773" for a Type-Part# database value of BLU-81773.

RTRIM

Trims away trailing spaces (any spaces on the right side) from the supplied string.

RTRIM(string)

```
LTRIM(" George ")
```

returns " George" (the leading space remains).

SPACE

Returns a string consisting of the number of space characters specified in the numeric argument.

SPACE(number)

```
"Tableau" + SPACE(5) + "Software"
```

will return "Tableau   Software" (with five spaces appearing between the two words).

STARTSWITH

Determines whether the value in the first string argument starts with the value in the second string argument. If so, the function returns True. Otherwise, it returns False.

STARTSWITH(string, substring)

```
IF STARTSWITH([Type-Part#], "BLU") THEN
        "BluRay Media"
ELSE
        "Other Media"
END
```

will determine if the Type-Part# database field starts with the characters BLU. If so, "BluRay Media" will be returned. Otherwise, the result will be "Other Media."

TRIM

Trims trailing spaces from the beginning and ending of the supplied string.

TRIM(string)

```
TRIM(" George ")
```

returns "George".

UPPER

Converts the supplied string to uppercase letters.

UPPER(string)

```
UPPER("GeOrgE")
```

returns "GEORGE".

Date Functions

These functions perform date operations and return various results (either dates or numbers). Depending on the function, they accept a combination of date, string, or numeric arguments.

Many date functions expect a date-part argument, which is a specific string value that must be supplied:

- "year"
- "quarter"
- "month"
- "dayofyear"
- "day"
- "weekday"
- "week"
- "hour"
- "minute"
- "second"

DATEADD

Returns a date/time before or after the date supplied in the third argument, based on the number of "intervals" supplied in the second argument. The type of interval (days, weeks, and so forth) is determined by the string date-part supplied in the first argument.

DATEADD(date_part, interval, date)

```
DATEADD("month", 6, [Order Date-Time])
```

returns 4/1/2013 2:15:00 PM if the Order Date-Time database field contains October 1, 2012, 2:15 p.m.

DATEDIFF

Returns a numeric value indicating the number of "intervals" between the start_date argument and the end_date argument. The type of interval (days, weeks, and so forth) is determined by the string date-part supplied in the first argument.

DATEDIFF(date_part, start_date, end_date)

```
DATEDIFF("days", [Order Date], [Ship Date])
```

returns the numeric value 8 if the Order Date database field is 2/15/2013 and the Ship Date database field is 2/23/2013.

DATENAME

Returns a string value representing the spelled-out date_part supplied in the first argument of the date supplied in the second argument.

DATENAME(date_part, date)

```
DATENAME("month", [Order Date])
```

will return the string "March" if the Order Date database field is 3/10/2013.

DATEPART

Returns a numeric value indicating the date_part supplied in the first argument of the date supplied in the second argument.

DATEPART(date_part, date)

```
DATEPART("hour", [Sample Date-Time])
```

will return the numeric value 15 if the Sample Date-Time database field contains 3/10/2013 03:25:10 p.m.

DATETRUNC

Truncates, or rounds, the date supplied in the second argument to the date_part supplied in the first argument, returning a date value.

DATETRUNC(date_part, date)

```
DATETRUNC("quarter", [Order Date])
```

returns 1/1/2013 12:00:00 AM if the Order Date database field contains 3/10/2013 (the first date of the calendar quarter that 3/10/2103 falls in is 1/1/2013).

DAY

Returns a numeric value between 1 and 31 indicating the day of the month of the supplied date argument.

DAY(date)

```
DAY([Order Date])
```

returns a numeric 10 if the Order Date database field contains 3/10/2013.

ISDATE
Tests the supplied string argument and returns True if it can be converted to a date value with the DATE function. Otherwise, returns False.

ISDATE(string)

```
IF ISDATE([DateOrderedString]) THEN
      DATE([DateOrderedString])
ELSE
      DATE("01/01/1900")
END
```

will return the string database field DateOrderedString as a date value if it contains a string value that the DATE function can properly interpret. Otherwise, it will return the date value January 1, 1900.

Simply using

```
DATE([DateOrderedString])
```

will return a null if the supplied string argument does not contain a properly formatted date. By using ISDATE, null values may be avoided.

MAX
Returns either the latest date value of a supplied database field within the underlying set of data records if used with one argument, or the latest date value of two supplied values if used with two arguments.

MAX(date)
MAX(date1, date2)

```
MAX([Order Date])
```

returns 12/15/2012, if the latest Order Date in the underlying set of records is 12/15/2012.

```
MAX([Paid Date], [Invoice Due Date])
```

returns 5/10/2013 if the Paid Date database field contains 5/5/2013 and the Invoice Due Date database field contains 5/10/2013.

MIN
Returns either the earliest date value of a supplied database field within the underlying set of data records if used with one argument, or the earliest date value of two supplied values if used with two arguments.

MIN(date)
MIN(date1, date2)

```
MIN([Order Date])
```

returns 1/22/2012, if the earliest Order Date in the underlying set of records is 1/22/2012.

```
MIN([Paid Date], [Invoice Due Date])
```

returns 5/5/2013 if the Paid Date database field contains 5/5/2013 and the Invoice Due Date database field contains 5/10/2013.

MONTH

Returns a numeric value between 1 and 12 indicating the month of the supplied date argument.

MONTH(date)

```
MONTH([Order Date])
```

returns a numeric 3 if the Order Date database field contains 3/10/2013.

NOW

Returns a date/time value consisting of the current date and time as returned by the database. Although NOW doesn't require any arguments, parentheses are still required.

NOW()

```
NOW()
```

returns 5/30/2013 3:44:41 PM if executed on May 30, 2013, at 3:44:41 p.m.

TODAY

Returns a date value consisting of the current date as returned by the database. Although TODAY doesn't require any arguments, parentheses are still required.

TODAY()

```
DATEDIFF("day", [Due Date], TODAY())
```

returns a numeric value 33 if the Due Date database field is 4/27/2013 and the database server's current date is 5/30/2013.

Caution *NOW and TODAY retrieve values from the underlying database server, not your local Tableau client computer. If the database server you are using is set to a different time zone, you may not see the results you expect.*

YEAR

Returns a numeric value indicating the year of the supplied date argument.

YEAR(date)

```
YEAR([Order Date])
```

returns a numeric 2,013 if the Order Date database field contains 3/10/2013.

Type Conversion Functions

These functions convert from one data type to another.

DATE

Converts the supplied expression to a date value. The supplied expression may be a number (representing the number of days since 1/1/1900), string, or date/time value.

DATE(expression)

```
IF ISDATE([DateOrderedString]) THEN
        DATE([DateOrderedString])
ELSE
        DATE("01/01/1900")
END
```

will return the string database field DateOrderedString as a date value if it contains a string value that the DATE function can properly interpret. Otherwise, it will return the date value January 1, 1900.

Simply using

```
DATE([DateOrderedString])
```

will return a null if the supplied string argument does not contain a properly formatted date. By using ISDATE, null values may be avoided.

DATETIME

Converts the supplied expression to a date/time value. The supplied expression may be an integer or real number (representing the number of fractional days since 1/1/1900), string, or date/time value.

DATETIME(expression)

```
DATETIME([Order DateTime String])
```

returns the date/time value 2/10/2013 3:42:00 PM if the string value of the Order DateTime String database field contains the string "2013-02-10 15:42:00".

FLOAT

Converts the supplied string or number to a floating-point (noninteger) number.

FLOAT(expression)

```
FLOAT([Discount String])
```

will return the floating-point numeric value .08500 if the Discount String database field contains the string ".085".

INT

Converts the supplied string or number to an integer (whole) number. Any decimal values appearing in the original argument are ignored (truncated)—the result will not be rounded up.

INT(expression)

```
INT([Unit Price])
```

returns the whole number 7 if the floating-point Unit Price database field contains 7.75.

STR

Converts any value to a string.

STR(expression)

```
STR([Order DateTime])
```

returns the string value "2013-04-10 14:15:00" if the Order DateTime database field contains a date/time value of 4/10/2013 2:15 PM.

Logical Functions

These functions perform various logical tests, returning various values resulting from the tests. In some cases, comparison operators are used with these functions. Comparison operators recognized by Tableau include

- = or ==
- <
- >
- <=
- >=
- <> or !=

CASE

CASE defines an initial expression that is evaluated by one or more following WHEN tests. When a WHEN test is True, the corresponding THEN value is returned. An optional ELSE clause will return a value if all WHEN tests fail. If there is no ELSE clause and all WHEN tests fail, a null is returned.

CASE <expression> WHEN <value1> THEN <return1> ... *[ELSE <else>]* END

```
CASE LEFT([ProductType-SKU], 3)
      WHEN "HDW" THEN "Hardware"
      WHEN "SFT" THEN "Software"
      WHEN "ACC" THEN "Accessory"
END
```

will return "Software" for a ProductType-SKU value of "SFT-18385".

```
CASE LEFT([ProductType-SKU], 3)
      WHEN "HDW" THEN "Hardware"
      WHEN "SFT" THEN "Software"
      WHEN "ACC" THEN "Accessory"
END
```

will return null for a ProductType-SKU value of "APP-15432".

```
CASE LEFT([ProductType-SKU], 3)
      WHEN "HDW" THEN "Hardware"
      WHEN "SFT" THEN "Software"
      WHEN "ACC" THEN "Accessory"
      ELSE "Uncategorized"
END
```

will return "Uncategorized" for a ProductType-SKU value of "APP-15432".

IF

Performs the test specified in the first expression. If the test evaluates to True, returns the value specified in the THEN clause. Optionally, additional ELSIF/THEN tests may be executed to perform more tests if the first test fails. And, an optional ELSE clause may be added to return a result if all IF and ELSEIF tests fail.

IF <expression> THEN <then> [ELSEIF <expression2> THEN <then2>...] [ELSE <else>] END

```
IF LEFT([ProductType-SKU, 3) = "HDW" THEN
      "Hardware"
ELSEIF LEFT([ProductType-SKU, 3) = "SFT" THEN
      "Software"
```

```
ELSEIF LEFT([ProductType-SKU, 3) = "ACC" THEN
        "Accessory"
ELSEIF [ProductPrice] > 1000 THEN
        "Premium Category"
ELSE
        "Uncategorized"
END
```

will return "Premium Category" for the combination of a ProductType-SKU value of "APP-15432" and ProductPrice of 2,500.

Note *While the CASE construct (discussed prior to IF) provides similar logic that may be easier to read and maintain, it does not provide the ability to include more than one test or more than one data type in a test, as does IF.*

IFNULL

Tests whether the first expression evaluates to a null value. If so, the second expression is returned. If not, the first expression is returned.

IFNULL(expression1, expression2)

```
IFNULL([Unit Price] * [Discount], [Unit Price])
```

returns the calculated results of Unit Price multiplied by Discount if neither of the fields contains null. Otherwise, Unit Price is returned.

IIF

Performs the logic test specified in the first argument (the first argument may also be a Boolean field). If the test evaluates to True, returns the value supplied by the second Then argument. If the test evaluates to False, returns the values specified in the third Else argument. If the optional fourth Unknown argument is provided, it will be returned if the test evaluates to Unknown (perhaps because the test returns a null value).

IIF(test, then, else, *[unknown]*)

```
IIF([Discount] < 0, [Unit Price], [Unit Price] * [Discount], [Unit Price])
```

returns the value of Unit Price if the Discount is less than 0. Otherwise, returns the calculated results of Unit Price multiplied by Discount. If Discount is null, returns Unit Price.

ISDATE

Tests the supplied string argument and returns True if it can be converted to a date value with the DATE function. Otherwise, returns False.

ISDATE(string)

```
IF ISDATE([DateOrderedString]) THEN
        DATE([DateOrderedString])
ELSE
        DATE("01/01/1900")
END
```

will return the string database field DateOrderedString as a date value if it contains a string value that the DATE function can properly interpret. Otherwise, it will return the date value January 1, 1900.

Simply using

```
DATE([DateOrderedString])
```

will return a null if the supplied string argument does not contain a properly formatted date. By using ISDATE, null values may be avoided.

ISNULL

Returns True if the supplied expression evaluates to a null value. Otherwise, returns False.

ISNULL(expression)

```
IF ISNULL([Discount]) THEN
        [Unit Price]
ELSE
        [Unit Price] * [Discount]
END
```

returns the Unit Price if the Discount field is null. Otherwise, the calculated results of Unit Price multiplied by Discount are returned.

ZN

Returns the numeric value of the supplied number if it is not null. Otherwise, returns 0.

ZN(expression)

```
ZN([Salary])
```

returns 125,000 if the Salary database field contains the value 125,000. If the Salary database field contains a null value, the result will be 0 instead of a null.

Aggregate Functions

These functions perform in-calculation aggregation. While Tableau typically aggregates by default, these functions provide for more precise aggregation, if desired, within a calculated field.

Examples within this section are based on the sample data set illustrated in Figure A-1.

RowID	Product	Amount
1	SFT	24.50
2	SFT	85.45
3	HRD	1150.00
4	ACC	245.10
5	HRD	750.00
6	ACC	Null
7	SFT	249.00
8	ACC	9.25
9	SFT	750.00
10	ACC	12.50

Figure A-1   Sample data for aggregate functions

ATTR

Returns the value of the supplied expression if all rows in the group of data contain the same value. Otherwise, returns an asterisk (*).

ATTR(expression)

ATTR([Product])

returns * if there is no Product filter applied or Product is not added to a shelf. Otherwise, the value of Product is returned.

AVG

Returns the numeric average of the supplied numeric value.

AVG(number)

AVG([Amount])

returns 363.977777778. Note that a null value does not figure into the average calculation.

COUNT

Returns the numeric count of records based on the supplied expression (any data type is allowed).

COUNT(expression)

COUNT([RowID])

returns 10.

COUNT([Amount])

returns 9, as null values do not increment the COUNT function.

COUNTD

Returns the numeric count of distinct (or unique) records based on the supplied expression (any date type is allowed).

COUNTD(expression)

`COUNTD([RowID])`

returns 10, as RowID is unique.

`COUNTD([Amount])`

returns 8, as there are two occurrences of the same value, as well as a null value (which does not increment COUNTD).

`COUNTD([Product])`

returns 3, as there are three unique occurrences of a product type.

Note *COUNTD is not available when using Microsoft Excel, Microsoft Access, or text file data sources. If you wish to use the COUNTD function with these data sources, perform a data extract from these data sources (covered in Chapter 3), as COUNTD is available when using a data extract.*

MAX

Returns the largest numeric value, latest date, or last alphabetical value based on the supplied expression (any data type is allowed).

MAX(expression)

`MAX([Product])`

returns the string "SFT," as that is the last alphabetical value in the Product field.

`MAX([Amount])`

returns the number 1,150, the largest Amount value.

MEDIAN

Returns the numeric median of the supplied numeric value.

MEDIAN(number)

`MEDIAN([Amount])`

returns 245.1. Note that the null amount does not figure into the median calculation.

Note *MEDIAN is not available when using Microsoft Excel, Microsoft Access, or text file data sources. If you wish to use the MEDIAN function with these data sources, perform a data extract from these data sources (covered in Chapter 3), as MEDIAN is available when using a data extract.*

MIN

Returns the smallest numeric value, earliest date, or first alphabetical value based on the supplied expression (any data type is allowed).

MIN(expression)

```
MIN([Product])
```

returns the string "ACC," as that is the first alphabetical value in the Product field.

```
MIN([Amount])
```

returns the number 9.25, the smallest Amount value.

STDEV

Returns the standard deviation of the supplied numeric value.

STDEV(number)

```
STDEV([Amount])
```

returns 416.143059920.

STDEVP

Returns the population standard deviation of the supplied numeric value.

STDEVP(number)

```
STDEVP([Amount])
```

returns 392.343439484.

SUM

Returns the sum of the supplied numeric value.

SUM(expression)

```
SUM([Amount])
```

returns 3,275.8.

VAR

Returns the variance of the supplied numeric value.

VAR(number)

```
VAR([Amount])
```

returns 173,175.046319444.

VARP

Returns the population variance of the supplied numeric value.

VARP(number)

```
VARP([Amount])
```

returns 153,933.374506173.

Pass-Through Functions

While many functions in the Tableau formula language may look familiar to those who work with SQL databases, not every function or feature of an individual database server is provided in Tableau. Should you desire to call a native SQL function from your particular database server, Tableau provides a series of *pass-through functions*. These functions are not interpreted or modified by Tableau before being sent to the database server (hence, the name RAWSQL). As such, any native function available in your underlying SQL database may be used in a calculated field.

Pass-through functions are available for each data type that Tableau recognizes (real, integer, string, and others). There are also nonaggregate and aggregate versions of each pass-through function. Nonaggregate versions will be automatically aggregated by Tableau, as with standard database fields. Aggregate versions, which generally will be used when passing aggregate functions to the underlying database, will be not be reaggregated by Tableau.

You may pass as many arguments as necessary to the underlying SQL function. However, as the database may not be able to interpret Tableau's field-naming convention, you must add argument "placeholders" in the RAWSQL specified as the first argument. These placeholders are represented by a percent sign (%) followed by sequential numbers (the first argument will be %1, the fifth %5, and so on). You must then supply the actual Tableau field names to pass to the placeholders as additional arguments in the RAWSQL syntax.

For example, if you wish to return a random number from an underlying Microsoft SQL Server database, the following calculated field, using the SQL Server RAND function, may be used. Note that the RAND function makes use of an optional "seed" value. This is being supplied by a unique order ID number from Tableau.

```
RAWSQL_REAL("RAND(%1)",[Order ID])
```

If you uncheck Aggregate Measures from the Analysis drop-down menu, or add the unique Order ID to your visualization, Tableau will display the underlying random numbers from SQL Server. However, as with any other standard numeric database value, the random number calculated field will be aggregated as a SUM otherwise.

If you wish the pass-through function to make use of a value aggregated on the database server, use the AGG versions of the pass-through function. For example:

```
RAWSQLAGG_REAL("FLOOR(SUM(%1))",[Order Amount])
```

will subtotal the passed Order Amount field on the database server and return the results of the SQL Server native FLOOR function. Much as with standard calculated fields that use Tableau aggregate functions, calculated fields using AGG versions of pass-through functions will not be reaggregated by Tableau and will appear with an AGG indicator when used on the workspace.

RAWSQLAGG_BOOL

Returns a Boolean (True or False) result based on the supplied SQL expression. The result will not be reaggregated by Tableau.

RAWSQLAGG_BOOL("sql_expression", [argument1], ... [argumentN])

RAWSQLAGG_DATE

Returns a date result based on the supplied SQL expression. The result will not be reaggregated by Tableau.

RAWSQLAGG_DATE("sql_expression", [argument1], ... [argumentN])

RAWSQLAGG_DATETIME

Returns a date/time result based on the supplied SQL expression. The result will not be reaggregated by Tableau.

RAWSQLAGG_DATETIME("sql_expression", [argument1], ... [argumentN])

RAWSQLAGG_INT

Returns an integer (whole number) result based on the supplied SQL expression. The result will not be reaggregated by Tableau.

RAWSQLAGG_INT("sql_expression", [argument1], ... [argumentN])

RAWSQLAGG_REAL

Returns a real (fractional) result based on the supplied SQL expression. The result will not be reaggregated by Tableau.

RAWSQLAGG_REAL("sql_expression", [argument1], ... [argumentN])

RAWSQLAGG_STR

Returns a string result based on the supplied SQL expression. The result will not be reaggregated by Tableau.

RAWSQLAGG_STR("sql_expression", [argument1], ... [argumentN])

RAWSQL_BOOL

Returns a Boolean (True or False) result based on the supplied SQL expression.

RAWSQL_BOOL("sql_expression", [argument1], ... [argumentN])

RAWSQL_DATE

Returns a date result based on the supplied SQL expression.

RAWSQL_DATE("sql_expression", [argument1], ... [argumentN])

RAWSQL_DATETIME

Returns a date/time result based on the supplied SQL expression.

RAWSQL_DATETIME("sql_expression", [argument1], ... [argumentN])

RAWSQL_INT

Returns an integer (whole number) result based on the supplied SQL expression.

RAWSQL_INT("sql_expression", [argument1], ... [argumentN])

RAWSQL_REAL

Returns a real (fractional) result based on the supplied SQL expression.

RAWSQL_REAL("sql_expression", [argument1], ... [argumentN])

RAWSQL_STR

Returns a string result based on the supplied SQL expression.

RAWSQL_STR("sql_expression", [argument1], ... [argumentN])

User Functions

These functions retrieve user and group information from a connected Tableau Server. By using these functions, you may tailor your worksheet or dashboard behavior according to who is logged in to Tableau Server (see Chapter 9).

FULLNAME

Returns the full name of the current Tableau user. If logged into Tableau Server, the Tableau Server full name is returned. Otherwise, the domain/Windows user is returned. Even though this function accepts no arguments, the parentheses are required.

FULLNAME()

```
FULLNAME()
```

returns "George Peck" if the full name (not the user name) of the user currently logged in to Tableau Server is George Peck.

ISFULLNAME

Returns True if the supplied string argument is the same as the current FULLNAME (see the "FULLNAME" entry previously in this section). Otherwise, returns False.

ISFULLNAME(string)

```
ISFULLNAME("George Peck")
```

returns True if the user currently logged in to Tableau Server has a full name (not a user name) of "George Peck".

ISMEMBEROF

Returns True if the supplied string argument is the same as a Tableau Server group that the current user is a member of. Otherwise, returns False.

ISMEMBEROF(string)

```
IF ISMEMBEROF("HR") THEN
    STR([Salary])
ELSE
    "Not Available"
END
```

returns the string conversion of the Salary database field if the current user is a member of the HR group. Otherwise, returns "Not Available".

ISUSERNAME

Returns True if the supplied string argument is the same as the current USERNAME (see the "USERNAME" entry later in this section). Otherwise, returns False.

ISUSERNAME(string)

```
ISUSERNAME("GPeck")
```

returns True if the user currently logged in to Tableau Server has a user name (not a full name) of "GPeck".

USERDOMAIN

Returns the domain of the Tableau Server the current user is logged in to. If the user is not logged in to Tableau Server, the current Windows domain is returned. Even though this function accepts no arguments, the parentheses are required.

USERDOMAIN( )

```
USERDOMAIN()
```

returns "local" if the Tableau Server the user is currently logged in to is not in an Active Directory domain.

USERNAME

Returns the user name (not the full name) of the user currently logged in to Tableau Server. If the user is not logged in to Tableau Server, the Windows user name is returned. Even though this function accepts no arguments, the parentheses are required.

USERNAME( )

```
USERNAME()
```

returns "GPeck" if the user name (not the full name) of the user currently logged in to Tableau Server is GPeck.

```
USERNAME() = "Administrator" OR [Employee Login] = USERNAME()
```

when added to the Filters shelf, returns all records if the administrator is logged in. Otherwise, only returns records where the Employee Login database field matches the user name (not the full name) of the user currently logged in to Tableau Server.

Table Calculation Functions

These functions perform table calculation manipulation (see Chapter 7 for detailed information on table calculations). These functions force the calculated field they're in to evaluate after Tableau has returned an aggregated set of data from the underlying data source. As such, any field arguments provided must appear in aggregate (by way of SUM(), AVG(), or other aggregate functions described earlier in this appendix).

Any calculated field using these functions will automatically become a table calculation. As such, it will appear with a delta icon when used on the workspace. And, as with standard table calculations, *direction* and *scope* may be specified for the calculated field by way of the Compute Using option from the field's context menu (direction and scope are covered in detail in Chapter 7). The direction/scope choices will determine the "partition" the function applies to.

		Accessories	Hardware	Software
2012	October	350	550	250
	November	60	1,225	300
	December	1,025	660	300
2013	January	650	1,325	1,175
	February	300	260	200
	March	500	260	250

Figure A-2   Table calculation function example

The examples in this section are based on the text table illustrated in Figure A-2. For these examples, direction/scope has been set to Pane Down, indicating that table calculations will calculate from top to bottom, resetting at a new "pane," or year. As such, this example contains two partitions. Due to the Pane Down partition setting, only the first Accessories row is illustrated in the following examples.

FIRST

Returns the offset from the current position to the starting position in the partition. Even though this function accepts no arguments, the parentheses are required.

FIRST()

```
FIRST()
```

returns

Amount	Calc
350	0
60	-1
1,025	-2
650	0
300	-1
500	-2

INDEX

Returns the number of the current position in the partition. Even though this function accepts no arguments, the parentheses are required.

INDEX()

INDEX()

returns

Amount	Calc
350	1
60	2
1,025	3
650	1
300	2
500	3

LAST

Returns the offset from the current position to the ending position in the partition. Even though this function accepts no arguments, the parentheses are required.

LAST()

LAST()

returns

Amount	Calc
350	2
60	1
1,025	0
650	2
300	1
500	0

LOOKUP

Looks up another value from earlier in the partition (if the numeric offset argument is negative) or later in the partition (if the numeric offset is positive). The offset determines how many positions before or after the current position to retrieve. If offset is not supplied, the offset may be supplied with the "Relative To" option on the table calculation context menu.

LOOKUP(expression, *[offset]*)

```
LOOKUP(SUM([Amount]), -1)
```

returns

Amount	Calc
350	
60	350
1,025	60
650	
300	650
500	300

PREVIOUS_VALUE

Returns the value of the previous occurrence of the calculated field. If this is the first occurrence of the calculated field, the expression argument is returned. Otherwise, this function builds a cumulative value as it progresses through the data partition.

PREVIOUS_VALUE(expression)

```
PREVIOUS_VALUE(0) + SUM([Amount])
```

returns

Amount	Calc
350	350
60	410
1,025	1,435
650	650
300	950
500	1,450

RUNNING_AVG

Returns the running average of the supplied expression as of the current position in the partition.

RUNNING_AVG(expression)

```
RUNNING_AVG(SUM([Amount]))
```

returns

Amount	Calc
350	350
60	205
1,025	478.333333333
650	650
300	475
500	483.333333333

RUNNING_COUNT

Returns the running count of the supplied expression as of the current position in the partition.

RUNNING_COUNT(expression)

```
RUNNING_COUNT(SUM([Amount]))
```

returns

Amount	Calc
350	1
60	2
1,025	3
650	1
300	2
500	3

RUNNING_MAX

Returns the running maximum of the supplied expression as of the current position in the partition.

RUNNING_MAX(expression)

```
RUNNING_MAX(SUM([Amount]))
```

returns

Amount	Calc
350	350
60	350
1,025	1,025
650	650
300	650
500	650

RUNNING_MIN

Returns the running minimum of the supplied expression as of the current position in the partition.

RUNNING_MIN(expression)

```
RUNNING_MIN(SUM([Amount]))
```

returns

Amount	Calc
350	350
60	60
1,025	60
650	650
300	300
500	300

RUNNING_SUM

Returns the running sum of the supplied expression as of the current position in the partition.

RUNNING_SUM(expression)

```
RUNNING_SUM(SUM([Amount]))
```

returns

Amount	Calc
350	350
60	410
1,025	1,435
650	650
300	950
500	1,450

SIZE

Returns the number of positions in the partition. Even though this function accepts no arguments, the parentheses are required.

SIZE()

```
SIZE()
```

returns

Amount	Calc
350	3
60	3
1,025	3
650	3
300	3
500	3

TOTAL

Returns the total sum of the supplied expression over the partition.

TOTAL(expression)

`TOTAL(SUM([Amount]))`

returns

Amount	Calc
350	1,435
60	1,435
1,025	1,435
650	1,450
300	1,450
500	1,450

WINDOW_AVG

Returns the overall average of the supplied expression over the partition (referred to as the "window"). If optional numeric start and end arguments are supplied, the average is reduced to that range.

WINDOW_AVG(expression, *[start, end]*)

`WINDOW_AVG(SUM([Amount]))`

returns

Amount	Calc
350	478.333333333
60	478.333333333
1,025	478.333333333
650	483.333333333
300	483.333333333
500	483.333333333

`WINDOW_AVG(SUM([Amount]),0,LAST()-1)`

returns

Amount	Calc
350	205
60	60
1,025	
650	475
300	300
500	

WINDOW_COUNT

Returns the overall count of the supplied expression over the partition (referred to as the "window"). If optional numeric start and end arguments are supplied, the count is reduced to that range.

WINDOW_COUNT(expression, *[start, end]*)

WINDOW_COUNT(SUM([Amount]))

returns

Amount	Calc
350	3
60	3
1,025	3
650	3
300	3
500	3

WINDOW_COUNT(SUM([Amount]),0,LAST()-1)

returns

Amount	Calc
350	2
60	1
1,025	0
650	2
300	1
500	0

WINDOW_MAX

Returns the overall maximum of the supplied expression over the partition (referred to as the "window"). If optional numeric start and end arguments are supplied, the maximum is reduced to that range.

WINDOW_MAX(expression, *[start, end]*)

```
WINDOW_MAX(SUM([Amount]))
```

returns

Amount	Calc
350	1,025
60	1,025
1,025	1,025
650	650
300	650
500	650

```
WINDOW_MAX(SUM([Amount]),0,LAST()-1)
```

returns

Amount	Calc
350	350
60	60
1,025	
650	650
300	300
500	

WINDOW_MEDIAN

Returns the overall median of the supplied expression over the partition (referred to as the "window"). If optional numeric start and end arguments are supplied, the median is reduced to that range.

WINDOW_MEDIAN(expression, *[start, end]*)

`WINDOW_MEDIAN(SUM([Amount]))`

returns

Amount	Calc
350	350
60	350
1,025	350
650	500
300	500
500	500

`WINDOW_MEDIAN(SUM([Amount]),0,LAST()-1)`

returns

Amount	Calc
350	205
60	60
1,025	
650	475
300	300
500	

WINDOW_MIN

Returns the overall minimum of the supplied expression over the partition (referred to as the "window"). If optional numeric start and end arguments are supplied, the minimum is reduced to that range.

WINDOW_MIN(expression, *[start, end]*)

`WINDOW_MIN(SUM([Amount]))`

returns

Amount	Calc
350	60
60	60
1,025	60
650	300
300	300
500	300

```
WINDOW_MIN(SUM([Amount]),0,LAST()-1)
```

returns

Amount	Calc
350	60
60	60
1,025	
650	300
300	300
500	

WINDOW_STDEV

Returns the overall standard deviation of the supplied expression over the partition (referred to as the "window"). If optional numeric start and end arguments are supplied, the standard deviation is reduced to that range.

WINDOW_STDEV(expression, *[start, end]*)

```
WINDOW_STDEV(SUM([Amount]))
```

returns

Amount	Calc
350	495.134661818
60	495.134661818
1,025	495.134661818
650	175.594229214
300	175.594229214
500	175.594229214

```
WINDOW_STDEV(SUM([Amount]),0,LAST()-1)
```

returns

Amount	Calc
350	205.060966544
60	
1,025	
650	247.487373415
300	
500	

WINDOW_STDEVP

Returns the overall population standard deviation of the supplied expression over the partition (referred to as the "window"). If optional numeric start and end arguments are supplied, the population standard deviation is reduced to that range.

WINDOW_STDEVP(expression, *[start, end]*)

```
WINDOW_STDEVP(SUM([Amount]))
```

returns

Amount	Calc
350	404.275758473
60	404.275758473
1,025	404.275758473
650	143.372087784
300	143.372087784
500	143.372087784

```
WINDOW_STDEVP(SUM([Amount])),0,LAST()-1)
```

returns

Amount	Calc
350	145
60	0
1,025	
650	175
300	0
500	

WINDOW_SUM

Returns the overall sum of the supplied expression over the partition (referred to as the "window"). If optional numeric start and end arguments are supplied, the sum is reduced to that range.

WINDOW_SUM(expression, *[start, end]*)

```
WINDOW_SUM(SUM([Amount]))
```

returns

Amount	Calc
350	1,435
60	1,435
1,025	1,435
650	1,450
300	1,450
500	1,450

```
WINDOW_SUM(SUM([Amount]),0,LAST()-1)
```

returns

Amount	Calc
350	410
60	60
1,025	
650	950
300	300
500	

WINDOW_VAR

Returns the overall variance of the supplied expression over the partition (referred to as the "window"). If optional numeric start and end arguments are supplied, the variance is reduced to that range.

WINDOW_VAR(expression, *[start, end]*)

```
WINDOW_VAR(SUM([Amount]))
```

returns

Amount	Calc
350	245,158.33333
60	245,158.33333
1,025	245,158.33333
650	30,833.33333
300	30,833.33333
500	30,833.33333

```
WINDOW_VAR(SUM([Amount]),0,LAST()-1)
```

returns

Amount	Calc
350	42,050
60	
1,025	
650	61,250
300	
500	

WINDOW_VARP

Returns the overall population variance of the supplied expression over the partition (referred to as the "window"). If optional numeric start and end arguments are supplied, the population variance is reduced to that range.

WINDOW_VARP(expression, [start, end])

```
WINDOW_VARP(SUM([Amount]))
```

returns

Amount	Calc
350	163,439
60	163,439
1,025	163,439
650	20,556
300	20,556
500	20,556

```
WINDOW_VARP(SUM([Amount]),0,LAST()-1)
```

returns

Amount	Calc
350	21,025
60	0
1,025	
650	30,625
300	0
500	

Index

Symbols

= (equals), 247
== (equals), 247
/ (division), 158
> (greater than), 247
>= (greater than or equal to), 247
< (less than), 247
<= (less than or equal to), 247
* (multiplication), 158
( ) (parentheses), 158
+ (plus)
    numeric calculations using, 158
    using for strings and numbers, 158
[ ] (square brackets), 157
- (subtraction), 158
!= symbol, 247
<> symbol, 247

A

ABS function, 231
Access. *See* Microsoft Access
ACOS function, 231
actions. *See also specific type of action*
    dashboard, 202–209
    filter, 112–115, 202, 204–207
    highlight, 112, 115–117, 202, 203–204
    methods initiating, 112, 202
    URL, 112, 118–120, 202, 207–209
    worksheet, 112–120
Actions drop-down menu, 112
Add/Edit Field Mapping dialog box, 64
Add/Edit Permissions dialog box, 219
Add From Field button (Edit Parameter dialog box), 109
Add Table dialog box, 36
Add WMS Server Connection dialog box, 144

addressing in table calculations, 171
aggregate functions, 250–254
    about, 250–251
    ATTR, 251
    AVG, 251
    COUNT, 251
    COUNTD, 252
    creating aggregated numeric values, 155
    MAX, 252
    MEDIAN, 252–253
    MIN, 234, 240, 244–245, 253
    STDEV, 253
    STDEVP, 253
    SUM, 163, 165, 253
    VAR, 254
    VARP, 254
aggregated numeric values. *See also* aggregate functions
    calculated fields using, 163–165
    filtering, 99–100
    functions creating, 155
Android devices, 221, 228
Apply Filter To Worksheets dialog box, 102
area annotations, 82
area charts, 71–73, 74
area code data, 125, 128–130
area zoom mode, 141
arguments. *See also* functions
    including in SQL pass-through functions, 254–256
    using in functions, 155, 231
ASCII function, 236
ASIN function, 231–232
ATAN function, 232
ATTR function, 251
authenticating external data sources, 220
AVG function, 251

axes
    adding references lines to, 179
    charts using dual, 23–24
    comparing measures on shared, 23–24
    highlighting with references bands,
        181–182
    references lines denoting point on,
        180–181
    table calculations for right and left,
        176–177

B

Background Image dialog box, 151–153
background maps
    about, 140–141
    choosing options for, 144–145
    customizing images for, 151–153
    selecting, 122–123
bar charts
    as component in bullet graph, 85
    converting to line/area charts, 72
    creating, 69–71
    histogram using binned field, 166–167
    illustrated, 6
BI Magic Quadrant, 80
binned fields, 166–167
blank dashboard element, 200
box plot chart, 88–92
    defined, 89
    with whiskers, 90–91
broken link icons, 63
bubble charts, 83, 84–85
built-in functions. See functions
bullet graph charts, 85–88

C

Calculated Field dialog box, 150, 151, 156, 177,
        178, 224
calculated fields. See also table calculation
        functions
    binned fields, 166–167
    creating, 156–157
    data aggregation for, 163–165
    date/time calculations, 160–161
    defined, 155
    naming, 157
    numeric calculations for, 157–158
    operators for, 155
    setting custom dates, 161–162
    testing logic for, 162–165
    using table calculations, 167–179
cards. See also Marks card
    about, 5
    color legends for, 14–15

CASE function, 163, 248, 249
case sensitivity
    converting strings to proper case, 159
    Tableau's, 163
CBSA (Core Based Statistical Area) data, 125
CHAR function, 237
charts, 69–94. See also axes; and specific chart type
    adding mark labels to, 18
    applying table calculations with any, 176
    bar, 6, 69–71
    blending data for, 60–65
    box plot, 88–92
    bubble, 83–85
    bullet graph, 85–88
    choosing mark types for, 13
    combination, 29
    comparing measures on shared axis, 23–24
    converting bar to line/area, 72
    creating with Show Me, 9, 11–12
    design flow for, 5–8
    dimension headers in, 10
    dual axis, 26–28
    forecasting, 73–74
    line/area, 71–73, 74
    pie, 74–76
    scatter plot, 16, 80–83
    stacked bar, 7
    text table or crosstab, 17–18, 76–80
    Tree Map, 92–94
    word cloud, 94
Choose Source Folder dialog box, 135
city geocoding data, 125, 128–130
Clipboard. See also copying data
    adding data using, 40–43
    copying worksheet images to, 214
color
    adding to card shapes, 17
    charting dimensions with, 70
    combining on Marks card, 15
    increasing line chart data with, 71–72
combined sets, 54
company logos, 201
computed sets, 50
concatenating
    fields, 39–40
    string data, 159
Connect To Data drop-down menu, 31–32
Connection dialog boxes, 33–34
connections. See data sources
constant sets, 50
CONTAINS function, 237
coordinate systems
    generating customized, 149–151
    plotting latitude/longitude as X/Y,
        122, 124

Copy Image dialog box, 214
copying data
    as crosstab chart, 212
    from web-based data sources, 40–43
    from worksheet and dashboard, 213
Core Based Statistical Area (CBSA) data, 125
COS function, 232
COT function, 232
COUNT function, 251
COUNTD function, 252
COUNTID function, 252
country/region data, 126
county data, 126
Create Bins dialog box, 167
Create Custom Date dialog box, 162
Create Group dialog box, 47
Create Hierarchy dialog box, 45
Create Parameter dialog box, 107–108
Create Set dialog box, 50–51, 54
crosstab (text table) charts, 76–80
    adding table calculations to, 167–176
    best uses for, 80
    copying data as, 212
    exporting data to Excel, 213
    using, 17–18, 76–77, 79–80
    using multiple measures, 78–79
.csv files
    extending geographic roles with,
        132–133, 134
    importing custom geocoding as, 135–138
custom background images, 148–153
    generating X/Y coordinates for, 149–151
    illustrated, 149
custom dates, 161–162
customizing
    background images, 148–153
    Clipboard data, 41–42
    data views, 38–55
    geographic roles, 131–138

━━ **D** ━━

dashboard actions
    defined, 202
    filter actions, 202, 204–207
    highlight actions, 202, 203–204
    initiating, 202–203
    types of, 202
    URL actions, 202, 207–209
Dashboard drop-down menu, 215
dashboards, 187–209. *See also* dashboard actions
    adding text to, 200
    blank element for, 200
    copying data from, 213
    creating, 187–188

deleting duplicate quick filters for, 198
    embedding web pages in, 201
    exporting as image, 215
    floating placement for, 188, 196–197
    function of Tableau, 187
    images for, 200–201
    initiating actions with hovering, 112, 118,
        202, 203
    layout containers for, 198–200
    placement of images in, 201
    printing to .pdf files, 211–212
    resizing on worksheets, 195
    sharing published views of, 219
    sizing elements of, 195, 201–202
    tiled placement for, 188, 189–195
    working with worksheet elements
        appearing on, 197–198
    worksheet vs. dashboard actions, 120
data. *See also* aggregated numeric values; data
    sources; filtering data; publishing data to web
    blending, 38, 60–65
    copying, cutting, and pasting, 40–43,
        212, 213
    filtering by user, 222–226
    functions for converting data types,
        246–247
    manipulating dimension string, 158–160
    marks for scatter plot, 81–83
    reading in Tableau Reader, 215–216
    retrieving with NOW and TODAY
        functions, 245
    storing and refreshing extracted
        Tableau, 58
    types of geographic fields, 125–126
    using different axis scales for, 27
data blending
    about, 60
    table joins vs., 60
    using, 38, 60–65
Data Connection dialog box, 56
data connections. *See* data sources
Data Extract file, 56
data layers, 142, 143
data sources, 31–68. *See also* extracted data;
    web-based data sources
    adding/joining tables from same
        database, 35–37
    authenticating external, 220
    building hierarchies in, 43, 44–45
    changing default map source, 141
    choosing, 33–34, 56
    connecting workbook to, 2, 31–35
    creating metadata groups, 45–49
    customizing view of, 38–40, 43–55
    cutting and pasting data in Tableau, 40–43

data sources (cont.)
  downloading drivers for, 34
  extracting data from, 55–59
  filtering worksheets sharing, 102
  importing custom geographic roles as, 135–138
  maintaining relationship to source of extracted data, 59
  modifying default field assignments, 38
  modifying field appearance, 43
  relation of data extract to original, 58
  replacing, 66–68
  saved, 2, 3
  saving as .tds file, 53–55
  setting up primary and secondary, 61–63
  simplifying, 38
  types of available, 32–33
  uploading for Tableau Server workbooks, 220
  using Connect To Data drop-down menu, 31–32
  using data blending, 38, 60–65
  using in set/out set feature with Excel and Access, 53
Data window
  about, 3–4
  calculated fields displayed in, 157
  combining sets in, 54
  creating parameters from, 107
  dragging Measure Names and Measure Values fields to, 26
  illustrated, 3
  modifying data groups in, 46–47
  using data blending in, 60–65
databases. See also data sources; tables
  adding/joining tables from same, 35–37
  blending data from different, 38, 60–65
  extracting data from, 55–59
  joining on common fields, 35, 36–37
  moving from test to production, 66–68
  presenting all or relevant values in, 105
date. See also date functions
  calculating, 160–161
  converting expressions to time and, 246
  creating custom, 161–162
  filtering data by, 97, 105
  functions for, 242–246
  quick filters by, 105
  using SQL pass-through functions for, 255, 256
date functions, 242–246
  about, 242
  DATE, 160, 246
  DATEADD, 242
  DATEDIFF, 243
  DATENAME, 243

DATEPART, 243
DATETRUNC, 243
DAY, 243–244
ISDATE, 238, 244, 249–250
MAX, 233, 239–240, 244, 252
MIN, 234, 240, 244–245, 253
MONTH, 245
NOW, 245
TODAY, 245
YEAR, 246
DATEADD function, 160–161, 242
DATEDIFF function, 243
DATENAME function, 243
DATEPART function, 161, 243
DATETIME function, 246
DATETRUNC function, 161, 243
DAY function, 243–244
DEGREES function, 232
Describe Trend Model dialog box, 186
dimension headers, 10, 46
dimension members
  combining into group, 45–46
  defined, 10
  using constant sets of, 50–51
  working with group, 47–48
dimensions. See also dimension members
  basing trend lines on measures and, 184
  building hierarchies of, 43, 44–45
  changing from horizontal to vertical bar charts, 69
  charting with color, 70
  defined, 3
  editing cut-and-paste data, 41–43
  headers for, 10, 46
  manipulating string data for, 158–160
  mapping geographic, 121–122, 139–140
  measure vs., 10–11
  modifying for scatter plot charts, 81–82
  naming for primary and secondary data sources, 62–63
  recategorizing as measure, 38
  setting up bullet graph, 86, 87
  specifying conditions for filtering data, 98–99
direction of field, 258
disaggregating scatter plot data, 81–82
downloading data source drivers, 34
Drop Field dialog box, 161
dual axis charts, 26–28

E

Edit Colors dialog box, 15
Edit Filter Action dialog box, 114, 207
Edit Highlight Action dialog box, 116
Edit Location dialog box, 127, 130

Edit Parameter dialog box, 109
Edit Reference Line dialog box, 89, 92, 180, 181, 183
Edit Set dialog box, 52
Edit Shape dialog box, 16, 17
Edit URL Action dialog, 119, 208
editing
    data groups in Data window, 46–47
    default field assignments, 38
    dimensions, 41–43
    field appearance, 43
    measures, 41–43, 80
    misinterpreted geocoded fields, 124–125, 126–128
    mismatched location values, 127, 130
    scatter plot chart dimensions, 81–82
    trend lines, 185
ELSE keyword, 162–163
ELSEIF keyword, 162–163
END keyword, 162–163
ENDSWITH function, 237
EP function, 233
errors
    creating trend lines, 184
    data blending dimension name mismatches, 64–66
    geocoding assignment, 124–125
    matching dimensions for data sources, 62–63
    opening workbooks in Tableau Reader, 215
    saving data from remote connections, 55
    using plus sign for strings and numbers in same formula, 158
Excel. *See* Microsoft Excel
Export Data To Access dialog box, 214
exporting
    crosstab data to Excel, 213
    dashboards as image files, 215
    data to Access .mdb file, 213
    data to Tableau Reader, 215–216
    publishing data to web, 216–229
    worksheet data, 212–214
    worksheet images, 213–215
    worksheets and dashboards, 211–215
expressions
    converting to date and time, 246
    defining contents of computed sets with formulaic, 50
Extract Data dialog box, 57
Extract sub-menu, 59
extracted data, 55–59
    creating as .tde file, 54–55
    extracting before using COUNTD and MEDIAN, 252, 253

    maintaining relationship to original data source, 59
    refreshing extracted, 220
    in set/out of set feature for, 53
    storing and refreshing, 58
    using from large databases, 55

F

fields. *See also* calculated fields; geocoded fields
    binned, 166–167
    changing properties of, 19
    creating parameter from calculated, 107
    editing misinterpreted geocoded, 124–125, 126–128
    filtering calculated, 100
    generating customized coordinate systems, 149–151
    geocoded, 124–138
    globe icon indicating geographic, 121, 122, 124
    hiding, renaming, and combining, 39–40
    including in pass-through functions, 254
    joining databases on common, 35, 36–37
    modifying appearance of, 43
    naming, 39, 157
    recategorizing dimensions and measures, 38
    selecting from Format window, 20–21
files. *See also* .csv files
    COUNTD function unavailable in text, 252
    .csv, 135–138
    exporting dashboards as image, 215
    exporting image, 215
    .mdb, 213
    .pdf, 211–212
    saving Clipboard data as tab-delimited, 42–43
    .tde, 55–59
    .tds, 53–55
    .tms, 144
    .twbx, 138, 215–216
Filled Map marks, 147
filter actions
    adding, 112–115
    adding to dashboards, 204–207
    defined, 112, 202
Filter dialog box, 7, 96, 97, 98, 99, 100, 101, 106
filtering data, 95–105
    count for, 97
    date for, 97, 105
    defined, 95
    filtering out mismatched geocoding, 128
    hard coding in worksheets, 95–101

filtering data *(cont.)*
    interactively, 101, 103
    measures, 100–101
    setting conditions for, 98–99
    user ID for, 222–226
    wildcard options for, 98
filters. *See also* filter actions; Filters shelf
    creating Tableau Server user, 222–226
    quick, 103–105
    removing, 96
    sharing among worksheets, 102
    using top, 99–101, 106
Filters shelf
    applying filters to worksheets, 102
    including interactive filters on, 101, 103
    working with, 96–97
FIND function, 238
FIRST function, 259
FLOAT function, 247
floating dashboards
    designing, 196–197
    layout containers and, 199
    using, 188
folders
    choosing data source, 135
    My Tableau Repository, 54–55
Forecast Options dialog box, 74
forecasting charts, 73–74
Format window, 20
formatting visualizations, 20–22
formulas. *See* calculated fields
FULLNAME function, 257
functions, 231–272. *See also specific type of function*
    about, 155
    aggregate, 250–254
    calculated fields using table calculation, 176–179
    date, 242–246
    displaying hints of built-in, 157
    found in Calculated Field dialog box, 156
    logical, 247–250
    number, 231–236
    pass-through, 254–256
    string, 236–242
    table calculation, 258–272
    type conversion, 246–247
    user, 256–258
    using, 231

G

geocoded fields, 124–138
    choosing mark types for, 145–148
    customizing geographic roles, 131–138
    defined, 124
    editing, 124–125, 126–128
    filtering out mismatched, 128
    importing custom geocoding roles, 135–138
    removing imported custom geocoding, 138
    resolving ambiguities in geographic hierarchy, 128–130
    types of geographic data for, 125–126
geographic dimensions
    globe icon indicating, 121, 122
    mapping, 121–122, 139–140
Geographic Role context menu, 137
geographic roles
    assigning latitude/longitude values to, 139–140
    correcting misidentified, 124–125
    customizing, 131–138
    importing custom .csv, 135–138
    requirements for customizing, 132–133
groups
    creating metadata, 45–49
    creating visual, 48–49
    defined, 45
    dimension headers for creating, 46
    functions retrieving data for, 256–258
    modifying in Data window, 46–47

H

Heat Map, 15, 16
hiding fields, 39
hierarchies
    building metadata, 43, 44–45
    defined, 44
    displaying in tree maps, 92–94
    resolving ambiguities in geographic, 128–130
highlight actions
    creating, 115–117
    defined, 112
    using, 202, 203–204
hovering, 112, 118, 202, 203

I

icons
    broken link, 63
    globe, 121, 122, 124
IF function, 162–163, 248–249
If-Then-Else logic, 162–163
IFNULL function, 249
IIF function, 248–249
images
    copying worksheet to Clipboard as, 214
    customizing for background maps, 148–153
    exporting dashboards as single, 215
    exporting worksheet, 213–215
    placing on dashboards, 196, 201
    selecting for dashboards, 200–201

Import Custom Geocoding dialog box, 135, 138
importing custom geocoding roles, 135–138
INDEX function, 260
INT function, 247
interacting with viewer, 95–120
    enabling worksheet actions, 112–120
    filtering data, 95–105
    initiating dashboard actions, 112, 118,
        202–203
    using parameters, 106–111
interactive filtering, 101, 103
ISDATE function, 238, 244, 249–250
ISFULLNAME function, 257
ISMEMBEROF function, 257
ISNULL function, 250
ISUSERNAME function, 257

J

joining
    data blending vs. data, 60
    databases on common fields, 35, 36–37

K

keywords
    adding for workbooks, 219
    ELSE, 162–163
    ELSEIF, 162–163
    MAX, 165
    THEN, 162–163

L

labels
    adding to pie wedges, 75
    automatically added for multiple
        measures, 18
LAST function, 260
latitude/longitude
    default for mismatched geographic
        values, 28
    determining city's, 128–130
    mapping to geographic dimensions,
        139–140
    placement in .csv file, 133, 134
    plotting as X/Y coordinates, 122, 124
layout containers, 198–200
LEFT function, 160, 238–239
legends, 196
LEN function, 239
line/area charts, 71–73, 74
LN function, 233
locations
    editing mismatched values for, 127, 130
    geocoding information for, 125, 126

LOG function, 233
logic. *See also* logical functions
    comparison operators testing, 247
    testing fields with If-Then-Else, 162–163
logical functions, 247–250
    CASE, 163, 248, 249
    comparison operators for, 247
    IF, 162–163, 248–249
    IFNULL, 249
    IIF, 248–249
    ISDATE, 249–250
    ISNULL, 250
    ZN, 250
logical operators, 155
LOOKUP function, 261
LOWER function, 239
LTRIM function, 239

M

map layers, 142
maps, 121–153. *See also* background maps;
    geocoded fields
    background, 122–123, 140–141, 144–145
    choosing mark types for, 145–148
    connecting to Web Map Services,
        143–145
    creating, 121–123
    illustrated, 123
    map and data layers, 142–143
    mapping custom background images,
        148–153
    mapping latitude/longitude to
        dimensions on, 139–140
    mark types used on, 13
    nongeocoded fields on, 146
    offline, 141
    using geocoded fields, 124–138
    using Pie mark type on, 75–76
marks. *See also* Marks card
    adding color to shaped, 17
    annotations for, 82
    background map for X/Y coordinate
        map, 122
    choosing mapping, 145–148
    displaying default position for
        mismatched geographic values, 28
    Filled Map, 147
    labels for, 18
    Pie, 147–148
    pre-selecting for server workbooks, 220
    selecting actions with, 112, 202
    shaped, 16–17
    types used on maps, 13, 75–76
    using variable sizes of, 15–16, 76

Marks card
    about, 5
    changing field properties on, 19
    color-coding shapes on, 17
    color options for, 14–15
    converting bar to line/area charts with, 72
    creating stacked bar charts with, 7
    mark types used on, 12–13
    Multi-Measure, 28–29
    selecting text for tables on, 18
    setting up pie charts using, 74–76
    shape selections from, 16–17
    using variable mark sizes on, 15–16, 76
MAX function, 233, 239–240, 244, 252
MAX keyword, 165
.mdb files, 213
measures, 22–29
    adding to dual axis charts, 26–28
    basing reference lines on, 181
    basing trend lines on dimensions and, 184
    changing from horizontal to vertical bar
        charts, 69
    comparing multiple, 22–23
    creating dual axis charts, 26–28
    crosstab charts using multiple, 78–79
    defined, 3
    dimension vs., 10–11
    editing, 41–43, 80
    filtering on, 100–101
    labeling multiple fields for, 18
    modifying for scatter plot charts, 81–82
    Multi-Measure Marks card, 28–29
    quick filters based on numeric, 105
    recategorizing as dimension, 38
    setting up bullet graph, 86, 87
    shared axis charts using multiple, 23–24
    swapping to new shelves, 80
    using Measure Names and Measure
        Values fields, 24–26
    values of, 11
MEDIAN function, 252–253
menus
    Actions drop-down menu, 112
    Connect To Data drop-down menu,
        31–32
    Dashboard drop-down menu, 215
    Extract sub-menu, 59
    selecting actions from, 112, 202
    Server drop-down menu, 222
    Totals drop-down menu, 77
metadata
    building hierarchies of, 43, 44–45
    creating visual groups of, 48–49
    defined, 38
    grouping, 45–49

organizing in sets, 50–53
saving and sharing, 53–55
Metropolitan Statistical Area (MSA) data, 125
Microsoft Access
    COUNTD function unavailable in, 252
    MEDIAN function unavailable in, 253
    uploading data sources to Tableau
        Server, 220
    using in set/out of set feature with, 53
Microsoft Excel
    COUNTD function unavailable in, 252
    exporting crosstab data to, 213
    uploading data sources to Tableau
        Server, 220
    using in set/out of set feature with, 53
Microsoft SQL Server, 55, 66–68
Microsoft SQL Server Connection dialog box,
    33, 35
MID function, 160, 240
MIN function, 234, 240, 244–245, 253
mobile apps, 221, 227–228
mobile browsers, 221, 228
MONTH function, 245
MSA (Metropolitan Statistical Area) data, 125
Multi-Measure Marks card, 28–29
Multiple Tables radio button, (Connection dialog
    box), 35–36
My Tableau Repository folder, 54–55

N

naming
    calculated fields, 157
    dimensions for data sources, 62–63
    fields, 39
    mismatched blending dimensions, 64–65
    worksheets, 7–8, 187
nongeocoded fields in maps, 146
NOW function, 245
null values, 159–160
number functions, 231–236
    about, 231
    ABS, 231
    ACOS, 231
    ASIN, 231–232
    ATAN, 232
    COS, 232
    COT, 232
    DEGREES, 232
    EP, 233
    LN, 233
    LOG, 233
    MAX, 233, 239–240, 244, 252
    MIN, 234, 240, 244–245, 253
    PI, 234

POWER, 234
RADIANS, 234
ROUND, 235
SIGN, 235
SIN, 235
SQRT, 235
SQUARE, 236
TAN, 236
ZN, 236

O

offline maps, 141
online maps, 141
operators
    comparison, 247
    functions vs., 155
    numeric, 157
    order of precedence for, 158
    using in calculated fields, 155
Oracle databases, 55
order of precedence, 158

P

parameters, 106–111
    creating, 106–109
    defined, 106
    displaying on worksheet, 109–110
    selecting in Calculated Field dialog
        box, 156
    using in worksheet, 110–111
    workbook uses for, 106
parsing strings, 158
partitioning table calculations, 171
pass-through functions, 254–256
    about, 254–255
    RAWSQLAGG_BOOL, 255
    RAWSQLAGG_DATE, 255
    RAWSQLAGG_DATETIME, 255
    RAWSQLAGG_INT, 255
    RAWSQLAGG_REAL, 255
    RAWSQLAGG_STR, 256
    RAWSQL_BOOL function, 256
    RAWSQL_DATE, 256
    RAWSQL_DATETIME, 256
    RAWSQL_INT, 256
    RAWSQL_REAL, 256
    RAWSQL_STR, 256
permissions
    accessing Tableau Server data using user
        IDs, 222–226
    setting for published workbooks, 219
Personal Edition, 32
PI function, 234
pie charts, 74–76

Pie marks, 147–148
point annotations, 82
postal codes, 126, 136
POWER function, 234
PREVIOUS_VALUE function, 261
primary data sources, 61–65
printing to .pdf files, 211–212
Professional Edition, 32
project categories for workbooks, 219
proper case for strings, 159
properties for mark fields, 19
Publish Workbook Results dialog box, 221
Publish Workbook To Tableau Server dialog box,
    218–219
publishing data to web, 216–229
    options for, 216
    Tableau Online for, 216, 218–221
    Tableau Public for, 216, 217
    Tableau Server for, 216

Q

quick filters, 103–105
    based on numeric measures, 105
    eliminating duplicate filters for
        dashboards, 198
    presenting all or relevant values with, 105
    removing, 104
Quick Table Calculation option
    Pane (Across) option, 172, 175
    Pane (Down) option, 172, 175
    Table (Across) option, 172, 173
    Table (Across then Down) option,
        172, 174
    Table (Down) option, 172, 174
    using, 169–170, 172

R

RADIANS function, 234
RAWSQLAGG_BOOL function, 255
RAWSQLAGG_DATE function, 255
RAWSQLAGG_DATETIME function, 255
RAWSQLAGG_INT function, 255
RAWSQLAGG_REAL function, 255
RAWSQLAGG_STR function, 256
RAWSQL_BOOL function, 256
RAWSQL_DATE function, 256
RAWSQL_DATETIME function, 256
RAWSQL_INT function, 256
RAWSQL_REAL function, 256
RAWSQL_STR function, 256
reference lines
    adding, 89, 91
    defined, 179
    using single, 180–181

references bands
    defined, 179
    highlighting range on numeric axis with, 181–182
    references distribution vs., 182
references distribution
    defined, 179
    displaying, 182–183
    illustrated, 183
    references bands vs., 182
refreshing extracted data, 58–59
relationships
    maintaining with original data, 59
    renaming mismatched dimensions, 63–64
Relationships dialog box, 63
removing
    filters, 96
    imported custom geocoding, 138
    quick filters, 104
renaming. *See* naming
Replace Data Source dialog box, 67
replacing data sources, 66–68
resetting maps, 141
RIGHT function, 160, 240–241
ROUND function, 235
RTRIM function, 241
RUNNING_AVG function, 262
RUNNING_COUNT function, 262
RUNNING_MAX function, 263
RUNNING_MIN function, 263
RUNNING_SUM function, 264

S

Salesforce Connection dialog box, 34
Save To Web dialog box, 217
saving
    Clipboard data in tab-delimited file, 42–43
    data sources, 2, 3
    .tds files, 53–55
    .twbx workbook files, 215–216
    workbooks to Tableau Public server, 217
    worksheets, 8
scatter plot charts
    about, 16
    bubble charts vs., 83
    creating effective, 80–83
    disaggregating data on, 81–82
    trend lines for, 82
Scheduling & Authentication dialog box, 220
scope of field, 258
secondary data sources, 61–65
Server drop-down menu, 222

sets
    combined, 54
    In/Out feature of, 52–53
    organizing metadata in, 50–53
shapes
    adding custom, 17
    selecting from Marks card, 16–17
shelves
    about, 5
    comparing multiple measures on, 22–23
    dragging groups to, 47
    editing measures added to wrong, 80
    using Filters shelf, 96–97
Show Me
    box plot unavailable in, 89
    creating Bullet Graph in, 86
    creating charts with, 9, 11–12
    gauges unavailable in, 87
    illustrated, 11
SIGN function, 235
SIN function, 235
single references lines, 180–181
Single Table radio button, (Connection dialog box), 35, 36
SIZE function, 264
sizing
    dashboards and their elements, 195, 201–202
    marks, 15–16, 76
    objects with layout containers, 198–200
small multiples visualizations, 82–83
smartphone devices, 221, 228
source data. *See* data sources
SPACE function, 241
SQL Server, 33, 35, 55, 66–68
SQRT function, 235
SQUARE function, 236
stacked area charts, 72
stacked bar charts, 7, 69–70
Start Page, 2
STARTSWITH functions, 241
state/province data, 126
STDEV function, 253
STDEVP function, 253
STR function, 160, 247
string functions, 236–242
    about, 236
    ASCII, 236
    CHAR, 237
    CONTAINS, 237
    ENDSWITH, 237
    FIND, 238
    ISDATE, 238, 244, 249–250
    LEFT, 160, 238–239
    LEN, 239

LOWER, 239
LTRIM, 239
MAX, 233, 239–240, 244, 252
MID, 240
MIN, 234, 240, 244–245, 253
RIGHT, 240–241
RTRIM, 241
SPACE, 241
STARTSWITH, 241
TRIM, 241
UPPER, 242
string literals, 158
strings
converting to number, 158
converting to proper case, 159
detecting null values in, 159–160
functions for, 236–242
SUM function, 163, 165, 253
Swap button, 69, 80
syntax for calculated field, 157

━━━ **T** ━━━

Table Calculation dialog box, 172, 176
table calculation functions, 258–272
about, 258–259
example of, 259
FIRST, 259
INDEX, 260
LAST, 260
LOOKUP, 261
PREVIOUS_VALUE, 261
RUNNING_AVG, 262
RUNNING_COUNT, 262
RUNNING_MAX, 263
RUNNING_MIN, 263
RUNNING_SUM, 264
SIZE, 264
TOTAL, 265
WINDOW_AVG, 265
WINDOW_COUNT, 266
WINDOW_MAX, 266–267
WINDOW_MEDIAN, 267–268
WINDOW_MIN, 268–269
WINDOW_STDEV, 269
WINDOW_STDEVP, 270
WINDOW_SUM, 270–271
WINDOW_VAR, 271–272
WINDOW_VARP, 271–272
table calculations, 167–179. *See also* table
calculation functions
adding to crosstab charts, 167–176
addressing vs. partitioning in, 171
drop-down lists for, 172
two-pass, 177

Tableau
about, 1–3
analyzing data in, 38
app for iPad, 221, 227–228
calling SQL functions in, 254–255
case sensitivity in, 159, 163
creating Tableau Public account, 217
dashboards in, 187
data aggregation used by, 163–165
data sources supported by, 32–33
developing design flow for charts in, 5–8
downloading drivers for data sources, 34
forecasting charts in, 73–74
iPad app for, 221, 227–228
limitations of Tableau Reader, 216
mapping concepts in, 121–123
Start Page for, 2
user interface for, 3–6
Tableau Data Extract (.tde) files, 55–59
Tableau Data Source (.tds) files, 53–55
Tableau Map Source (.tms) files, 144
Tableau Online
pre-selecting marks for server
workbooks, 220
setting permissions for worksheets
on, 219
web-based publishing with, 216,
218–221
Tableau Packaged Workbook (.twbx) files, 138,
215–216
Tableau Public, 216, 217
Tableau Reader, 215–216
Tableau Server
creating ID-based user filters, 222–226
pre-selecting marks for server
workbooks, 220
setting permissions for worksheets on, 219
showing worksheets as tabs on, 220
storing and refreshing extracts on, 58
Tableau Public version of, 216, 217
web-based publishing with, 216, 218–221
tables. *See also* axes; table calculations
adding and joining multiple, 35–37
data blending vs. table joins, 60
functions for calculating, 258–272
selecting from data sources, 34–35
text, 17–18, 76–80
tag clouds, 94
TAN function, 236
.tde (Tableau Data Extract) files, 55–59
.tds (Tableau Data Source) files, 53–55
testing
calculated field logic, 162–163
migrating test databases to production
databases, 66–68

text
    adding to dashboards, 200
    using with floating dashboards, 196
text table (crosstab) charts
    best uses for, 80
    creating, 76–80
    using, 17–18
THEN keyword, 162–163
tiled dashboards
    aligning elements in, 188
    designing, 189–195
    using layout containers for, 199
time. *See also* date functions
    calculated fields for date and, 160–161
    converting expressions to date and, 246
    functions for date and, 242–246
    quick filters for, 105
    using SQL pass-through functions for,
      255, 256
.tms (Tableau Map Source) files, 144
tooltips, 19
top filters, 99–101, 106
TOTAL function, 265
Totals drop-down menu, 77
totals for crosstab charts, 77
Tree Map charts, 92–94
Trend Line Options dialog box, 185
trend lines
    adding to scatter plot charts, 82
    creating, 184–185
    defined, 184
TRIM function, 241
.twbx (Tableau Packaged Workbook) files, 138,
    215–216
two-pass table calculations, 176–177
type conversion functions, 246–247
    DATE, 160, 246
    DATETIME, 246
    FLOAT, 247
    INT, 247
    STR, 247

U

ungrouping
    dimension members, 47
    visual groupings, 49
uploading workbook data sources, 220
UPPER function, 242
URL actions
    defined, 112, 202
    initiating from dashboard, 207–209
    launching web pages with, 118–120

URLs
    embedding web pages using, 201
    selecting images on web server using,
      200–201
U.S. congressional districts, 126
User Filter dialog box, 223
user functions, 256–258
    FULLNAME, 257
    ISFULLNAME, 257
    ISMEMBEROF, 257
    ISUSERNAME, 257
    USERDOMAIN, 258
    USERNAME, 258
user interface. *See also* Data window; Marks card;
    menus
    features of, 3–6
    illustrated, 2
    tooltips, 19
USERDOMAIN function, 258
USERNAME function, 258
users. *See also* interacting with viewer
    filtering data for specific, 222–226
    functions retrieving data for, 256–258
    setting permissions for published
      workbooks, 219
    Tableau interface for, 3–6

V

VAR function, 254
VARP function, 254
versions and Tableau data sources, 32–33
views
    customizing data, 38–55
    sharing published workbook and
      dashboard, 219
visual grouping, using, 48–49
visualizations, 9–29, 211–229. *See also* charts
    annotating, 82
    basic and predefined, 2
    color options for Marks card, 14–15
    comparing multiple measures, 22–23
    dimensions and measure for, 10–11
    dual axis charts, 26–28
    exporting worksheets and dashboards,
      211–215
    filtering data for, 95
    formatting options, 20–22
    mark types for, 12–13
    Multi-Measure Marks card for, 28–29
    printing worksheets as .pdfs, 211–212
    publishing data to web, 216–229
    shapes for, 16–17

shared axis charts for, 23–24
sharing with in Tableau Reader, 215–216
small multiples, 82–83
text tables, 17–18, 76–80
tooltips, 19
using Measure Names and Measure
    Values fields, 24–26
variable mark sizes for, 15–16, 76
viewing with mobile apps and browsers,
    221, 227–228
VizQL, 1

━━━ **W** ━━━

warning dialog box. *See* errors
web-based data sources. *See also* publishing data
  to web
    copying data from, 40–43
    dialog boxes for, 33–34
    embedding web pages in dashboard, 201
    updating Web Page element when URL
        action initiated, 209
    viewing HTML5 mobile browsers,
        221, 228
Web Map Services (WMS), 141, 143–145
whiskers, 90, 91
wildcards, 98
WINDOW_AVG function, 265
WINDOW_COUNT function, 266
WINDOW_MAX function, 266–267
WINDOW_MEDIAN function, 267–268
WINDOW_MIN function, 268–269
WINDOW_STDEV function, 269
WINDOW_STDEVP function, 270
WINDOW_SUM function, 270–271
WINDOW_VAR function, 271–272
WINDOW_VARP function, 271–272
WMS (Web Map Services), 141, 143–145
word clouds, 94
workbooks. *See also* data sources; worksheets
    about, 3
    connecting to data source, 2, 31–35
    creating new, 2–3
    designing dashboards for, 188
    importing custom geocoding from
        current, 138
    maintaining relationship to source of
        extracted data, 59
    moving from test to production databases,
        66–68
    opening, 2
    pre-selecting marks for server, 220

project categories for, 219
publishing to Tableau Server and Tableau
    Online, 216, 218–221
saving as .twbx files, 215–216
saving to Tableau Public server, 217
sharing published views of, 219
using parameters in, 106
worksheet actions, 112–120
    adding filter actions, 112–115
    creating highlight actions, 115–117
    dashboard actions vs., 120
    initiating with hovering, 112
    launching web pages with URL actions,
        118–120
    types of, 112
Worksheet drop-down menu, 212, 213
worksheets. *See also* worksheet actions
    about, 3
    blending data from multiple, 60
    copying data as crosstab chart, 212
    copying data from dashboard and, 213
    displaying parameters on, 109–110
    dropping fields on shelves, 5
    exporting data from, 212–214
    filtering data for, 95–101
    grouping metadata on, 46–49
    hard coding filtering in, 95–101
    mobile access to, 227–229
    naming, 7–8, 187
    parameters in, 110–111
    printing to .pdf files, 211–212
    saving, 8
    sharing filters among, 102
    showing as tabs on Tableau Server, 220
    tiled dashboards for, 188, 189–195
    using with floating dashboards, 196
workspaces, 161–162

━━━ **X** ━━━

X/Y coordinates
    generating for custom images, 149–151
    plotting latitude/longitude as, 122, 124

━━━ **Y** ━━━

YEAR function, 246

━━━ **Z** ━━━

ZIP codes, 126, 128–130
ZN function, 236, 250
zoom in/out on maps, 141

LICENSE AGREEMENT

THIS PRODUCT (THE "PRODUCT") CONTAINS PROPRIETARY SOFTWARE, DATA AND INFORMATION (INCLUDING DOCUMENTATION) OWNED BY McGRAW-HILL EDUCATION AND ITS LICENSORS. YOUR RIGHT TO USE THE PRODUCT IS GOVERNED BY THE TERMS AND CONDITIONS OF THIS AGREEMENT.

LICENSE: Throughout this License Agreement, "you" shall mean either the individual or the entity whose agent opens this package. You are granted a non-exclusive and non-transferable license to use the Product subject to the following terms:

(i) If you have licensed a single user version of the Product, the Product may only be used on a single computer (i.e., a single CPU). If you licensed and paid the fee applicable to a local area network or wide area network version of the Product, you are subject to the terms of the following subparagraph (ii).

(ii) If you have licensed a local area network version, you may use the Product on unlimited workstations located in one single building selected by you that is served by such local area network. If you have licensed a wide area network version, you may use the Product on unlimited workstations located in multiple buildings on the same site selected by you that is served by such wide area network; provided, however, that any building will not be considered located in the same site if it is more than five (5) miles away from any building included in such site. In addition, you may only use a local area or wide area network version of the Product on one single server. If you wish to use the Product on more than one server, you must obtain written authorization from McGraw-Hill Education and pay additional fees.

(iii) You may make one copy of the Product for back-up purposes only and you must maintain an accurate record as to the location of the back-up at all times.

COPYRIGHT; RESTRICTIONS ON USE AND TRANSFER: All rights (including copyright) in and to the Product are owned by McGraw-Hill Education and its licensors. You are the owner of the enclosed disc on which the Product is recorded. You may not use, copy, decompile, disassemble, reverse engineer, modify, reproduce, create derivative works, transmit, distribute, sublicense, store in a database or retrieval system of any kind, rent or transfer the Product, or any portion thereof, in any form or by any means (including electronically or otherwise) except as expressly provided for in this License Agreement. You must reproduce the copyright notices, trademark notices, legends and logos of McGraw-Hill Education and its licensors that appear on the Product on the back-up copy of the Product which you are permitted to make hereunder. All rights in the Product not expressly granted herein are reserved by McGraw-Hill Education and its licensors.

TERM: This License Agreement is effective until terminated. It will terminate if you fail to comply with any term or condition of this License Agreement. Upon termination, you are obligated to return to McGraw-Hill Education the Product together with all copies thereof and to purge all copies of the Product included in any and all servers and computer facilities.

DISCLAIMER OF WARRANTY: THE PRODUCT AND THE BACK-UP COPY ARE LICENSED "AS IS." McGRAW-HILL EDUCATION, ITS LICENSORS AND THE AUTHORS MAKE NO WARRANTIES, EXPRESS OR IMPLIED, AS TO THE RESULTS TO BE OBTAINED BY ANY PERSON OR ENTITY FROM USE OF THE PRODUCT, ANY INFORMATION OR DATA INCLUDED THEREIN AND/OR ANY TECHNICAL SUPPORT SERVICES PROVIDED HEREUNDER, IF ANY ("TECHNICAL SUPPORT SERVICES"). McGRAW-HILL EDUCATION, ITS LICENSORS AND THE AUTHORS MAKE NO EXPRESS OR IMPLIED WARRANTIES OF MERCHANTABILITY OR FITNESS FOR A PARTICULAR PURPOSE OR USE WITH RESPECT TO THE PRODUCT. McGRAW-HILL EDUCATION, ITS LICENSORS, AND THE AUTHORS MAKE NO GUARANTEE THAT YOU WILL PASS ANY CERTIFICATION EXAM WHATSOEVER BY USING THIS PRODUCT. NEITHER McGRAW-HILL EDUCATION, ANY OF ITS LICENSORS NOR THE AUTHORS WARRANT THAT THE FUNCTIONS CONTAINED IN THE PRODUCT WILL MEET YOUR REQUIREMENTS OR THAT THE OPERATION OF THE PRODUCT WILL BE UNINTERRUPTED OR ERROR FREE. YOU ASSUME THE ENTIRE RISK WITH RESPECT TO THE QUALITY AND PERFORMANCE OF THE PRODUCT.

LIMITED WARRANTY FOR DISC: To the original licensee only, McGraw-Hill Education warrants that the enclosed disc on which the Product is recorded is free from defects in materials and workmanship under normal use and service for a period of ninety (90) days from the date of purchase. In the event of a defect in the disc covered by the foregoing warranty, McGraw-Hill Education will replace the disc.

LIMITATION OF LIABILITY: NEITHER McGRAW-HILL EDUCATION, ITS LICENSORS NOR THE AUTHORS SHALL BE LIABLE FOR ANY INDIRECT, SPECIAL OR CONSEQUENTIAL DAMAGES, SUCH AS BUT NOT LIMITED TO, LOSS OF ANTICIPATED PROFITS OR BENEFITS, RESULTING FROM THE USE OR INABILITY TO USE THE PRODUCT EVEN IF ANY OF THEM HAS BEEN ADVISED OF THE POSSIBILITY OF SUCH DAMAGES. THIS LIMITATION OF LIABILITY SHALL APPLY TO ANY CLAIM OR CAUSE WHATSOEVER WHETHER SUCH CLAIM OR CAUSE ARISES IN CONTRACT, TORT, OR OTHERWISE. Some states do not allow the exclusion or limitation of indirect, special or consequential damages, so the above limitation may not apply to you.

U.S. GOVERNMENT RESTRICTED RIGHTS: Any software included in the Product is provided with restricted rights subject to subparagraphs (c), (1) and (2) of the Commercial Computer Software-Restricted Rights clause at 48 C.F.R. 52.227-19. The terms of this Agreement applicable to the use of the data in the Product are those under which the data are generally made available to the general public by McGraw-Hill Education. Except as provided herein, no reproduction, use, or disclosure rights are granted with respect to the data included in the Product and no right to modify or create derivative works from any such data is hereby granted.

GENERAL: This License Agreement constitutes the entire agreement between the parties relating to the Product. The terms of any Purchase Order shall have no effect on the terms of this License Agreement. Failure of McGraw-Hill Education to insist at any time on strict compliance with this License Agreement shall not constitute a waiver of any rights under this License Agreement. This License Agreement shall be construed and governed in accordance with the laws of the State of New York. If any provision of this License Agreement is held to be contrary to law, that provision will be enforced to the maximum extent permissible and the remaining provisions will remain in full force and effect.